THE SUBTLE KNOT

THE SUBTLE KNOT

GREENWOOD PRESS PUBLISHERS

NEW YORK   1968

THE SUBTLE KNOT

*Creative Scepticism
in Seventeenth-Century England*

by

MARGARET L. WILEY

our blood labours to beget
Spirits, as like soules as it can,
Because such fingers need to knit
That subtile knot, which makes us man . . .
JOHN DONNE 'The Extasie'

GREENWOOD PRESS, PUBLISHERS

NEW YORK   **1968**

Originally printed in 1952 by Unwin Brothers Ltd., London

Reprinted with the permission of
George Allen & Unwin, Ltd.

First Greenwood reprinting, 1968

Library of Congress catalogue card number: 68-54994

Printed in the United States of America

TO
RODERICK MARSHALL

FOREWORD

SINCE 'all experience is an arch,' one normally spends more of his time looking through it than examining its composition. Yet the individual would be both blind and ungrateful who did not try, on occasion, to call the roll of those influences upon his thought and life of which he is most aware, realizing all the while, of course, that one neither knows what he is nor dares to lay at the door of others the responsibility for what he has thus far become.

This book, for better or for worse, is one of the results of the kind of home my parents and grandparents provided, in which both literature and religion were made abundantly available, without either's having been strained through the sieve of dogma, and where actions spoke louder than words. It stems also from approximately eight years of listening, during youth, to the literate and inspired sermons of the late Dr. Harold H. Griffis in Portland, Oregon, and from an overlapping period of six years of listening to the equally literate and inspired lectures of the late Professor Barry Cerf at Reed College, who made accessible hitherto unexplored realms of the world's literature, philosophy and religion and who struggled persistently, often against stubborn resistance, to bring some order out of the chaos of my undergraduate mind. It was Professor George Williamson who, in a course in seventeenth-century literature at the University of Oregon, first suggested that a study of the co-existing scepticism and faith of the seventeenth century might enable me to make a pattern out of certain trends which I had appreciated without being able to identify. In spite of the dangers inherent in such a topic, Professor Kenneth B. Murdock at Harvard undertook to stand by and offer both moral and bibliographical assistance while I struggled to write something which would satisfy both my own intellectual needs and the standards of a great university. His continuing faith in the project has been invaluable. The very practical suggestion that I should publish separate

7

articles on the five sceptics before bringing out the book was made by Dr. Helen C. White of the University of Wisconsin.

To professional philosophers I am indebted for more light than I have been able to make constructive use of, notably to Professor Arthur O. Lovejoy of Johns Hopkins University and to the late Professor Felix Kaufmann of the Graduate Faculty, New School for Social Research.

Most of the ideas in this book have been beaten into their present shape by conversations with long-suffering friends, teachers and students during the past twenty-five years, for this is the only way one can become articulate. Those individuals who have survived this process will recognize bits of conversation reflected here and there; the others have been perhaps mercifully spared the embarrassment of being held even remotely responsible for the following pages.

My deep gratitude is due to the Oregon Branch of the American Association of University Women for a fellowship grant in 1937–38, which provided the necessary leisure for research and for the re-evaluation of old ideas.

Permission has been granted by the editors of *The Hibbert Journal*, the *Journal of the History of Ideas*, and *The Western Humanities Review* for the inclusion of portions of the book which have already appeared in the form of articles.

BROOKLYN COLLEGE   M. L. W.
December, 1950

CONTENTS

CHAPTER I

PROLEGOMENA TO
THE DEFINITION OF SCEPTICISM

IF Chekhov's judgment that every artist has an axe to grind is valid for the creators, it has an even greater validity for those who scan their creations and who seek to interpret literary trends and identify patterns of thought. Among this second group, the critics, it is practically impossible to conceal the axe, and it often turns out to be double-bitted; therefore one may as well at the outset declare his weapons and confess how he came by them.

This book, as honestly as I can now account for its genesis, seems to have been the result of the interplay of two forces—one my own experience in learning how to live and the other my sharing the recorded experience of others. This latter, if one has been fortunate in his guides, is always proved upon the pulses, and out of that process is born one's conception of the nature of truth and one's convictions about the way it can be attained. Thus it is not quite accurate to say one is taught by what he reads. Rather does he ingest, like the amoeba, whatever in his environment seems life-sustaining, rejecting such foreign matter as he cannot use. Perhaps the whole problem of education, then, is to increase the range of the individual's susceptibility so that he may recognize the potentialities of larger and larger areas of his environment; but to suggest this is already to have slipped beyond description and into performance—like Chaucer's Pardoner.

As the interaction between living and reading went on, I discovered myself powerfully drawn toward the poets and prose writers of seventeenth-century England and gave as an 'official' explanation the judgment that in this century the three areas overlapped in which my chief interest lay—literature, philosophy, and religion. Behind this academic façade, however, was the fact that I had caught sight, in the thought of these writers, of a pattern which was gradually forming itself in my own living. They spoke to me because our experience seemed made of the same stuff, and to expatiate on their meaning was to make the meaning of my own experience clearer and more explicit. The specific anomaly which I had set myself to study, on a hint from Louis Bredvold (in *The Intellectual Milieu of John Dryden*), was the coexistence of faith and scepticism in the same seventeenth-century writers. But as I explored this apparent contradiction and as I sought out the meaning of 'scepticism' (the simpler of the two terms to define), I concluded that here was a word which, if rehabilitated, might serve the same purpose as the colouring carried in the life-rafts of planes—to mark an area on the ocean of truth where something precious was floating. The word came to stand for a process of truth-seeking which seemed to carry its own immunity against the most deadly enemy of truth-seekers, the virus of dogmatism.

In order to be sure that I was not merely creating my own solipsistic language, I began scrutinizing the use which others had made of the word. Of the two principal and widely separated meanings, I discovered that one appeared to be an eighteenth-century corruption of the other. The appearance of this corrupted meaning, soon after the Restoration, threw a new light upon the nature of eighteenth-century thought and marked the end of the period which had attracted me because what I now called scepticism was in flower there.

Happily I came across many writers, both obscure and well-known, who were heading in my direction, toward the use of 'scepticism' in what appears to be its original meaning—enough to encourage me to explore the historical origins of the term and to show how its pattern, set by the Greeks and revived in the Renaissance, recurred in prominent seventeenth-century writers and might perhaps account for the vigour and attractiveness of their thought and also for its essential soundness.

Such an investigation, at our stage of the world's spiritual development, can scarcely constitute a mere academic exercise. It is fraught with all the urgency with which sufferers from an incurable disease turn to each new panacea. Scepticism is not here set forth as such a panacea (this would be a very unsceptical procedure), but it is rather used as a rallying-point about which to organize one individual's insights into the meaning of truth in so far as they seem to be borne out by others who have cut a significant jagged path across the history of human thought.

The most important single technique to be learned from the sceptics is that of wresting from unpromising materials the very building-stones of truth. The seventeenth-century sceptics were continually transforming the philosophic confusion of their age and the upthrusts of pessimism and heresy into the components of the kind of faith which at least enabled them to come to terms with their world and to do their work in it with calmness and dignity. They had learned the secret of taking the obvious next step, instead of railing against the fate of having been set down in an uncongenial age. Theirs was a wisdom which had been prefigured in the words of the apostle, 'The word is nigh thee, even in thy mouth, and in thy heart.' It seemed to me that instead of bewailing the world's unbelief or its secularism, one might more profitably show in these very attitudes the hitherto unrecognized seeds of spiritual power. It is reasonable to suppose that having turned in despair from simple and direct methods, our generation might be willing to venture its last throw on the chance that this paradoxical wresting of victory from defeat may constitute our only means to salvation. The use which the seventeenth century often made of the sceptical method to blunt the edge of intellectual and spiritual disaster—requiring like Jacob a blessing from the dark angel of schism—may teach us how to deal with the growing unbelief and secularism of our day and force from it great riches.

Before undertaking a systematic historical survey of scepticism, it seems well to reproduce if we can, in miniature, the kind of hit or miss beating about the field, out of which exploration there grew the above convictions regarding the nature and importance of scepticism. For the philosopher, such a procedure would be intellectually indefensible, but what we are concerned with here is in keeping the concept as close to experience as possible since it is in the field of literature rather than of formal philosophy that we should like to trace its outlines. Therefore whatever byways of technical philosophy may lure us in this investigation, let us remain true to our original intent—to sketch in roughly the outlines of the pattern of thought known as scepticism so that we may recognize it wherever it occurs in literature and learn what wisdom we can from the men who have experimented with it. Such a mission is to be undertaken in the spirit of a great historian of ideas, who describes thus the relation between the fields of philosophy and literature:

> The interest of the history of literature is largely as a record of the movement of ideas—of the ideas which have affected men's imaginations and emotions and behavior. And the ideas in serious reflective literature are, of course, in great part philosophical ideas in dilution—to change the figure, growths from seed scattered by great philosophic systems which themselves, perhaps, have ceased to be.[1]

In trying to identify the particular growth under discussion here, what concerns the literary critic is the anguish of intellectual despair and the possibility of wresting from that a new conception of truth and not, as in the case of the philosopher, the epistemological concomitants of that despair.

The Sceptic Experience

In order to set the tone of this discussion and to have before us at least one concrete example of what we mean by scepticism, let us look at some words of Socrates which lie along the triple watershed of literature, philosophy and religion. After having avowed that 'the god' bids him stand forth as one who is a devotee of wisdom and a questioner of all the world, he says it would be strange if he quit his post because of the fear of death.

14

For the fear of death, my friends, is only another form of appearing wise when we are foolish and of seeming to know what we know not. No mortal knoweth of death whether it be not the greatest of all good things to man, yet do men fear it as knowing it to be the greatest of evils. And is not this that most culpable ignorance which pretends to know what it knows not?[2]

A consideration of these words will set the problem of scepticism against its proper background of human experience, for it is to such situations as this that the sceptic keeps returning.

What appears on the surface here is a rare willingness to relinquish dogmatism in an area where it is reinforced by fear. To find something akin to this ultimate suspension of judgment we should need to go to the parallel words of Jesus, 'Thy will, not mine, be done.' There is in these two the same launching out into an unknown but compelling future, the same hope that truth will be the ultimate terminus; and in their utterances are subsumed all the cries of nescience from Montaigne's '*Que sais-je?*' to Oliver Cromwell's 'I beseech you, in the bowels of Christ, think it possible you may be mistaken.'[3] Lying just beneath the surface, like a hidden rock set there to wreck the unwary dogmatist, is the implied paradox, in the case of both Jesus and Socrates, that death may be a good and not an evil. The intellectual humility generated by this realization pervades the whole passage, and along with this there is a certain naïve wonder which flees before the breath of dogmatism.

Diogenes Laertius in his brief life of Pyrrho recognizes this as the authentic experience of scepticism. After outlining the chief features of Pyrrhonism, he says that some people hold Homer to be the founder of scepticism since to philosophical questions he gave different answers at different times and since he was never definite nor dogmatic. Euripides, too, he includes among others who are called sceptics, and he quotes these lines from the dramatist:

> Who knoweth if to die be but to live,
> And that called life by mortals be but death?[4]

The precedent of Diogenes, unacceptable as he is to historians of philosophy, would seem to be at least partial justification for our concentrating upon the scepticism to be found among men of letters. There it seems to touch human experience at many points, and so it becomes relevant for a wider area of thought than does philosophical scepticism.

Scepticism—Process or Result?

One difficulty which has always been encountered by historians of free thought is the tendency of their readers to mistake a process for conclusions. Since the sceptic and the freethinker often coincide, the same situation obtains for historians of scepticism. (J. M. Robertson observes that the terms *sceptic* and *freethinker* have often been applied interchangeably as terms of opprobrium for those 'who doubted where doubt was most resented and most resisted.')5 The siren-call of comfortable conclusions has lured many an intellectual mariner from his turbulent and precarious course. Adam Farrar in *A Critical History of Free-thought in Reference to the Christian Religion* points out the difference between 'free thinking,' as used by Collins early in the eighteenth century to designate a dynamic method, and 'free thought' as the nineteenth century's label for the codified results of this method. Collins' term implied 'the freedom of the mode of inquiry rather than the character of the conclusions attained.'6 It seems almost impossible for such words as *free thought* and *scepticism* to remain long as the designation for a process rather than for its conclusions; and because of this human propensity for the static, dogmatism is a persistent threat to scepticism. It is natural that men should feel much more comfortable and secure when a word stands for certain results rather than for a set of mind or for the direction of an ongoing movement. Nevertheless, the scepticism we are trying to define enthrones a process in the belief that as soon as the sceptic halts and begins to draw rigid conclusions, he is no longer a sceptic.

John Owen, who wrote in the late nineteenth century, has done the most fruitful and impressive work in clarifying the meaning of scepticism as it defines broad movements of thought rather than narrow philosophical systems. In an essay prefixed to his 1885 edition of Joseph Glanvill's *Scepsis Scientifica*, Owen says:

> But although he styled his thought *sceptical*, and himself a *sceptic*, Glanvill did not employ those terms in the commonly received sense of wanton or unreasonable disbelief, but in the classical meaning of enquiry and judicial suspense. . . . It [*skepsis*] is best described as the principle opposed to excessive dogma, whether in Philosophy, Science, or Religion.[7]

Then in a footnote Owen explores, as he has so consistently done, the sources of our modern confusion regarding the term.

> Some mode of discrimination between Skepticism in its proper and primary sense of Enquiry, and in its perverted but usual sense of disbelief or Negation, seems urgently needed. . . . The persistent confusion that occurs between Suspense and Negation, even in accredited works on Philosophy, is not very complimentary to the progress of human thought. Few persons seem able to realize that *Skepsis* is as much opposed to Dogmatic Negation as to Dogmatic Affirmation.[8]

It is not unusual to discover an individual, in whatever age, swinging from a positive dogmatism to a negative one—from a narrow, dogmatic theology, for example, to an equally dogmatic rejection of all theology, from a rigidly held political dogmatism of the right to an equally rigid dogmatism of the left. What is rarer is to find one who holds both positive and negative dogmatisms in suspense and drives forward toward a truth which is beyond them.

The progressive (or should we say 'processive'?) quality of scepticism is further underscored by Owen in the preface to *The Religious Aspects of Scepticism*:

> It is surely time that the Skeptic or philosophical inquirer should be distinguished from the dogmatic Agnostic, or Negationist; and that Positive and Negative Dogmas, when dealing with speculative

subjects in which absolute certitude is inconceivable, should be regarded as similar in essence and object however different in form.[9]

Thus all dogmatisms, however superficially different from each other, are to be set over against the seeking and inquiring nature of scepticism, which remains itself only so long as it does not succumb to the tyranny of results and conclusions.

The question of whether the sceptic ever reaches any kind of decision is one which cannot be answered until there is more concrete evidence of sceptical thought before us. Suffice it to state categorically here (before all the evidence is in) that the emphasis of the sceptic, because he is interested in breaking up the narrow moulds of dogmatisms, is upon the means he is using to arrive at a decision rather than upon the decision itself. A significant spiritual law seems to be operative in this domain. Its presence has been recognized by more than one thinker. Francis Bacon once said, 'He that would begin in certainties shall end in doubts; but if he be content to begin with doubts and have patience a while he shall end in certainties.'[10] A similar progression is noted three hundred years later by Alfred Hodder, under the philosophical influence of Josiah Royce and F. H. Bradley:

> There are people who care for processes and people who care only for results: it is the wisdom of centuries that to those who care for processes, results shall be added, and that from those who care for results only shall be taken even that which they have.[11]

Definitions of Scepticism

Having established the instrumental rather than the terminal character of scepticism, let us consider quite apart from their historical sequence, several definitions, all of which point in the same general direction. Almost every writer on scepticism pauses to call attention to the loss of the word's original meaning and to the necessity of recovering that. William Mitchell says that Emerson in his essay on Montaigne used the word in its 'oldest, largest and noblest sense,' for the Greek σκεπτεσθαι means 'to consider, inquire, look into, examine, look at, observe, fix one's eyes upon.'[12] The slant of Mitchell's own definition in the direction of religion is apparent at once. 'By skepticism therefore in this essay is meant the spirit of inquiry, of earnest doubt, of hesitation and indecision in embracing Christian truth.'[13] Although this is not a completely satisfactory definition for our purposes, it contains the germ of what is most important in scepticism. Mitchell follows this with an explanation which is remarkable for its treatment of what we have called literary scepticism in terms which are entirely appropriate to the material involved.

> It [skepticism] would seem, rather, to mark that transition stage between the faith of childhood and the faith of manhood. There comes a period, an epoch, a moment in our lives when we have neither the one nor the other. The past is gone and with it the faith of the past; the future is not yet here. . . . Truth seems far away and the search for truth involves a struggle. The skeptical moment therefore lies in this very struggle of the human soul in its search for truth. It is the feeling of bewilderment and drift, the discovery that we have lost our moorings, the desolation, emptiness and loneliness which are sure to follow. . . . It is a fact of the individual experience, a phase of life which meets us everywhere, a fact written deep in our spiritual history, and a fact which meets us in the larger life about us, in biography, in literature, and social movements, in human life as a whole.[14]

It is this kind of experience which Socrates, in the words previously quoted, had somehow maintained beyond his youth, as an insurance against the blight of dogmatism. Far from indicating arrested development, this ability of Socrates at a moment of crisis to reach back into his adolescence for light and guidance is evidence that he had maintained a genuine sceptic flexibility of spirit. For what he does when confronted with death is to strip himself of preconceived notions and set himself back at the gateway of his maturity, where in comparative intellectual innocence he can make a fresh start in the direction of truth, counting not himself 'already to have apprehended.' It is the intimacy of scepticism and faith in such an experience which prompts speculation as to their proper relationship.

Scepticism and Faith

Whereas some have seen faith as the terminus of scepticism, others, like Emerson, see scepticism as a kind of language made use of to step down the revelations of faith so that they may be apprehended by the mass of men. Hence the misunderstanding which always greets the prophet.

> Great believers are always reckoned infidels, impracticable, fantastic, atheistic, and really men of no account. The spiritualist finds himself driven to express his faith by a series of skepticisms.[15]

Farther on in the same essay Emerson expresses this notion on another plane of experience. He conceives of scepticism as a self-transcending phase of the search for truth. He is convinced that once he has progressed further, he will understand the coming together of what now seems disparate, but until he arrives at that deeper insight he must maintain his scepticism.

> George Fox saw that there was 'an ocean of darkness, and death; but withal an infinite ocean of light and love which flowed over that of darkness.'. . . I play with the miscellany of facts, and take those superficial views which we call skepticism; but I know that they will presently appear to me in that order which makes skepticism impossible.[16]

This variant of Emerson's is predicated upon shifting the meaning of scepticism once the truth is in sight and so kicking away the ladder by which one has risen. But perhaps it is in the nature of scepticism to destroy itself; perhaps that is the only fate consistent with its nature.

In analysing the relationship of scepticism and faith, two such dissimilar minds as those of Josiah Royce and T. S. Eliot show a common perception that somehow in the sceptic process, doubt if honestly pursued undergoes a metamorphosis and so becomes an essential component of whatever faith the individual is able to achieve. Says Royce:

> Philosophic truth, as such, comes to us first under the form of doubt; and we never can be very near it in our search unless, for a

longer or shorter time, we have come to despair of it altogether. First, then, the despair of a thorough-going doubt, and then the discovery that this doubt contains in its bosom the truth that we are sworn to discover, however we can—this is the typical philosophic experience.[17]

Eliot, describing the same process with a slightly different angle of vision, makes clear among other things the relation of terminal to instrumental scepticism and the possibility of the whole cycle's being consummated in faith.

> For every man who thinks and lives by thought must have his own scepticism, that which stops at the question, that which ends in denial, or that which leads to faith and which is somehow integrated into the faith which transcends it.[18]

We shall see that in the scepticism of seventeenth-century England the integration of scepticism into faith is the most distinctive and significant phase of the process.

Sceptic Action

The action which the sceptic indulges in, however, is rarely the result of conclusions intellectually arrived at. More often it is undertaken in order to break a logical deadlock, and indeed the action itself may be as near as the sceptic ever comes to a conclusion. C. B. Wheeler has accurately described the intermediate process by which the sceptic utilizes probability as a basis for action when he cannot determine where the truth lies.

> Of course, on many subjects he is driven to suspend his judgment and forced to wait a while for further evidence: but in the majority of cases, he finds that there is a balance of probabilities on one side or the other, and he will follow the turn of the scale, being, of course, quite prepared to jump from one pan to the other if fresh facts come to light. This he will have to do pretty often if he is honestly in search of truth.[19]

It is because of this practice that the sceptic is berated for his inconsistency, which is far removed from the petty dogmatisms of men, and thus difficult for them to understand. This inconsistency is the kind which made Donne say, 'For by tomorrow I may think so too' and which was echoed two centuries later by Emerson's 'A foolish consistency is the hob-goblin of little minds.'[20]

Owen notes that however men protest being required to act without having arrived at conclusions, most of their action is built upon less than absolute certainty.

> Few men seem to realize how much the ordinary beliefs, nay, even the resolutions and decisive acts of their lives, depend, not upon demonstrated certainties, but upon a greater or less amount of reasonable probabilities.[21]

He goes on to connect with this observation the conclusion of Cardinal Newman:

> 'Probability is the Rule of Life.' Hence [says Owen] we might define Skepticism as THE RELIGION OF TRUTH, as implying the attitude of cautious hesitation and reverential constraint before the infinite shrine wherein Truth has her dwelling.[22]

'A wary and pious discretion' is the phrase we shall find Sir Thomas Browne using to illuminate the attitude Owen is here describing. It involves not the grovelling worship of some vague metaphysical entity, but that combination of awe and caution which renders the truth-seeker at once humble and open-minded, and which enables him to handle with supreme tact the most diverse concepts.

Emerson found himself at one of those points in history at which, dogmatism having become oppressive, the cleansing and lightening of scepticism was indicated, and he took the task upon himself. In this undertaking he found Montaigne to be one of the most congenial souls among his predecessors, and in his essay on Montaigne he sketches with his usual percipience the outlines of the genuine sceptic.

> This then is the ground of the skeptic—this of consideration, of self-containing; not at all of unbelief; not at all of universal denying, nor of universal doubting—doubting even that he doubts; least of

all of scoffing and profligate jeering at all that is stable and good. These are no more his moods than are those of religion and philosophy. He is the considerer, the prudent taking in sail, counting stock, husbanding his means, believing that a man has too many enemies than that he can afford to be his own foe; that we cannot give ourselves too many advantages in this unequal conflict, with powers so vast and unweariable ranged on one side, and this little conceited vulnerable popinjay that a man is, bobbing up and down into every danger, on the other. It is a position taken up for better defence, as of more safety, and one that can be maintained; and it is one of more opportunity and range: as, when we build a house, the rule is to set it not too high nor too low, under the wind, but out of the dirt.[23]

This is one of the most flawless and winning portraits of the sceptic, and it illustrates in addition the tendency of all defenders of scepticism to feel that they are merely advocating what every right-minded seeker of the truth is aiming toward. Emerson is one with the other definers of scepticism in insisting that, far from representing an alien discipline, it constitutes one important phase in the normal development of the human spirit.

Every superior mind will pass through this domain of equilibration,—I should rather say, will know how to avail himself of the checks and balances in nature, as a natural weapon against the exaggeration and formalism of bigots and blockheads.

Skepticism is the attitude assumed by the student in relation to the particulars which society adores, but which he sees to be reverend only in their tendency and spirit. The ground occupied by the skeptic is the vestibule of the temple. Society does not like to have any breath of question blown on the existing order. But the interrogation of custom at all points is an inevitable stage in the growth of every superior mind, and is the evidence of its perception of the flowing power which remains itself in all changes.[24]

Perhaps the most important portion of this definition is the perception that when the sceptic clashes with society, it is because he is considering objects in view of 'their tendency and spirit' while society insists upon their intrinsic value. Here, once more, is the opposition between process and result. The sceptic picks up and lays down the dogmatisms of men according to what their tendency is and to whether they forward or obstruct his progress toward the highest truth he can conceive.

In the essay on 'Self-Reliance' there is a striking illustration of how this principle operates.

> In your metaphysics you have denied personality to the Deity, yet when the devout motions of the soul come, yield to them heart and life, though they should clothe God with shape and color. Leave your theory, as Joseph his coat in the hand of the harlot, and flee.[25]

Here is another point at which mysticism and scepticism lie very close to each other. Both require a flexibility which veers to receive the truth from whatever direction it blows. Emerson's upholding of paradox is a kind of objectification of this experience. As in the case of 'a foolish consistency,' this will look to the world like a perverse and irresponsible shifting of position. But to the sceptic, with his eye on the farthest horizon, or even on the unapproachable stars, all this is merely necessary tacking. What does it matter if he angles now to port and now to starboard so long as his goal, though perhaps unseen, is fixed?

> Let a man learn to look for the permanent in the mutable and fleeting; let him learn to bear the disappearance of things he was wont to reverence without losing his reverence; let him learn that he is here, not to work, but to be worked upon; and that, though abyss open under abyss and opinion displace opinion, all are at last contained in the Eternal Cause:
> 'If my bark sink, 'tis to another sea.'[26]

Among the Cambridge Platonists of the seventeenth century we shall find the same coupling of certainty with flexibility. This is the source of a kind of recklessness characteristic of sceptics, whose confidence in the existence and power of truth matches their conviction that they have not yet apprehended it. Witness Richard Baxter's faith that 'nothing is so *certainly* known as God and yet nothing so imperfectly.'[27]

Yet in their moments of insight the mystics have stood firm in support of their own vision.

There is one other phase of so-called skepticism which demands at least a reference. . . . It is what we shall call the skepticism of faith: the skepticism of those spiritual natures to whom the invisible world is so real and so near that the traditional interpreters of it are an intrusion and an obstacle. Such a skeptic was James Martineau in the nineteenth century, Martin Luther in the sixteenth, Savonarola in the twelfth, Paul in the first. . . . They refused to accept the dogmas in which the faith of the world had been enshrined because their own faith had outgrown these dogmas. . . . Living with God face to face, they have cared little for the pictures which other men have taken of him. Such is the skepticism of the mystic. . . . It is a skepticism born of a faith sometimes too audacious to be a safe guide to others, sometimes too egotistic to be a safe guide to him who possesses it.[28]

This is the kind of scepticism which we have seen Emerson calling for, the scepticism which undergirds his remarkable self-reliance.

The Scepticism of Santayana

The most colourful of modern philosophical sceptics and the one whose scepticism is most distinctive is George Santayana. By the very force of his style he verges on literary scepticism; yet there is one factor which cuts him off from the creative scepticism which flourished in seventeenth-century England, and that is the narrowness and literalness with which he interprets scepticism and consequently his complete philosophical detachment. Far from employing the sceptic method to reach the truth about this world, Santayana makes of it a kind of insurance against involvement. He feels that the richest philosophies are the most sceptical, for therein 'the mind is not . . . tethered in its home paddock, but ranges at will over the wilderness of being.'[29] This richness, far from representing a cross-section of the world's meaning, is rather a patina or a thin inlay which has no functional relationship to what is real.

The sceptic, then, as a consequence of carrying his scepticism to the greatest lengths, finds himself in the presence of more luminous and less equivocal objects than does the working and believing mind; only these objects are without meaning, they are only what they are obviously, all surface. . . . Scepticism therefore suspends all knowledge worthy of the name, all that transitive and presumptive knowledge of facts which is a form of belief; and instead it bestows intuition of ideas, contemplative, aesthetic, dialectical, arbitrary.[30]

Although in the light of the complex entity which scepticism became in the seventeenth century Santayana seems to be merely making things easier for himself by restricting his field of operation, he does touch upon a fundamental aspect of scepticism applicable also in the seventeenth century, the difficulty of maintaining an equipoise.

Scepticism is not concerned to abolish ideas; it can relish the variety and order of a pictured world, or of any number of them in succession, without any of the qualms and exclusions proper to dogmatism. Its case is simply not to credit these ideas, not to posit any of these fancied worlds, nor this ghostly mind imagined as viewing them. The attitude of the sceptic is not inconsistent; it is merely difficult, because it is hard for the greedy intellect to keep its cake without eating it.[31]

In this rarified atmosphere, however, there is little except the paradoxical nature of the process to suggest the rugged and agonizing attempts of seventeenth-century sceptics to make the separate worlds of their consciousness cohere if not coincide. In this respect they essayed a task which Santayana long ago abandoned as impossible. They tried to work out the implications of scepticism for their life considered as a whole, whereas he restricts it to one specific function in the intellectual process of truth-seeking. But the piquancy of his style is irresistible.

Scepticism is an exercise, not a life; it is a discipline fit to purify the mind of prejudice and render it all the more apt, when the time comes, to believe and to act wisely; and meantime the pure sceptic need take no offence at the multiplicity of images that crowd upon him if he is scrupulous not to trust them and to assert nothing at their prompting. Scepticism is the chastity of the intellect, and it is shameful to surrender it too soon or to the first comer: there is nobility in preserving it coolly and proudly through a long youth, until at last, in the ripeness of instinct and discretion, it can be safely exchanged for fidelity and happiness.[32]

What this figure does not make clear is that there has to be a perennial relinquishing of intellectual chastity and a perennial renewal of it. Unlike the analogous physical sequence, these two phases must alternate endlessly if there is to be a movement toward truths which are untainted by dogmatism.

Scepticism and Truth

It is a frequent practice among writers on scepticism to use the two terms, 'scepticism' and 'truth,' in juxtaposition. Mitchell says that 'truth, like character, must be fought for. Skepticism is the wrestling for truth. . . . Skepticism is the assertion of man's individual freedom in the search for truth.'[33] C. B. Wheeler, writing in the *Westminster Review*, plays up the search for truth as the dominant factor determining the quality of a man's scepticism. He chides the faint-heartedness of those religionists who would set up their own idols before the temple of truth.

> How many of the people who are termed religious are ready to subscribe to the Rajah's maxim: 'There is no religion higher than truth'?[34]

There are two important elements of scepticism, both related to the search for truth, which are touched upon in another of Mitchell's definitions—the sceptic awareness of dualisms and the emphasis upon the active and the ethical.

> The skeptic is one who stops bewildered at what we may call a split in truth, and that split, that gulf, comes in the divorce which we too often make between religion and morality. . . . It [the mind] longs for religious peace and comfort, but is not willing to obtain these at the sacrifice of its own moral ideals. It gives up religion as a

system in order that it may hold fast to morality as a *life*, and in that very act it gains for itself consistency and strength. . . . The ethical impulse of skepticism, therefore, its moral quality, is its redeeming force, the very power by which the skeptic himself returns to religion.[35]

Not all sceptics will agree concerning the name of this split in truth, but no sceptic whom we have yet encountered is insensitive to its presence. Indeed this very quality at once reinforces the sceptic's nescience and is incorporated, in the form of paradox, into his ultimate conception of truth.

In reaction against narrow dogmatisms, the sceptic strives for a complete absence of discrimination among the various ways of knowing. This, he feels, is the only way he can be sure of not missing an important element of truth.

> Tous nos moyens de connaître ont leur valeur, la raison théorique et la raison pratique, le libre examen et la tradition. Nous repoussons toutes les doctrines exclusives, tout ce qui appauvrit l'esprit humain, tout ce qui diminue notre foi et notre amour. Rien ne nous parait plus funeste que cette étroitesse d'esprit qui supprime sans façon tout un ordre de faits et d'idées.[36]

By the very nature of this method one cannot yet have traced the outlines of the kind of truth which will ultimately be achieved; but the sceptic has a far better chance than the dogmatist of coming upon this truth and of recognizing it when he sees it. This open-mindedness of scepticism does not imply any incapacity for conviction, but only a persistence beyond the point at which most thinkers settle back into conclusions. Something of the perennial challenge and the compelling attraction of a truth which is undelineated and yet unquestioned is expressed by Paul Elmer More as he picks up and makes legitimate use of a phrase from Sir Thomas Browne, 'And thus I teach my haggard and unreclaimed reason to stoop unto the lure of faith.'

> Adventure is not the search for something new, or the ambition to create that which does not already exist. In the past, whether it be the voyage of discovery over the estranging seas or the risk of

physical comfort for a peace of spirit, always, if it ends in success, it has been the searching for something, unknown indeed, set there, a truth awaiting the courageous explorer, and so the lure of faith is the hope that by venturing forth a man shall come at last to a reality that is beckoning out of the unknown and to a waiting land of the spirit.[37]

Such are the heights to which scepticism, in the sense in which we are trying to define it, can lead. That anyone should fear the effect of this kind of scepticism upon the truths of religion argues an arbitrary delimiting of those truths to correspond to the stature of man's mind. Owen rightly insists that only by means of the sceptical method can religion achieve its full power.

It [the skeptical method] demands that freedom of outlook and speculative research which is the inalienable prerogative of Thought, and which is both allied with and presupposes that entire absence of bias or preconception implied by Suspense. This, in the true analysis of religious and spiritual insight, is but another way of saying that so far from destroying, Skeptical thought gives new birth and energy to the religious faculty. . . . On the other hand it destroys the germs of that conceit, narrowness, surcharged individuality and Dogmatic exclusiveness, which of all evils incident to Religion, is undoubtedly the greatest.[38]

It may have been noted that thus far in this discussion the word 'truth' has been used rather generally and with no attempt at a definition. Although it would be presumptuous to propose here a brief and casual answer to Pilate's question, our general position must be clarified. When we say that seventeenth-century scepticism affords an important insight into the nature of truth, we mean by truth the end term of a process of free inquiry, the limit toward which all investigation pursued in the spirit of those equally profound words of Socrates and of Jesus is heading.[39] There is an illuminating passage in the Gospel of John, variously interpreted according to each exegete's pet theory, which we may venture to use here because it is a means of pointing up the conception of truth manifest throughout this discussion. Jesus had been questioning the consistency of the Jews' rejection of him since they claimed that their authority derived from Abraham. He felt that since he was preaching what he had received from his Father, God, there could be no conflict with what Abraham, also a man of God, had delivered. But his opponents kept insisting doggedly upon the authority of Abraham and upon their descent from him. Finally Jesus, for whom God and the truth seem to have been interchangeable symbols ('He that sent me is true'), urging them to embrace a larger truth than any they had yet envisioned, said, 'Ye shall know the truth, and the truth shall make you free.'[40] Previously he had admitted his complete subservience to truth, no matter where it might lead him, when he said, 'I do nothing of myself but as my Father hath taught me.' What he was urging upon the Jews was the necessity of breaking away from a narrow, dogmatic conception of the truth in favour of a larger, continually expanding vision; and this is precisely the kind of advice which the sceptics are always giving. The consequent freedom which they achieve is maintained only so long as they are practising sceptics. When, through metaphysical fear or spiritual laziness, they relinquish the sceptic method, they lose at once their freedom and the entrée to truth.

Just as the principle of simplicity employed by scientists states that of competing theories the truest is the one which accounts for most facts in the simplest manner, so we should propose an analogous principle in the field of literary, philosophical, and religious ideas, that he who leaves the fewest facts out of account—contradictory though they be—is the man who is closest to the truth. To try to maintain his grasp upon all those facts which his experience has brought him is the almost superhuman task which the sceptic has set himself. Therefore progress toward the kind of truth we are talking about may be represented not as a two-dimensional plotted curve flowing from left to right, but as a series of concentric spheres, through each of which the individual moves out into a new freedom and a new expansiveness, ever approaching the uncharted empyrean as a limit.

CHAPTER II

AN HISTORICAL DEFINITION OF SCEPTICISM

⚹

HAVING looked at the sceptical experience relatively divorced from time and space, we can now turn to its historical manifestations and have a basis for understanding them as well as for justifying our use of the term *scepticism*. To look closely at the origins of a sceptical philosophy among the Greeks, to touch lightly on its mediaeval manifestations, and to see its rebirth in the Renaissance will provide a kind of historical ballast to prevent the ship of this discussion from keeling over with the weight of airy speculation.

Greek Scepticism

Like most other philosophies, scepticism had its origins in that seed-bed of human thought which the Greeks maintained through four centuries. Alfred Benn has called attention to the fact that scepticism as a philosophical principle was alien to early Greek thought[1] but that as the Greeks became more sophisticated and critical, scepticism was a natural consequence. It took several forms, beginning with the questioning of Greek mythology. From there it moved toward suspicion concerning the reality of sensible appearances. In the field of personal relations the habit of questioning and the growing intellectual doubts led to contemptuous references to opinions held by other philosophers. Perhaps these opinions rested on as uncertain foundations as one's own. All these culminated in 'occasional lamentations over the difficulty of getting at any truth at all.'[2] Benn rightly points out that this latter phase was the one to be emphasized in modern times, whenever scepticism was not merely a passing mood from which men relapsed into dogmatisms.

Pyrrho

The first period of Greek thought which was self-consciously sceptical came to a focus in the teachings of Pyrrho about 300 B.C., although later sceptics often trace the origin of their ideas to Socrates. As is customary with sceptics, Pyrrho's reaction against the dogmatism of his day led him to question the whole process of knowing. The further he investigated, the more convinced he became that man could never achieve truth by means of his natural faculties. Not only are sense impressions unreliable, he felt, but since every statement can be contradicted, it is impossible by reasoning to know the truth about things in themselves.

> Whatever property may be attributed to a thing, with equal justice the opposite may be predicated.[3]

According to Diogenes Laertius,

> he denied that anything was honourable or dishonourable, just or unjust. And so, universally, he held that there is nothing really existent, but custom and convention govern human action; for no single thing is in itself any more this than that.[4]

Isosothenia is the term for this equilibrium of evidence. Here Pyrrho was not imposing an elaborate theory of his own but was pushing to its ultimate conclusion an observation which has been made by every individual who has launched out in search of truth.

> Pyrrho . . . grasped the conscious sense of ignorance inherent in the minds of all men, penetrated to its source, and applied it relentlessly where other men faltered or drew back.[5]

What Pyrrho found on the other side of this epistemological despair is what distinguishes him from others and probably what keeps his philosophy perennially alive and attractive. If each opinion can be balanced by its opposite, the only logical conclusion will be *epoché*, the abstinence from forming an opinion. It is at this point that the sceptic is either left in a painful state of suspended animation or by the addition of a *je ne sais quoi*, passes over into *ataraxia*, the imperturbability which is said to follow suspension of judgment like its shadow.

Some historians of scepticism, notably Brochard, have emphasized the Hindu influence upon Pyrrho, who is known to have gone to India with Alexander's army, in the company of Anaxarchus, who was a follower of Democritus. It has been established that Pyrrho did bring back from this expedition one illustration of the unreliability of sense impressions which was not previously found among the sceptics. They had long recognized the fact that a straight stick will look bent if submerged in water, but it remained for Pyrrho to add the example of a coiled rope which seems at first glance to be a serpent. The Hastings *Encyclopaedia of Religion and Ethics* further develops this Oriental influence until Pyrrho becomes 'a sort of Buddhist arhat, not so much a sceptic as an ascetic or quietist.'[6] Diogenes lends support to this by noting Pyrrho's desire to withdraw from the world and live in solitude after he had heard an Indian reproach Anaxarchus,

> telling him that he would never be able to teach others what is good while he himself danced attendance on kings in their courts.[7]

Although Pyrrho maintained a reputation for withdrawal, it is significant that his followers are always emphasizing the empirical and that although he denied having a *philosophia*, he admitted having an *agōgē*, a manner of life. What this manner of life aimed at is illustrated by the story of Pyrrho's observing during a storm at sea that a pig was eating placidly, unaffected by the chaos about him. So, he felt, should man maintain an unperturbed state in the world.[8]

Diogenes hints at another ingredient of Pyrrho's scepticism when he says, 'According to some authorities the end proposed by the Sceptics is insensibility; according to others, gentleness.'[9] This bears out the ambivalence we have noted, between withdrawal and involvement. But it is of farther-reaching significance that out of *epoché* and *ataraxia* there should emerge a gentleness toward other human beings, who are recognized as equally ignorant of the truth and equally destined to seek it out.

33

Another important element in Pyrrho's scepticism is emphasized by Mary Patrick, who says that his suspension of judgment
for the time being was supplemented by his open mind toward
future discoveries.[10] This we have seen is one of the positive
elements in scepticism which ensures its continual flourishing.
The seventeenth century made striking use of it in the form of
progressive revelation, which holds that all the truth has not yet
been delivered to man. There is a curiously contemporary relevance in Diogenes' list of the kinds of Pyrrhonists:

> Zetetics or seekers because they were ever seeking truth, Sceptics
> or inquirers because they were always looking for a solution and
> never finding one, Ephectics or doubters because of the state of
> mind which followed their inquiry, I mean, suspense of judgment,
> and finally Aporetics or those in perplexity, for not only they but
> even the dogmatic philosophers themselves in their turn were often
> perplexed.[11]

It would perhaps be difficult to hit upon a passage in the history
of philosophy which so comes home to us today as this one, for
are we not all unacknowledged Aporetics—those in perplexity?

The New Academy

Arcesilaus and Carneades, in the New Academy, made an
attempt to perpetuate certain elements of Platonic scepticism,
which by this time was being recognized as their legitimate
ancestor. It was the Plato of the earlier dialogues whom they
took as their master. Cicero, a later member of the same tradition,
says they regarded themselves as followers of Socrates. Paul
Elmer More remarks in this connection that Socrates' equation,
virtue equals knowledge, if taken in one sense, leads to 'a
rationalism or a metaphysic, quite incompatible with scepticism,
while taken in another way (with the emphasis upon action) it
leads to reasonableness and a kind of intuition which consort
easily with scepticism.'[12] More considers that Socrates, because
of his concern with right action, is a rare example of 'the union of
scepticism and spiritual affirmation.'

34

His nescience was not the cry of despair, but of effort, buoyant, continuous, and untiring; we might compare it to the conviction of moral and spiritual imperfection which so many earnest religionists possess, and which not only incites to perfection, but itself increases, *pari passu*, with every successive advance in that direction.[13]

The New Academy made more explicit Pyrrho's intuition of nescience and affirmed that since we can have no real knowledge of objects as they are, all our knowledge is subjective, relative, and therefore probable instead of absolute. Carneades picked up this concept of probability and insisted that it was just as adequate for action as was absolute truth, which could provide no more security for practical ends than could probability. Carneades further worked out a graded system of probability in his search for some ethical criteria. His three grades were: the probable; the probable and undisputed; and the probable, undisputed, and tested.[14] We shall see later an analogous progression worked out by Richard Baxter in the seventeenth century.

Carneades' practical application of his doctrine of probability brought down upon him the wrath of Cato when in about 150 B.C. Carneades went to Rome as an ambassador from Athens. He there made, according to Pliny the Elder, two philosophical orations in which on the one hand he eulogized justice, and on the other he maintained it was merely conventional.[15] Cato saw a practical danger in this kind of scepticism, which was based not on the absolute but on the probable.

Members of the New Academy not only acquiesced in nescience, but they seemed to glory in it. They flaunted before the world their conviction that neither the senses nor the reason can carry man beyond the circle of appearances. They stated dogmatically that things are incomprehensible. Carneades, following in the footsteps of Pyrrho with his ten modes of perplexity,[16] set up a list of antinomies to reinforce this generalization, a list, moreover, which Augustine was to make use of later.

Sextus Empiricus

The third great phase of Greek scepticism was operative just before the Christian era and extended into the first century. Here Sextus Empiricus is the most important name. Both he and Anesidemus thought that the New Academy was too radical and that Carneades and his followers had merely substituted a new dogmatism. for an old one. Sextus Empiricus proposed to take more seriously the key words, *isosothenia*, *epoché* and *ataraxia*. The assertion that nothing could be known must be balanced by its opposite in order to maintain true scepticism.

> He terms it the equilibration or perpetual counterpoising of antagonistic ideas and arguments by means of which a man may arrive at suspense, and afterwards at Ataraxia, or complete mental serenity.[17]

The New Academics had been content with one-half of a dualism, and Sextus proposed to embrace both halves though the process should result in his own *Zerissenheit*. Despair, for example, was denounced because it implied a knowledge that the world is evil, and no sceptic could allow himself the luxury of that 'inverted and sullen dogmatism.'[18] In its psychological twist, this is very like the words of Socrates condemning the dogmatism that death is an evil. Thus Sextus puts a greater emphasis than his predecessors upon paradox and antinomy, employed always in the service of *ataraxia*, that peace of mind which the sceptics shared as an ideal with Stoics and Epicureans and which, he held, could not be achieved as long as dogmas were maintained.

> If the philosophic axioms of the two systems [Epicureanism and Stoicism] contradict one another, it may be thence inferred that the aim of both may be attained independently of any dogmatic view, in short, knowledge may be despaired of in order to pass from a recognition of ignorance to a general indifference to everything and to an unconditional repose of mind. Thus scepticism is connected with stoicism and epicureanism as the third chief form of the philosophy of that age. [19]

By maintaining scepticism as an attitude and not a doctrine, Sextus tried to avoid the pitfalls of both stoics and epicureans and of previous sceptics.

The story which is told of the painter Apelles is significant, especially for its illustration of the growing complexity of scepticism. He was trying to paint a picture of horses who had been racing, and he found after many attempts that he could not paint realistically the foam about their mouths. Finally, in desperation, he threw his sponge at the picture, and there was the foam, exactly as he had tried to represent it.[20]

> Thus the Sceptics were never able to attain to ataraxia by examining the anomaly between the phenomena and the things of thought, but it came to them of its own accord just when they despaired of finding it.[21]

The Knot

This experience is in a way prophetic of all modern scepticism, for it adumbrates that paradoxical quality of truth which we have chosen to symbolize by 'the subtle knot' and which was to act like a spiritual hormone in maintaining the vigour of scepticism. The experience, rare but not abnormal, of finding that a complete despair of truth and a moment of thorough non-attachment to dogmatisms may somehow generate new and enlarged insights —this experience may rightly be called sceptical, as exemplified in the words of Socrates and of Jesus, quoted above. One of the most striking and often perplexing of 'the seven last words' is Jesus' quotation from the twenty-second Psalm, 'Eloi, Eloi, lama sabachthani?' . . . 'My God, my God, why hast thou forsaken me?' The whole experience of the crucifixion seems humanly consistent if this is taken as the sceptic nadir, the point at which new insights may be achieved because the individual has relinquished all of what he previously considered to be the truth. He is here undergoing the mystic's dark night of the soul. Paradox is merely the superficial designation, the intellectual formula for an experience whose complexity is matched only by the complexity of the human being. The practical result of scepticism has always been, as in the case of Pyrrho, a tender regard for characteristically human values. Benn cites as 'the two principal tendencies exhibited by all future scepticism: devotion to humanity issuing in exclusive attention to human interests and great mildness in the treatment of human beings.'[22] Emphasis upon the human being as an inexplicable and yet undeniable conjunction of opposites remains at the heart of scepticism, and it is for this reason that the symbol of the knot is appropriate.

> As our blood labours to beget
> Spirits, as like soules as it can,
> Because such fingers need to knit
> That subtile knot, which makes us man:
> So must pure lovers soules descend
> T'affections, and to faculties,
> Which sense may reach and apprehend,
> Else a great Prince in prison lies.[23]

The background of this passage in technical philosophy will become apparent when we consider the 'animal-spirits' of Descartes.[24] It is sufficient here to note that there is implied a species of anti-intellectualism. What 'makes us man' is not the pure, untainted spirit, since until spirit is incarnated, until 'the Word (becomes) flesh and (dwells) among us,' 'a great Prince in prison lies.' Hence a continuing intellectual humility is provided for as a result of contemplating the mystery of man's duality in oneness.

The Middle Ages

Every layman knows that the Middle Ages was not a period notable for the presence of scepticism in any organized form. But as Stoicism and Epicureanism went underground during these centuries, to emerge vigorously during the Renaissance, so it was with scepticism. All we can do here, short of writing a history of scepticism, is to indicate its outcroppings and to show that they bear a direct relation to the scepticism of the Greeks, even though the precise connection is often irretrievably lost. This will make easier the discerning of scepticism in the thought of seventeenth-century England, where again religion was in the saddle.

In tracing sceptical elements in Christian thought during the first and second centuries, Eugene de Faye states in *The Hibbert Journal* that because of the influence of scepticism, with its corrosive criticism, thinkers became so uncertain of reason that they tended to seek out authorities for every statement they made. Some of the schools invoked Socrates, and Philo the Jew went back to the Pentateuch. No one dared to think for himself because scepticism had made men timorous. One result of this negative criticism was the promotion of a kind of religious mysticism. Since reason was despaired of, men sought a supernatural substitute. This phenomenon of 'despair mysticism' lurks in the shadows wherever scepticism is practised, but always in the guise of a camp-follower. In modern times the Roman Church has condemned it as fideism. Faye shows how through Clement of Alexandria and Origen, two outstanding representatives of second-century Christian thought, Greek scepticism combined with the Hebraic tradition. Both men show a preference for moral problems over metaphysical conundrums, a condition which we have seen to characterize the later Greek sceptics.

Augustine

The scepticism of Augustine is continually being referred to by historians of thought, but apparently no one has yet ferreted out either its sources or its implications. Owen says that the scepticism of Sextus Empiricus had much the same effect upon Augustine as the essays of Montaigne had upon Pascal. The result in both cases was 'a kind of mystic Dogmatism attained . . . by passing through a course of philosophical Free-thought.'[25] Patrick says that the scepticism of Augustine was an impetus to sceptical thought during the Italian Renaissance.[26] Perhaps the most light is thrown on his contribution by Lovejoy, who says:

> The significance of the decision—concretely manifested in the rejection of the temper and doctrines of the Gnostics by Plotinus and, more dramatically, in Augustine's conversion from Manichaeism—in favor of a fruitful inconsistency, was not to become

39

clearly apparent until modern times, nor, indeed, in its entirety, until the eighteenth century.[27]

'A fruitful inconsistency' will be seen to correspond on its paradoxical side with 'the subtle knot.' If Augustine, as Lovejoy suggests, relinquished a thin, logical consistency for a rich and productive incomprehension, he was following the kind of sceptical pattern which begins to emerge from our previous discussion. His avowed influence on later sceptics supports this.

Arnobius

Arnobius in the fourth century has been singled out as a 'Christian sceptic.'[28] What he did in *Adversos Nationes* was, like Pascal, to try to rear a system of faith on his pessimism about human nature and his scepticism about the possibility of knowledge. Margaret Leigh says that Augustine may have been the intermediary between the Greek sceptics and Arnobius, who stresses the impotence and corruption of man and the feebleness of his intellect.

> 'What,' he asks [ii. 7], 'are we able to know by our own power, even if all ages were given up to research?'[29]

This is the genuine mark of the sceptic, but like his predecessors Arnobius is jolted out of his extreme and withdrawn scepticism by the necessity for action, and he decides that it is better to adopt a hypothesis which leads to hope than one which leads to despair. Since Christianity makes morality worth while, again like Pascal in his wager, he is willing to admit his ignorance and substitute faith for reason. There are as many ways, legitimate and illegitimate, of making this substitution as there are sceptics, and some day the analysis of these methods will show striking results. In yet another aspect of his scepticism Arnobius reveals his antecedents: 'There is nothing left to us but to act on probabilities.'[30] Carneades had his mediaeval avatar.

Abelard

One of the best known of mediaeval sceptics and one who caused the Church much embarrassment was Abelard. The very title of his book, *Sic et Non,* would put him in the sceptic camp, even if we knew nothing else about him. He carried on the tradition of the complex and paradoxical nature of truth, and went so far as to assert that ultimate truth is unattainable and that opinion and probability are therefore the most reliable guides. Like many sceptics, aware of the pre-eminence of human values, he is assembling the stones for an irenic.

> There would soon, he wisely observes, be an end of controversies if men would agree to recognize the inevitable nature of such divergences, and if we were able to defend the use of the same words with different implications.[31]

This is the kind of function which we shall see Richard Baxter and Jeremy Taylor performing for their generations. Perhaps it bears out Benn's contention that scepticism issues in a devotion to humanity and a mildness in treating men.

Michael Roberts points to the danger inherent in Abelard's activity, and makes it clear why the structure of scholastic thought was raised in no small part as a bulwark against the unsettling activity of such thinkers.

> In his famous treatise, *Sic et Non,* Abelard cites the passages from the Scriptures and the Fathers for and against important topics, 'in order to train the mind to vigorous and healthy doubt.' It is not surprising that Christian philosophers thought his work more likely to undermine the Faith than to reinforce it, and sought to discredit not only the doctrines of Roscellinus, but also every attempt to treat the problems of words and their meanings with philosophic wariness. Things, men, God, stones, and persons of the Trinity were real, and that was that.[32]

Allying Abelard with an outstanding thinker before and after his day, Farrar points up his real function in the history of thought.

> Abelard's *Sic et Non* recalls Zeno's *Paradoxes* and Kant's *Antinomies.* . . . Abelard's doubt is really the inquiry which is the first step to faith; the criticism which precedes the constructive process, negation before affirmation.[33]

Dualism

Between the negation and the affirmation lies the realm in which dualisms are elaborated; and these, as might be expected, point back to the Greeks and ahead to the moderns. Historians of ideas have noted the confluence in the Middle Ages of Platonistic and Jewish streams of thought.

> The influence of the *Timaeus* and of the Neoplatonic dialectic, mediated chiefly through the Pseudo-Dionysius, combined with the authority of Genesis to constrain the medieval theologian to affirm a real generation of a real universe of particular existents and to identify deity with self-expansive and creative energy.[34]

Lovejoy traces to this phenomenon most of the intellectual and spiritual tensions of mediaevalism. The Absolute and Immutable was for ever partaking of the particular and the changing. Thus the Platonic dialectic perpetuated itself and exerted over succeeding generations of thinkers a more pervasive power than among its Greek contemporaries. Augustine is usually pointed to as the mediaeval thinker who brought this dualism to a focus,[35] and thereby maintained a tradition which Descartes found ready to his hand. Meanwhile, in Thomas Aquinas there had been an attempt to sort out and distinguish a concept such as that of matter and form from the antithesis of matter and spirit. By the time of Descartes, form and spirit tended to become one, and man took his place midway between matter on the one hand and heavenly beings on the other. The character of 'the subtle knot' had been established.

Some mediaeval sceptics put the chief emphasis, along with their Greek forebears, on the empirical and the ethical rather than on the epistemological. Indeed, this is often one way of breaking an intellectual impasse.

> A tendency had already shown itself, in certain mediaeval mystics, to emphasize a moral rather than a metaphysical approach to 'truth.' From Hugo of St. Victor (d. 1141) we have the saying: *'Tantum de veritate quisque potest videre, quantum ipse est'*; and from Richard of St. Victor (d. 1173): *'In tantum Deus cognoscitur in*

quantum amatur.' The attitude here implied is an obvious corrective to excessive intellectualism in any form, and has bearings on issues wider than those of scriptural interpretation.[36]

To this exhibit should be added the characteristic pronouncement of William of Occam, who would give *carte blanche* to all seekers.

> With a similarly clear sense of justice and humanity, he pronounces all truth-seekers to be *ipso facto* exempt from the charge of heresy, considering that their attitude of seeking conflicts with the assumption of their holding any erroneous doctrine.[37]

Nicholas of Cusa

The mediaeval thinker of sceptical tendencies who seems most significant and attractive in view of the later development of scepticism is Nicholas of Cusa. His favourite philosophical contention was

> to vindicate that *docta ignorantia* which consists in knowing that we do not know. Any antinomy which reflection seemed to reveal served his purpose; it was one more welcome instance of the identity of opposites. And it was precisely in order to exemplify the identity of opposites that Cusanus endeavored to show, by whatever arguments came to his hand, that the concepts of 'centre' and 'circumference,' as applied to the universe, have no clear and distinct meaning.[38]

Lovejoy recalls here the difficulty which Abelard encountered in pressing for a definition of terms.

> The notion of the *coincidentia oppositorum*, of the meeting of extremes in the Absolute, was an essential part of nearly all medieval theology, as it had been of Neoplatonism; what Dean Inge has delicately termed 'the fluidity and interpenetration of concepts in the spiritual world,' or in plainer language, the permissibility and even necessity of contradicting oneself when one spoke of God, was a principle commonly enough recognized, though the benefits of it were not usually extended to theological opponents. The slight uneasiness which the application of such a principle left in the mind could be, and by the scholastic theologian usually was,

alleviated by the explanation that the seemingly contradictory terms were used in a *sensus eminentior*—that is to say, that they did not have their usual meanings, nor any other meaning which the human mind could understand.[39]

Nicholas of Cusa, who had been thinking his own way to a reconciliation of opposites, came into inevitable conflict with the temporizing doctrines of the Church. By contrast, his conclusions stand out with the force and beauty of all independent thinking.

It is a universe of contrasts, contradictions, antitheses, anomalies, and there must be some secret of ultimate reconciliation. There must be a region where oppositions blend into each other, where contradictions merge into the larger truth, where all is concordant and consistent, because all coalesces into a final unity. Nicholas identified this Absolute with God, as every religious thinker must. God is absolute Truth, absolute Goodness, absolute Being, and all that is many and diverse in the universe is one and the same in His absolute unity and His absolute identity. The whole doctrine of the coincidence of contraries is, in fact, an elaboration of the essential principle of the *theologia negatavia*. The superexistence of God can only be expressed by negations, because it surpasses all our positive conceptions, and in it all the contradictions of finite existence fall away into ineffable unity.[40]

Like so many of his sceptical brethren, Nicholas of Cusa drives forward toward unity on all fronts, and so provides a solid metaphysical underpinning for an irenic. This bears a close relationship to the syncretism which is often the outcome of the sceptic method.

The whole of his thought, political, philosophical, and theological alike, is marked by a persistent method of intellectual reconciliation and by a passion for unity. He was the advocate of unity in the political system of Europe; he was the apostle of unity amid the ecclesiastical dissensions of Christendom; and he was the philosopher of unity also, who consistently sought to see the beginning and the end of all things, the real existence, as hidden in the super-essential Unity of God.[41]

The Renaissance

If it were necessary at the beginning of our investigation of Renaissance scepticism to justify our sometimes straying from the narrow path of what philosophers call scepticism, we could appeal to a statement of Bredvold, who found himself in a similar situation.

> Many of these developments do not interest the metaphysician who is concerned with skepticism purely as a dialectic; he would reject them as not skeptical at all in the strict philosophical sense. But the historian is not permitted to be so selective in his method. Ideas which in their origins were unrelated may by the accident of history come to be associated, and thus sometimes gain in profundity, sometimes even receive new significance and intention.[42]

We shall continue, therefore, to relate ideas which seem to belong together as parts of an emerging pattern in the hope that the resultant picture will justify the means employed to compose it.

Considered historically, the scepticism of the Renaissance derived principally from the Greeks rather than from mediaeval sceptics, whom we have seen to be off the beaten path. Yet it seems likely to suppose that if scepticism had not somehow been kept alive during the Middle Ages, its legatees in the Renaissance would have been less disposed to an awareness of its value.

Incidental to his discussion of atheism in the English Renaissance, George Buckley shows that Pyrrhonism underwent a healthy Renaissance revival, especially in France, whence it spread to England. In the early part of the period the classical source was Cicero's *Academic Questions*, while later it was Sextus Empiricus and his *Pyrrhonic Sketches*. Evidence consists both of books written in support of Pyrrhonism and of those attempting to refute it.

In 1527 Henry Cornelius Agrippa of Nettesheim published his *De Incertitudine Scientiarum*, which was translated into English in 1568 and which asserted the vanity of all learning.[43] It has been established that Agrippa derived his ideas principally from Nicholas of Cusa.

45

Quod si audendum est verum fatere, tam est scientiarum ominum periculosa inconstansque traditio, ut longe tutius sit ignorare quam scire.[44]

Nihil homini pestilentius contingere potest quiam scientia: haec est vera illa pestis, quae totum ac omne hominum genus ad unum subvertit, quae omnem innocentiam expulit, & nos tot peccatorum generabus mortique fecit obnoxios, quae fidei lumen extinxit, animas nostras in profundas coniiciens tenebras, quae veritatem damnans, errores in altissimo throno collacavit.[45]

Agrippa, like many another sceptic, exhausted by the effort to know, concluded that he had been following an *ignis fatuus*, that his chief purpose was to be and not to know. He could at least exemplify the good which he might never be able to define intellectually.

Vera enim beatitudo non consistit in bonorum cognitione, sed in vita bona: non in intelligere, sed in intellectu vivere: neque enim bona intelligentia, sed bona voluntas coniungit homines deo, nec aliud efficiunt disciplinae foris adhibitae, nisi quia conditionem nobis quandam purgatoriam adhibent, ad beatitudinem aliquid conducentem, non tamen rationem ipsam auq nobis beatitudo compleatur, nisi eis adsit & vita, in ipsam bonorum translata naturam.[46]

There are at least two well-defined streams which have their source in the writings of Agrippa. One leads off in the direction of paradox. Bredvold says of Agrippa's work,

Its importance lies chiefly in that it was regarded by its later readers as an addition to the literature of *paradox*, a literary *genre* which frequently became a vehicle for skeptical thought and added to the spicy flavor of the modern skeptics from Montaigne down.[47]

Sixteenth- and seventeenth-century literature in England is full of paradoxes, ranging from the flippant to the profound. These examples from the *Orthodoxe Paradoxes* of Ralph Venning are typical:

He believes that the two extreames of being, matter and spirit be in man, and yet he believes that man is but one being.[48]

He knowes that he can never attaine to the perfection of God; and yet he labours *to be perfect, as God is perfect.*[49]

The other stream of influence from Agrippa connects him with such English authors as Fulke Greville, whose *Treatise of Humane Learning*, stemming from Pyrrho through Sextus Empiricus, arrives at conclusions coincident with those of Agrippa. Both men, believing that the attitude of the Pyrrhonist was justified by original sin, turned the weapons of Pyrrhonism against human learning, which had often proved inimical to Christianity. Both preached a return to the lowly followers of Christ and praised them for renouncing worldly traditions in order to draw their wisdom from an incorruptible source above. Fulke Greville, like the Greek sceptics, advocated the suspension of judgment, but unlike the Academicians, he did not conclude that truth was unknown and unknowable.[50] He emphasized what was to be an important ingredient in seventeenth-century scepticism, that man, precisely because he does not yet know, ought to go on forever seeking.

Pyrrhonism in France

Among the French books listed by Buckley as written to stem the tide of Pyrrhonism are the following:

1538, Sadolet, *Phaedrus*,
1546, Sant-Gelais, *Avertissement sur les jugements d'astrologie*,
1558, Guy de Brues, *Dialogues contre les nouveau academiciens*, and the third book of Rabelais' *Pantagruel*.[51]

Omer Talon in 1548 published his *Academia*, a defence of Pyrrhonism in which he justifies Ramus and condemns Aristotle.[52] This was based on Cicero's *Academic Questions*, and had as its purpose

to deliver opinionated men, enslaved by fixed philosophical beliefs and reduced to a shameful servitude, to make them understand that

47

true philosophy approaches things freely and openly and is not enchained to one opinion or to one author.53

Bacon was another workman in this same anti-Aristotelian tradition, and he too was urged on by sceptical drives.

To Bacon the logic-spinning of the schoolmen was a kind of forbidden knowledge; it was a presumptuous attempt to read the secret purposes of God, and to force his works into conformity with the laws of the human mind. This was for him the real *hubris*, this metaphysical arrogance, which 'disdains to dwell upon particulars,' and confidently explains all things by syllogism. The true humility is the attribute of the Baconian scientist, who is content to come forth into the light of things, and let nature be his teacher. 'Nor could we hope to succeed, if we arrogantly searched for the sciences in the narrow cells of the human understanding, and not submissively in the wider world.' Access to the kingdom of man, which is founded on the sciences, resembles 'that to the kingdom of heaven, where no admission is conceded except to children.'54

In 1562 Henri Etienne published his Latin translation of the *Pyrrhonic Sketches* of Sextus Empiricus. This is said to be 'one of the finest summaries not only of Pyrrhonism but of skeptical thought in general that the century affords,'55 and was probably used by Montaigne in his 'Apology for Raymond Sebond.' Thinkers of the Renaissance had a natural affinity for Pyrrhonism because its conclusions were the inevitable result of the new learning which was being thrown open to them.

It was the revelation of this infinite variety of men and beliefs that shocked the more active minds of Europe out of their complacency and rendered them critical of their own creeds and even of their own mental habits. To this state of mind Pyrrhonism easily adjusted itself, for it was a philosophy that built on the variety that had so impressed the men of the Renaissance and concluded from it that the truth is still unknown.56

Hence the additional emphasis which the Renaissance put upon seeking, in a world where so much had already been uncovered.

Yet the Renaissance would not have been true to its own scepticism if it had not produced, as the result of its seeking, a corrective to unbridled intellectual enthusiasm.

The false modern emphasis on the bold confidence and rebellious energy of the Renaissance has ignored the great mass of writing which perpetuated Hebraic, classical, and medieval pessimism, and the religious or naturalistic pessimism inherent in life itself was reinforced by this belief in a dying world and by the paralysing effects of science and of sceptical and conflicting philosophies. It is of course the emotional and imaginative realization of these ideas which awakens the greatest strains in Renaissance literature. From Sackville to Spenser, from Shakespeare, Raleigh, and Donne to Browne and Shirley, men are haunted by the spectres of devouring time and change, the brevity, misery, and vanity of life, the littleness of man in the cosmic panorama. Even Alexander, in his vast and unreadable *Dooms-day*, can achieve one great line, 'To scorne Corruption, and to mocke the Dust.'[57]

Deism

When the Renaissance man looked up from his books, which had presented him with the heterogeneous beliefs and opinions of other men, living and dead, he was ripe not only for Pyrrhonism but for deism, whose influence, according to Buckley, reached him via Stoicism.

The classics might make him a better moralist or a keener philosopher, and some of them might seem superficially to be bolstering up his Christianity, but the event was to show that good moralists and keen philosophers were not always good Christians, and that Christianity supported by pagan thought developed a disconcerting tendency to be neither paganism nor Christianity, but a new thing that was known in course of time as natural religion or 'deism.'[58]

Pyrrhonism had encouraged not only a doubt of religious revelation but a comparison of all religions.

From this came inevitably the observation that all creeds have many points in common and, in time, the attempt to rediscover and reconstruct the original belief from which the separate religions were

supposed to have varied. And from this observation and this attempt
I think it not too much to say were derived in a straight line the
lofty, detached skepticism of Montaigne and the deism of Lord
Herbert.[59]

This observation is reinforced by Douglas Bush, who shows that
the obverse side of the deism and scepticism of the age was its
Christian humanism.

> The working philosophy inherited by those authors was the
> Christian humanism which during the Middle Ages and the Renais-
> sance had fused Christian faith and pagan reason into a stable frame-
> work of religious, ethical, political, economic, and cultural thought.
> That tradition, the main European tradition, comes from Plato and
> Cicero down through Erasmus and others to such men as Spenser,
> Hooker, Daniel, Chapman, and Jonson—and, though less obvi-
> ously, Shakespeare. Its central religious and philosophic doctrine is
> order, order in the individual soul, in society, and in the cosmos.
> To mention two large elements of that doctrine which we meet
> everywhere in the seventeenth century, one is the concept of 'right
> reason,' the eternal and harmonious law of God and nature written
> in every human mind and heart; the other is that of the great chain
> of being, the hierarchical order which descends from God through
> angels and men to plants and stones, which at once distinguishes
> and unites all levels of existence.[60]

What we shall find most interesting in the seventeenth century
is the disruptive forces rather than those which made for a calm
and ordered world-picture; therefore we shall put less emphasis
upon right reason and the chain of being (elements which were
to have their full flowering in the eighteenth century) than upon
nescience and dualism and paradox—forces which if they do not
explain, go far to account for the vigorous intellectual and spiritual
life of the century.

Bush sees Shakespeare presaging, by his very lack of confidence
in man's goodness and greatness, the spiritual turmoil of the
century in which he died.

> Shakespeare and the rest know, as Pico had said, that man may
> sink to the brute or rise to the divine. With a simultaneous double

vision they see man as both a god and a beast. That double vision
is, to be sure, the mark of the greatest writers of all ages, especially
the ancients; but the Christian religion intensified the paradox by
exalting man's sense of his divinity and deepening his sense of
bestiality.[61]

That such an insight belongs to the main stream of scepticism
needs no other proof than Pascal's assertion that man is in danger
whenever he forgets either his greatness or his insignificance.

Italian Scepticism

The fact that scepticism was also in the air in Italy during the
Renaissance is important not so much for its direct bearing upon
seventeenth-century scepticism in England as for its helping to
determine the locus of a climate of opinion. We shall see reflections of the positions taken by these Italians when we come to
scrutinize sceptics of the seventeenth century. Evidences of
'influence' are not necessary, for the experience of one sceptic
illuminates the experience of all the rest. It is clear from the
spiritual antecedents of Pico della Mirandola that he exemplifies
the kind of scepticism which we have been trying to define.

He divided all philosophers into three groups: the dogmatists,
who affirm; the academics, who deny and therefore are but negative
or inverted dogmatists; and the skeptics or Pyrrhonians, who
neither affirm nor deny, but doubt. He declared himself an adherent
of the last sect, and borrowed his whole method of argument from
Sextus Empiricus, whose work he had met with in manuscript.[62]

As we turn from this solid generalization to the method of
another Italian, the psychology of the genuine sceptic comes
home to us. Of Guicciardini, Owen says,

His method in politics and history thus resembled the equi-
poising of divergent views which distinguished the theology of
Thomas Aquinas, Abelard, and Peter Lombard. Nor did he adopt
these Pro and Con exercises merely as a kind of youthful gymnastic,
as some writers have thought; but because the twofold method
formed an integral portion and manifestation of his cautious, far-

seeing, comprehensive intellect. To such an extent did he carry this method of investigation into human affairs that, as he himself confesses, when he had decided upon and adopted a given opinion or line of conduct, though with the utmost determination—for in practical matters he was anything but an irresolute man—he experienced afterwards a half-consciousness of repentance as the rejected alternations continued to present themselves to his reflective and ever busy intellect.[63]

Dualism, which may often appear cold and intellectual, is in fact only the inadequate label for this kind of experience, which must have been common to thousands of men who have never heard of scepticism.

It is interesting to note that although Pomponazzi and Petrarch split over the doctrines of Averroes and his double truth, each moved in the direction of an important area of scepticism.

The self-same argument on which Pomponazzi founded his doubt of immortality, is the basis of his belief in the powerlessness of the reason to attain or comprehend truth. 'The human intellect,' he says, 'cannot comprehend abstract things, being as it is of a dual nature, and placed between brutish and abstract intelligences; it can only perceive by means of the senses, and for that reason cannot apprehend itself. Hence it is unable to obtain a knowledge of the universal as it exists in itself and simply; and can only do so by means of the particular.'[64]

This shows at once an awareness of 'the subtle knot' and a proclivity for empiricism. Petrarch's scepticism allies him with men who used it as a support for their religion but used it seriously and responsibly and not like the fideists.

Averroism represented to him a blind, pedantic, self-conceited philosophy, to which he opposes Christianity as a system based on humility and conscious ignorance, and as a cultus which placed ethical practice above speculation. On this point Petrarca shares largely the same skeptical aspect of the Christian faith which impressed itself on other Christian skeptics, such as Huet, Le Vayer, and Pascal—I mean its insistence on humility and self-distrust, and its opposition to intellectual and spiritual pride.[65]

Petrarch's conviction of his own ignorance acted as a spur and not as a soporific. It is this which impels men toward faith in a progressive revelation.

We must not, however, attribute to Petrarca a preference for doubt, or suspense, considered as an end in itself, except when the principle of activity or energy is left in it, and it becomes, as in the case of Sokrates and others, a stimulus to inquiry. In other cases he regards it not from an absolute but from a relative point of view. Ignorance was his armour against the omniscience of scholasticism and the dogmatism of the Church, just as it was that of Sokrates from the sciolists and obscurantists of Athens. 'In many things,' says Petrarca, speaking of the vaunted wisdom of the schools, 'ignorance is the highest knowledge—the commencement of all science.'[66]

Is it perhaps a kind of semantic despair which perennially drives sceptics from the search for knowledge into the arms of action?

Giordano Bruno is a key figure among Italian sceptics of the Renaissance because he combined several important phases of scepticism. Influenced, like his contemporary Campanella, by the doctrines of Nicholas of Cusa, he displayed the kind of ardour for truth-seeking which is in the best sceptic tradition.

'Per amor de la vera sapienza, e studio de la vera contemplatione m'affatico, mi cruccio, e mi tormento.'[67]

There are echoes of both Bacon and Descartes (if an echo can be said to precede the sound which causes it) in Bruno's prescription for the philosopher.

He who wishes to philosophize, says Bruno, must begin by doubting of all things. Nay, he must continue in this path, for destruction must go hand in hand with construction, analysis with synthesis; at least until reason, the free light from heaven, sees her path clear and open before her.[68]

As a footnote to this statement we must include the wry comment of Lovejoy:

The intrinsically contradictory nature of the general medieval conception of God, which is present but judiciously obscured and minimized in a writer like Thomas Aquinas, is by Bruno ostentatiously paraded; for him, in one very characteristic mood, the greater the paradox, the better the doctrine.[69]

The reason sceptics are given to this kind of seeming perversity is that they have caught sight of the knot at the centre of truth and that in the exhilaration of this insight, they are in danger of idolizing the knot as truth itself. The example of Bruno reminds Owen that there are two equally effective ways of destroying dogma.

He is therefore an illustration of the truth that breadth of culture, eclecticism and toleration will subserve the same purpose as negation in undermining any narrow system of dogma. Indeed of the two it is the more effective and lasting method: the true opposite to dogma being not negation, which may be just as dogmatic as assertion, but latitudinarianism, freedom of research, and full toleration for all sincere and rationally attained conclusions.[70]

This suggests the functional relationship between scepticism and toleration, with all the implications which follow in the wake of such an insight.

Erasmus and Galileo

We should like to set here, out of the dust of critical controversy, the pronouncements of two men not usually linked together, Erasmus and Galileo, pronouncements which show the variety and profundity of Renaissance nescience. Both attitudes are central to the sceptic position; the difference between them is one of temperament. Erasmus, asserting that what men have in common is more important than the points on which they differ, is willing to hold his judgment in suspension 'against that day.'

We have defined so much that without danger to our salvation might have remained unknown or undecided. . . . The essentials of our religion are peace and unanimity. These can hardly exist unless

54

we make definitions about as few points as possible and leave many questions to individual judgment. Numerous problems are now postponed until the oecumenical council. It would be much better to put off such questions till the time when the glass shall be removed and the darkness cleared away, and we shall see God face to face.[71]

The same ability to operate effectively in this world without having settled ultimate questions is evidenced by Galileo, though he does not appeal to the same far-off experience as Erasmus does.

> Galileo admitted that he knew nothing about the ultimate nature of the forces he was measuring; nothing about the cause of gravitation, or the origin of the Universe; he deemed it better, rather than to speculate on such high matters, 'to pronounce thatwise, ingenious and modest sentence, "I know it not".'[72]

Raleigh and Montaigne

A consideration of two other important Renaissance sceptics and the use they made of their openly recognized heritage from the Greeks will help to set the sceptical pattern so that we can apply it in the seventeenth century. Raleigh in England and Montaigne in France were both intrigued by Greek scepticism and saw it as a corrective for dogmatic tendencies in their own day. Raleigh in *The Sceptick* gave currency in England to the first three books of Sextus Empiricus' *Hypotyposes*, covering a discussion of the unreliability of sense impressions. The upshot of this was the usual sceptic conclusion, 'I may then report, how these things appear, but whether they are so indeed, I know not.'[73] There are comparable passages, developed at much greater length, in Montaigne's 'Apologie of Raymond Sebond.' The Renaissance played with this idea like a child with a new toy; and as if acquired characters could be inherited, men of the following century found scepticism in their blood-stream. The fathers had eaten sour grapes, and the children's teeth were set on edge. That Raleigh understood the essence of Pyrrhonism is evidenced by his definition of the sceptic.

The Sceptick doth neither affirm, neither denie any Position: but doubteth of it, and opposeth his Reasons against that which is affirmed or denied, to justifie his not Consenting.[74]

Montaigne goes beyond this bare definition to stress the ethical implications of scepticism and its culmination in ataraxy.

The profession of the Pyrrhonians is ever to waver, to doubt and to enquire; never to be assured of any thing, nor to take any warrant of himself [sic]. . . . Now this situation of their judgement, straight and inflexible, receiving all objects with application or consent, leads them unto their Ataraxia; which is the condition of a quiet and settled life, exempted from the agitations which we receive by the impression of the opinion and knowledge we imagine to have of things; whence proceed, feare, avarice, envie, immoderate desires, ambition, pride, superstition, love of novelties, rebellion, disobedience, obstinacie, and the greatest number of corporall evils: yea by that meane they are exempted from the jealousie of their owne discipline, for they contend but faintly: They feare nor revenge, nor contradiction in the disputations.[75]

Whoever shall imagine a perpetuall confession of ignorance, and a judgement upright and without staggering, to what occasion soever may chance; That man conceives the true Phyrrhonisme. . . . A mind warranted from prejudice, hath a marvellous preferment to tranquility.[76]

Both Raleigh and Montaigne are deeply convinced of man's essential ignorance. In a passage in his *History of the World* Raleigh shows his contempt for the intellectual arrogance of man.

But Man, to cover his ignorance in the least things, . . . cannot give a true reason for the Grass under his Feet, why it should be green rather than red, or of any other colour; . . . could never yet discover the way and reason of Natures working, in those which are far less noble Creatures than himself.[77]

According to Montaigne, man's search for wisdom throughout the ages has taught him only to know his own ignorance and weakness.

That ignorance which in us was naturall, we have with long study confirmed and averred. It hath happened unto those that are truly learned, as it hapneth unto eares of Corne, which as long as they are empty, grow and raise their head aloft, upright and stout; but if they once become full and bigge, with ripe Corne, they begin to humble and droope downeward. So men having tried, and sounded all, and in all this Chaos, and huge heape of learning and provision of so infinite different things, and found nothing that is substantiall firme and steadie, but all vanitie, have renounced their presumption and too late knowen their naturall condition.[78]

What complements the nescience of both men is their confidence that such an attitude will have an ultimate and eternal justification. For Raleigh this justification takes the form of the overarching wisdom of God, to which Erasmus appealed from the uncertainties of men.

Certainly, as all the Rivers in the World, though they have divers risings, and divers runnings, though they sometimes hide themselves for a while under Ground, and seem to be lost in Sea-like Lakes; do at last find, and fall into the great *Ocean*: so after all the searches that Humane capacity hath; and after all Philosophical contemplation and curiosity; in the necessity of this Infinite Power, all the Reason of Man ends and dissolves it self.[79]

For Montaigne, man's ignorance is the spur which goads him into seeking, a seeking whose very drive implies that this is not mere circular action. After lumping the Peripatetics, Epicureans, and Stoics together as dogmatists because they believed they had found the truth and after condemning Carneades and the Academics for their despair of truth, which ends in weakness, Montaigne settles upon Pyrrho and the Epechists as the worthiest of philosophers. These say

that they are still seeking after truth. These judge that those are infinitely deceived, who imagine they have found it, and that the second degree is over boldly vaine in affirming that mans power is altogether unable to attaine unto it. For to establish the measure of our strength, to know and distinguish of the difficulty of things is a great, a notable and extreme science, which they doubt whether man be capable thereof or no. . . . That ignorance, which knoweth, judgeth and condemneth it selfe, is not an absolute ignorance.[80]

Statements like this are touched with the breath of paradox which pervades all scepticism. Practically, paradox is often merely *ataraxia* viewed from another angle. Montaigne appropriately sets it down in the form of questions.

Is it not better to remaine in suspence, than to entangle himselfe in so many errours, that humane fantasie hath brought forth? Is it not better for a man to suspend his owne perswasion, than to meddle with these sedicious and quarrellous divisions?[81]

But when a man moves on, as he inevitably must, to make even tentative statements, they come out with a certain twist which is the hallmark of paradox, as in this conclusion of Raleigh's.

Although the Air which compasseth Adversity, be very obscure; yet therein we better discern GOD, than in that shining Light which environeth worldly Glory; through which, for the clearness thereof, there is no Vanity which escapeth our Sight.[82]

Both Raleigh and Montaigne, having been convinced that what men do is oftener closer to the truth than what they say, are extremely critical of Christians, whose performance rarely is in accord with the absolute truth which they profess. Says Montaigne,

If this raie of Divinitie did in any sort touch us, it would everie where appeare: Not only our words, but our actions, would beare some shew and lustre of it. Whatsoever should proceed from us, might be seene inlightned with this noble and matchlesse brightnes. We should blush for shame, that in humane sects, there was never any so factious, what difficultie or strangenesse soever his doctrine maintained, but would in some sort conforme his behaviors and square his life unto it: Whereas so divine and heavenly an institution never markes Christians but by the tongue. And will you see whether it be so? Compare but our manners unto a Turke or a

Pagan, and we must needs yeeld unto them: Whereas in respect of our religions superioritie, we ought by much, yea by an incomparable distance, out-shine them in excellencie: And well might a man say, *Are they so just, so charitable, and so good? Then must they be Christians.*[83]

The road which leads on to natural religion is being marked out here. Raleigh's words, likewise, are reminiscent of the recurrent sceptic emphasis on a life rather than on a creed.

> We profess that we know GOD; but by works we deny him. For Beatitude doth not consist in the knowledge of Divine things, but in a Divine life: for the Devils know them better than Men. . . . We are all (in effect) become Comedians in Religion; and while we act in gesture and voice, Divine vertues, in all the courses of our lives we renounce our Persons and the Parts we Play. For Charity, Justice, and Truth have but their being *in terms*, like the Philosophers *Materia prima.*[84]

The Sceptic Pattern

It seems reasonable to conclude on the basis of the evidence before us that scepticism follows a broadly marked-out pattern. This includes, in whatever order, a sense of the inadequacy of human knowledge, a consequent sensitivity to dualisms and contradictions, a concern with paradox as expressing the complexity of truth, a belief in the wholesome effect of doubt, and a conviction that where knowledge falters, a right life can supply the only legitimate confidence known to man.

CHAPTER III

SEVENTEENTH-CENTURY SCEPTICISM:
THE KNOT

AT one point in *Tom Jones*, where the action is becoming very complicated, Fielding despairs, as every realistic novelist must, of ever being able to furnish his readers an adequate picture of what is happening. He feels frustrated because he cannot relate a half-dozen incidents at once and finally resigns himself to telling only a part of the story, and telling that part one incident at a time.

The historian of that other foundling, scepticism, often finds himself in the same situation. Before he can discuss the appearance and significance of his subject, he must define it; yet a definition which disregards the appearance and significance will not be understandable. It is thus that we come finally to an analysis of Donne's poem, 'The Extasie,' which can serve as a kind of symbolic presentation of the scepticism of the seventeenth century. It is better, perhaps, boldly to undertake this task now than to keep on skirting it and shying away from it and yet needing its results on which to build. To delay further would be like holding up the painting because the plastering has not yet been done.

In 'The Extasie' Donne tells of the spiritual communion of two lovers who lie all day with joined hands and eyes. Any kindred spirit, understanding the language of the two souls, might have eavesdropped and been the purer for it. The lovers understand by this 'extasie' that their love is more than physical attraction. Their souls, each of which is of mixed origin, have mingled and, like transplanted violets, are strengthened as a result. An abler and less lonely soul is the result of the mixture of their two changeless spirits. But why should they 'forbear' their bodies since disembodied spirits would never have met in the first place? Even the influence of heaven reaches man through the medium of the air, which is physical. As the body strives to generate 'animal spirits' which reach upward toward the soul, so the soul must reach down toward the sensible unless the greater soul of their love is to remain locked in the air and so of no consequence. Let us turn then, says the poet, to our bodies in order that the mystery of love may be put into readable form. If the percipient lover who, before, overheard our silent communion were still looking on, he would see that little change had then taken place. The significant lines for our purposes are these:

> As our blood labours to beget
> Spirits,[1] as like soules as it can,
> Because such fingers need to knit
> That subtile knot, which makes us man:
> So must pure lovers soules descend
> T'affections, and to faculties,
> Which sense may reach and apprehend,
> Else a great Prince in prison lies.

How do these lines relate to the sceptic pattern as enunciated at the end of the last chapter? To be sure, there is little evidence here, and that only by indirection, of the poet's nescience. For that, we must wait until we can see the impact of the new learning upon him. But nescience is the only element of the sceptic pattern which is not explicitly to be found in this poem, and hence the poem is a fitting landmark of scepticism. 'The subtile knot which makes us men' represents not only an intellectual awareness of the fundamental dualism of body and spirit but a more than intellectual perception of the fact that the human entity, which is the prototype of all truth, is not simple and direct but complex and oblique. Hence simple truths about body or spirit cannot give the sense of the knotted whole, for the knot is something other than the two strands which compose it. The sceptic finds himself continually puzzled and humbled and perennially pulled back into the orbit of truth by the recognition of this fact. Hence the paradoxes by which he tries to keep himself and the world from forgetting it.

It is as if, too, this human knot were reproduced at another level by the action which man undertakes. In some ways the lovers lying motionless upon the bank may be possessed of a purely theoretical wisdom which Donne does not so much criticize or scorn as he feels the need of transcending. Only when this wisdom is put to work, when action results, does it become available to the world and so effective, 'else a great Prince in prison lies.' Here is the sceptic's feeling that one must act, in this paradoxical world (on the basis of mere probability, to be sure), if the resources generated by dualism and doubt are to be released from their imprisonment. This action, in itself, is as near as the sceptic will ever come to the knowledge whose lack first set him off on his quest. If he had believed knowledge to be achieved easily, he might never have been driven to creative action, of the kind which now gives him as a by-product whatever wisdom he may expect to attain. Seventeenth-century sceptics, who were usually churchmen, were always pointing to the superior worth of a life in comparison with a creed, and thereby implying the innocence of heresy. They were operating in the spirit of Jesus' words, 'If any man will do his will, he shall know of the doctrine.' Doing was not subject to the abuses of knowing, which was always suspect, both because its instruments were unreliable and because it fostered wrangling and bitterness, signs of the disunion which could not coexist with the oneness of truth. Once the balance turned toward doctrine rather than toward 'doing,' the creativity of scepticism had been eclipsed.

It is not to be argued that Donne was aware of the significance we have found in his poem or that he would have admitted its presence. It is nearer the truth to hold that the poem is an unconscious reflection of the climate of opinion in which its author lived.

Nature of the Seventeenth Century

This climate was strikingly different, in respect to scepticism, from what had prevailed during the earlier Renaissance. Previously men were more aware of their debt to Greek thought and therefore were quite conscious of the roots of their scepticism. By the seventeenth century, however, their eyes were fixed on the immediate creative problems confronting them—in the fields of poetry, preaching, spiritual autobiography, religious controversy, devotional writing, or the philosophy of science—and they paid less attention to where sceptical elements originated. The cultural streams of Hebraism and Hellenism had by this time coalesced so that the writer who showed an aptitude for scepticism could make the most of both worlds without always being aware from which source his scepticism stemmed. While this makes for a richer and more powerful, it also makes for a more obscured and involved kind of scepticism. As Bredvold points out, the historian of ideas in the seventeenth century must be sensitive to the presence of scepticism in no matter what unsuspected places it occurs.

> Skepticism in the seventeenth century cannot be appreciated as a historical force if it is defined narrowly as a philosophical system. It was protean in nature, as much a group of tendencies as a system. It had popular as well as learned traditions, and it appealed to the most heterogeneous authorities, both ancient and modern. . . . Thus the warnings issued by Solomon and St. Paul and the Church Fathers against the vanity of worldly knowledge might lead the pious Christian apologist to a respectful reading of Sextus Empiricus. Various medieval developments, such as Nominalism and mysticism, had already popularized a distrust of reason as an organ of religious knowledge. Among other influences of a disruptive nature may be mentioned the influx of Arabian thought and the attacks on Aristotle and on the syllogism.[2]

Since we have already ravelled out many of these components of scepticism, we should be able to match them in the multi-coloured fabric of the seventeenth century.

Whatever homogeneity obtains in seventeenth-century writing is closely linked to the fact that, after the *libido sciendi* of the Renaissance had run its course, the result was a serious and burning aspiration toward the attainment of truth. What men had grasped in the first enthusiasm of the new learning had now to be scrutinized; and before the stream of thought had begun to freeze into dogmatisms, there came a moment, just as in the life of most truth-seeking individuals, where the disinterested pursuit of truth was the prime concern of thinking men. This phenomenon makes the seventeenth century unlike any other in modern history in its passion for truth—religious, philosophical, and scientific. In what other century could Herbert of Cherbury, a very layman in philosophy, have published his *De Veritate* without having been accused of presumption or blasphemy? That an analysis of this sort did not appear unusual is perhaps why the scepticism which obtained then seems always to be approximating the ideal pattern for all truth-seeking. The century's fervour for religious truth was remarkably linked, through the medium of scepticism, with an ever-deepening movement toward tolerance.

In the seventeenth century, when the controversies with Catholicism had brought the central principle of Protestantism into clear relief, and when the highest genius of Europe still flowed in the channels of divinity, this love of truth was manifested in the greatest works of English theology to a degree which no other department of literature has ever equalled. . . . Chillingworth, drawing with a bold and unfaltering hand the line between certainties and probabilities, eliminating from theology the old conception of faith considered as an unreasoning acquiescence, and teaching that belief should always be strictly 'proportionable to the credibility of its motives';—these and such as these, even when they were themselves opposed to religious liberty, were its real founders. Their noble confidence in the power of truth, their ceaseless struggle against the empire of prejudice, their comprehensive views of the laws and limits of the reason, their fervent, passionate love of knowledge, and the majesty and dignity of their sentiments, all produced in England a tone of thought that was essentially opposed to persecution, and made their writings the perennial source by which even now the most heroic natures are invigorated.[3]

Such is the truth-seeking temper of seventeenth-century literature, and it is within writing produced under such auspices that we propose to trace the sceptic pattern.

In a century which included the bitter and tragical plays of Shakespeare and Glanvill's *Scepsis Scientifica*, the impact of Elizabethan melancholy, followed by the political disillusion of the Commonwealth, was more than could be countered by an easy optimism, even when that seemed to have a scientific foundation. Though Glanvill was moving in the direction of eighteenth-century simplicity, he was still aware of the knotted quality of truth, even though he was not tortured by it, as Shakespeare was. Early Elizabethans could be cheerful atheists in the security of their new-found intellectual freedom, but soon their wonder grew that truth could have so many faces, and confusion began to under-cut their easy dogmatisms. The seventeenth century bore the full burden of this shift in attitude and so won its designation as the beginning of the modern era, largely because the period was so rich in the kind of scepticism we have been defining. The very violence of its religious controversy bears testimony to the fact that, unlike the previous age, it was certain there was something in religion worth salvaging; and it was equally certain that the scientific philosophy could not be abandoned. What have the intellectual struggles of the western world from that day to this been concerned with if not this same dilemma? The seventeenth century, with its political upheavals which reached to men's very doorsteps, could not retire with its mistrust of all dogmatisms until it had worked out a satisfactory solution; and this may account for the central and creative role of action in the scepticism of the century. The complex and sturdy intellectual pattern which was worked out there is full of meaning for our own day, which as yet has not learned to cultivate its doubts and turn them into creative capital.

In view of the intellectual heritage of the seventeenth century as it related to scepticism, it is understandable that once men began to consider soberly the nature of the truth which they had previously embraced with such abandon, their chief problem should have been an epistemological one. From Donne to Dryden, thoughtful men ask, 'What do I know?'

> Sharing the critical spirit, yet conscious of its destructive results, they seek some valid authority, some standing-ground more firm than that which had served their fathers. Is the edifice of knowledge built by ancient genius the modern man's permanent home or is it his prison? In his view of the universe and God and man, shall he hold by the Bible, Aristotle, and Ptolemy, or by one of the confusing new theories?[4]

Such was the delayed impact of the new philosophy of the Renaissance upon men whose spiritual heritage came jointly from the Greeks and from the Hebrews. The kind of teacher cited by Bush may be taken as representative of the deep confusion of the age.

> Against Bacon's assertion that at the universities students learned nothing but to believe may be set such a tutor as Joseph Mede (possibly the 'old Damoetas' of 'Lycidas'), who was wont to greet his charges with '*Quid dubitas?* What Doubts have you met in your studies today?'[5]

By this time, doubt had lost its initial attractiveness and was beginning to cast a pall over the intellectual life; yet the hardier spirits of the age recognized that whoever stopped asking '*Quid dubitas?*' was irretrievably lost. It was this paradoxical situation which nurtured and gave its stamp to the scepticism of the seventeenth century. Again, 'the subtle knot' is its trade-mark.

Scepticism a Valid Term?

There will always be those who feel that in view of the preponderance of religious thought in the seventeenth century, it represents a wrenching of critical terms to call the period sceptical. Therefore before we apply the sceptic pattern to five outstanding writers of the period, we should like to sketch in a background against which their scepticism will be understandable. This we shall attempt to do by relying largely on secondary sources in order to demonstrate that in no matter what capacity modern critics treat the seventeenth century, they are remarkably unanimous in indicating the presence of exactly the kind of historically defined scepticism we have been discussing. It is necessary only to relate these incidental references in order to see the sceptical pattern emerging. We shall find it possible to substantiate each phase of the pattern, as we have outlined it above, either directly from the works of seventeenth-century writers or from their modern interpreters and by the way to demonstrate the far-reaching results and implications of the sceptic method.

Regardless of the shifting meanings of scepticism during the last three centuries, a great many critics have found it a useful word to apply to the seventeenth century, and the meanings implied in their usage have tended to cluster about the definition worked out above. Bredvold's comment on Dryden is significant for what it reflects of the intellectual temper of Dryden's immediate predecessors.

> He lived in an age of philosophical scepticism; every reader of any pretensions to cultivation knew Montaigne and Charron intimately, and almost every scholar had read Sextus Empiricus. Neither Dryden nor his age can be fully understood apart from this Pyrrhonism, diffused in every department of thought, lending itself to the most diverse purposes, appearing sometimes in strange guises and in the most unexpected places.[6]

A stricture of this sort is necessary principally because people have tended to think of the seventeenth century as either lost in the darkness of dogmatism or as serenely pursuing its religious way, untroubled by doubt and despair. Bush also finds that he must struggle against these misconceptions if he is to uncover the true complexity and the resultant power of the age.

To the thoroughly modern mind the period 1600–60 may seem to have belonged to the kingdom of darkness. Yet it was a period of conflict over great issues in the abstract as well as the national sphere, over the nature of reality and of God and man, the very foundations of knowledge and faith. For the first time in England many men were compelled to go behind the rubrics and formulas and work out their own philosophy. The results ranged from various types of mystical thought to sceptical naturalism. These philosophies were in the main outgrowths of, or—very rarely—reactions against, the all-embracing tradition of Christian humanism which the age inherited, the tradition of the rational wisdom and culture of antiquity purified and exalted and intensified by the Middle Ages, the Renaissance, the Reformation, and the Counter-Reformation. For the last time in England all these forces, in differing degrees but in climactic concentration, made up the basic texture of men's thinking. The consequence was rich variety and strength, almost wholly within the Christian frame.[7]

That the seventeenth century was trying to work out a rationale for the often conflicting philosophical and religious convictions which it had inherited from the Renaissance is further support for the contention that scepticism flourished then as it has never done before or since.

Leishman finds its necessary in introducing the metaphysical poets to warn his readers against considering that the period can be explained simply as an age of clear-cut optimism concerning man and his potentialities. Again and again we find critics insisting upon the inherent paradox of the century, and this too encourages us regarding the validity of our diagnosis and the justification of our adopting the symbol of the knot.

> There is in Elizabethan literature, and still more in the literature of the seventeenth century, a strain of meditation which is more characteristic of what we usually mean by the Middle Ages than of what we usually mean by the Renaissance. . . . The Middle Ages loved to dwell on the limitations of man, on the depth of his ignorance, the smallness of his knowledge, the slightness of his capacity to increase that knowledge. . . . They [men of the seventeenth

century] became sceptical about the possible attainments of human knowledge, and the new discoveries in astronomy and other sciences merely increased their scepticism. . . . Thus another characteristic mediaeval conception, the insignificance of human knowledge, was intensified by the Renaissance.[8]

In the field of technical philosophy, too, critics have noted that scepticism was in the ascendant. The widespread feeling that man could know almost nothing had sent philosophers back to their studies to re-examine the bases of their systems.

The two rival philosophies which now arose are generally placed in opposition to each other, as physical and mental respectively, that of Bacon being conversant with nature, that of Descartes with man. But in truth in one respect both were united. Each was analytical; each strove to lay down a general method for investigating the sphere of inquiry which it selected. Both were reactions against the dogmatic assumptions of former systems; both assumed the indispensable necessity of an entire revolution in the method of attaining knowledge. Accordingly, though differing widely in appealing to the external senses or the internal intuitions respectively, they both built philosophy in the criticism of first principles. Hence, independently of any particular corollaries from special parts of their systems, the influence of their spirit was to beget a critical, subjective, and analytical study of any topic.[9]

This procedure, involving a radical overhauling of the method of truth-seeking, could not fail to influence other kinds of writing being done in the period and to bring writers under the spell of its critical approach.

In another philosophical tangle, that represented by the struggle between Gassendi, the sensationalist, and Descartes, the idealist, scepticism stepped in to prune out excessive dogmatisms and thereby clarify the issue.

In the contests which arose between these two schools, the weak sides of both were alternately held up to view, and the baneful results exhibited, to which either of them, if rigidly followed out, would invariably lead. The juncture then had arrived, at which scepticism was needed to pull down, on either hand, what was weak and unsatisfactory in their respective principles; and accordingly, just at this juncture, scepticism actually made its appearance, to perform the work assigned it in the progress of human knowledge.[10]

Although Douglas Bush is likely to shy away from the word *sceptic* because it has retained so little of its historical meaning, even he cannot escape using it, with qualifications, to express the attitude of honest inquiry. He refers to Donne's reason as

> the restless, inquiring reason of the instinctive sceptic—if this last word may be used in a very limited and quite unmodern sense. Donne had realized the winding and craggy approach to truth. He had, with intellectual detachment, refused to make a decision until he had digested the whole body of controversy regarding Roman and Anglican claims. And even in the sermons the old demon of uncertainty may raise its head, not seriously to disturb his faith, but to ask what human knowledge is perfect and secure.[11]

Again, in characterizing Sir Thomas Browne's intellectual technique in *Religio Medici*, Bush finds it necessary to revert to the use of *sceptical*.

> Browne's attitude, of course, is not that of either the village atheist or the philosophic sceptic. Men like Montaigne and Donne might push on into libertine naturalism, but Browne's reason is much too 'soft and flexible,' 'extravagant and irregular' a vehicle to arrive anywhere; his favourite image is a circle. He has, nevertheless, breathed the air of a sceptical age, and his consciousness of the Zeitgeist, while it does not disturb his faith, is just strong enough to demand a positive statement of it.[12]

That pattern of Browne's thought which takes the form of a circle might find its justification in the circular knot of scepticism. For does not the progression from nescience to the ultimate illumination provided by the good life describe the locus of a circle—from 'What can I know?' to 'If any man will do his will, he shall know of the doctrine'; from the impossibility of *a priori* knowledge to the strange and unforeseen quality of whatever *a postiori* knowlege may emerge from creative activity? In the field of religious controversy, too, critics assign the word *sceptical* to thinkers like Chillingworth, the flower of whose scepticism bore fruit in an admirable tolerance. It has been noted that when we discuss scepticism in religion, we must make the important distinction between

> the sceptic who views religion dispassionately because his nature is not religious and to whom tolerance therefore presents no problem and the fine objectivity and tolerance which has been attained at rare intervals by men who are by nature deeply religious. Chillingworth belonged to this latter group and, laying as he did the intellectual basis of Latitudinarianism, the moderation of his view and his remarkable ability to suspend judgment were to contribute powerfully to the formation of an intellectual atmosphere in which philosophical tolerance might be achieved.[13]

Most men who belong in this second category have arrived there by passing through a dark night of the soul where they have grappled with genuine doubt and have come to terms with it.

> Chillingworth's thought is distinguished for its almost transparent honesty and for its deep-seated scepticism. His greatest work bears throughout the marks of a profound religious struggle through which the author was still passing, and exhibits that strength and honesty of character which enabled him to consider the controversial questions of his age with an Olympian calmness of spirit.[14]

Here is the quality into which Greek *ataraxia* had been transformed in the seventeenth century. That Chillingworth deserved the designation *sceptical* which Clarendon applied to him[15] is obvious from the use to which he put his sceptical principles.

> Chillingworth recurred constantly to the necessity for casting off authority and prejudice and for viewing the conflicting religious claims of the age with dispassion and scepticism.[16]
> He exalted dispassion and scepticism, arguing that these states of mind were the noblest of which man was capable and that only when man was in the enjoyment of them was he prepared to receive truth or to advance in its quest.[17]

These principles link Chillingworth in spirit to the sect which, in view of the scepticism of the age, had the most striking name, the Seekers (although he was not actually a member of this sect).

There was a sect of his [Cromwell's] time who were called 'Seekers,' because they believed in the need of perpetual search for truth. He had a sympathy for them. 'To be a Seeker,' he once wrote, 'is to be of the best sect after a finder, and such an one shall every faithful humble Seeker be in the end.' This may remind us of a saying of Jesus in a papyrus found in Egypt over thirty years ago: 'Let not him that seeketh cease till he find, and when he findeth he shall wonder, and having wondered he shall reign, and having reigned he shall rest.' Seeking; finding; wondering; reigning; resting—these words are, in a sense, an epitome of Cromwell's earthly course. But it is the word 'seeking' which is peculiarly characteristic. . . . He believed in the seeking mind. 'The mind is the man. If that be kept pure, a man signifies somewhat.' He believed that it was man's own business to keep the mind free.[18]

Even though these Seekers did not conform wholly to the sceptic pattern, their very presence in the century is a straw which shows how the wind is blowing.

These people have been spoken of as Seekers, or Religious Sceptics, but Edwards distinguished the Seekers and Waiters from the Sceptics and Questionists. But the Seekers questioned most things. They held that the Scriptures were uncertain, that the ministry of the existing churches was null and without authority, that the worship and ordinances of their day were vain, and that miracles would be necessary to re-establish faith. The true church was in the wilderness, the true worship, the true ministry, the true Scriptures, and the true ordinances had all been lost, and they were now groping and seeking for these.[19]

This is similar to Milton's assumption in *Areopagitica* that since the death of Christ, truth had been cut into myriad pieces and scattered like the body of Osiris. The logical outcome of this position should have been, and was in Milton's case, a sustained faith in a progressive revelation, whose end no man could envisage—the kind of end which Emerson and Whitman were driving toward with their redefinition of *scripture*.

In so far as this spirit had penetrated the thinking of the period, it neutralized whatever fear men had had of doubt and confusion. Francis Quarles is a case in point.

> In the search for truth man may fall into doubt and error, but Quarles looked upon honest scepticism with far greater favour than upon bigotry seated in irrationality. Doubt is a stage on the road to truth and hence cannot harm a man's soul.[20]

This is reminiscent of Occam's pronouncement that the man who is still searching should be absolved of all charges of heresy. It is noteworthy that this confidence implies that a man has survived his period of doubt or, if such periods are recurrent, that he has known a complete cycle, and not that he is still engulfed by it and merely hopes for a way out.

The experience of Henry More is not unusual in the seventeenth century and demonstrates one way in which scepticism could co-exist with faith.

> His intuitive assurance of God remained unshaken, but he passed through a phase of purely intellectual doubt, which he describes thus: 'And to speak all in a Word, Those almost whole Four Years which I spent in Studies of this kind, as to what concern'd those Matters which I chiefly desired to be satisfied about (for as to the Existence of a God, and the Duties of Morality, I never had the least Doubt), ended in nothing, in a manner, but mere Scepticism.'[21]

The man who thus worked his way, by the method of scepticism, toward truths which he had grasped intuitively exemplified one use which the religionist made of his heritage of Pyrrhonism. Another use, illustrated by John Hales, is very close to that of Browne—a kind of delaying action in which the sceptic practices his *isosothenia* and *epoché* against the day when as a result of this process, the truth will break upon him.

> 'In places of ambiguous and doubtful, or dark and intricate meaning, it is sufficient if we religiously admire and acknowledge

73

and confess, neither affirming nor denying either side. . . . It shall well befit our Christian modesty to participate somewhat of the sceptic.'[22]

Mysticism and Scepticism

Critics have been struck by the fact that, as in the quotations here cited from More and Hales, mysticism and scepticism often co-existed in the seventeenth century in the same individual. As we shall see, this fact is big with implication for the nature of both scepticism and mysticism. Helen White, in discussing English devotional literature in the period, says,

> It is a curious thing that the mystery of life is the hunting ground of both the sceptic and the mystic, the excuse of unfaith, the opportunity of faith.[23]

The writings of the Cambridge Platonists could all be used to footnote this observation; and although there is no time to develop the argument here, it could certainly be shown that they cultivated intensively that area shared by mysticism and scepticism. And this analysis, in turn, could contribute to a deeper understanding of both.

> Mysticism . . . was favoured at this time with a far greater share of attention, and was supported by far greater learning, than were the feeble efforts of incipient scepticism. The way to this was, perhaps, already paved by the efforts of Robert Fludd (born 1574, died 1637) to revive the fanatical doctrines of Paracelsus; but the more direct cause is to be found in the fact that many lofty minds, disgusted with Hobbism on the one hand, and unsatisfied with Cartesianism on the other, took refuge in the sublime philosophy of Plato, and devoted themselves with severe and ardent study to the elucidation of his writings.[23a]

The struggle of every critic of the seventeenth century with the term *scepticism* is only complicated by the fact that just as it is often found in combination with mysticism, so it is often allied with credulity. This is illustrated by what happens to

Morell in discussing Glanvill, where he must be careful to cover himself when using this dangerous word.

> The author, who in England most perfectly expressed the sceptical tendency of this age, was Joseph Glanville, court-preacher to King Charles the Second, whose work, entitled 'Scepsis Scientifica, or Confessed Ignorance the Way to Science, in an Essay of the Vanity of Dogmatizing and Confident Opinion,' was intended rather to controvert the pretensions of the Aristotelian and the Cartesian philosophy, than to involve the whole circumference of human knowledge in darkness and uncertainty.[24]

So, too, Lecky, joining a sizeable group of critics puzzled by the mingled scepticism and credulity of Glanvill, is forced to make it clear that by scepticism he does not mean dogmatic incredulity.

> To those who only know him as the defender of witchcraft, it may appear a somewhat startling paradox to say, that the predominating characteristic of the mind of Glanvil was an intense scepticism. He has even been termed by a modern critic 'the first English writer who had thrown scepticism into a definite form'; ... and if we regard this expression as simply implying a profound distrust of human faculties, and not at all the rejection of any distinct dogmatic system, the judgment can hardly be disputed. And certainly, it would be difficult to find a work displaying less of the credulity and superstition that are commonly attributed to the believers in witchcraft than the treatise on *The Vanity of Dogmatizing, or Confidence of Opinions*, in which Glanvil expounded his philosophical views.[25]

Moody Prior, writing in *Modern Philology*, undertakes to explain this dilemma.

> It was, however, a skepticism which took the form, not of the classical *epoché*—the suspension of belief—but of the tentative suspension of disbelief that was for Glanvill a necessary element of the scientific attitude. Hence the paradox that Glanvill believed in witches because he was a skeptic. Nor is this to be wondered at; for seventeenth-century scientists—impressed by the difficulty of discovering causes for natural phenomena; willing as a result of

the striking reversals of old views by new discoveries and the restoration of older theories that had once been discarded, to entertain any hypothesis until they were convinced that it was untenable; and ambitious enough to consider all obscure, trivial, or extraordinary events worthy of their serious attention—allowed their opposition to dogmatism to lead them to an extreme of scientific skepticism that at times verged closely on credulity. And it was particularly tempting and easy to call in the aid of this systematic opposition to dogmatism in the interest of an assumption for which they had such tender concern as the reality of spirit.[26]

In spite of the fact that men often lost their balance in this precarious operation, it argues well for their truth-seeking that they were bent upon incorporating all the facts, no matter how diverse and apparently irreconcilable. For a brief moment in the seventeenth century there was maintained, somehow, an almost complete openness to ideas, from whatever quarter; and if man soon lapsed into the dogmatism which brought witchcraft persecutions in its train, he had known, at least once, this unaccountable hospitality of spirit, which was destined to challenge and disturb him for ever. The mystic substratum of Glanvill's position is appreciated by Bush, even while he deplores its practical consequences.

> The consciousness of the immediate presence and active intervention of God in all the affairs of life and the universe is even stronger in the seventeenth century than in the sixteenth; it was heightened by Puritanism and by various forms of more or less mystical thought. This ultra-religious view of the world entailed, to be sure, a belief not only in the harmless science of astrology but in witchcraft, and the practical consequences of that belief were horrible; yet one could hardly accept God and His angels without accepting Satan and his.[27]

Nescience

Documentation for the nescience of the seventeenth century is not as extensive as for its perception of dualism and paradox, but it is continually implied by every other phase of the century's sceptical thought. For a motto this nescience might well take Donne's cry, 'Poore soule, in this thy flesh what dost thou know?'[28] The most famous detailed statement is undoubtedly contained in Donne's other lines from the 'Anatomie of the World':

> And new Philosophy calls all in doubt,
> The Element of fire is quite put out;
> The Sun is lost, and th'earth, and no mans wit
> Can well direct him where to looke for it.
> And freely men confesse that this world's spent,
> When in the Planets, and the Firmament
> They seeke so many new; then see that this
> Is crumbled out againe to his Atomies.
> 'Tis all in peeces, all cohaerance gone;
> All just supply, and all Relation:
> Prince, Subject, Father, Sonne, are things forgot,
> For every man alone thinkes he hath got
> To be a Phoenix, and that then can bee
> None of that kinde, of which he is, but hee.[29]

An experience like this, in which the individual feels that he is completely without a hitherto solid intellectual underpinning, always precedes the sceptic's long and sometimes unsuccessful trek toward certainty. Once he sees the implications of this experience, though he has proceeded no farther than a paradox, it is usual for the sceptic to recommend its being induced, where it does not occur naturally, as a kind of intellectual prophylaxis to prevent the decay which inevitably accompanies dogmatism.

It is with this motive that Richard Whitlock in his *Zootomia or Observations on the Present Manners of the English* recommends nescience both as a critique and as a spur to investigation. In discussing 'Reasons Independency,' he asks what would have happened if Columbus had stopped at the Pillars of Hercules, just because they seemed to some geographers of his day to represent the farthest bounds of their knowledge.

> I am perswaded nothing hath more continued such an Ignorance in the World, as Mens setting these terminating Bounds, and Pillars

to their Discoveries, *My Sense, My Reason*; So farre will I go, and no further: calling *Obstinacy* to an Opinion, *Solidity*; and humble *Ductility* after further Reason and Discovery, *Sceptick Inconstancy*.[30]

Only by admitting honestly his own ignorance is the truth-seeker freed for a venture into the unknown. Incidentally, there is evidence here that the meaning of *sceptic* was already confused in the seventeenth century. Whitlock encountered the same misunderstanding as Emerson was to encounter two centuries later, for in listing causes of intellectual slavery (on the pattern of Bacon's idols) he puts first,

> the *Marriage* (or *Espousall*, as the sage *Frenchman*) of our *Fancy*, or *Judgement* to some *Notions*, or *Men*; and this hath begot that peevish *Morosity* among men; that the more knowing *Man*, is to the very *Ignorant, Hereticall*, and to the *Smatterer* in Knowledge, *Paradoxicall*.[31]

Such is the price the sceptic always pays for being unwilling to rest in dogmatisms. Whitlock's prescription for intellectual health unites the wisdom of a Hebrew prophet with that of a metaphysical poet—thus illustrating his conception of the oneness of truth.

> It is an observation even here usefull, as well as in Divinity, to obey that Text, *Jerem.* 6.16. *Stand in the way and enquire for the old paths.* Stand in the old wayes, or enquire for them, before we enlarge our Discoveries of the new. And that inimitable Poets Rule is true in al mending of our Intellectuals.
> > —Doubt wisely, in strange way
> > To stand inquiring right, is not to stray:
> > To sleep, or run wrong, is.—[32]

If 'our Intellectuals' are ever to be mended, the sceptic is convinced that we must relinquish our grasp on what we hold to be the truth and by a kind of creative doubt make our way in the direction of the truth which beacons to us, ever so faintly. The unpardonable sin is to shirk this responsibility through complacency or blind dogmatism.

Daniel Whitby, five years after the century closed, presented with sympathy and understanding the position of classical scepticism, as a preliminary to advocating the necessity of Christianity.

> As for the Heathen *Philosophers*, let it be noted, 1st, That among the generality of them, all things were counted dubious and uncertain; the common issue of their search after their Duty to God and Man, and the foundation on which they do entirely depend, was mostly *Scepticism*, and the most knowing men were they who did renounce all knowledge of them. 'Tis easie, saith *Caecilius*, to manifest that in humane affairs, *omnia sunt dubia, incerta, suspensa*. All things are dubious and uncertain. The various apprehensions of wise men, saith *Cicero*, will justifie the doubtings and demurs of *Scepticks*, and it will then be sufficient to account them malepert. . . . It was this obscurity of things, saith He [Cicero] which brought *Socrates, Democritus, Anaxagoras, Empedocles*, and almost all the Antients, to the confession of their Ignorance, saying, *Nihil cognosci, nihil percipi posse*, nothing could be known or perceived, Truth lay buried in the deep, Men were held by Opinions and Ordinances, *Nihil veritati relinqui*, no place being left for Truth. Lastly, they said, *Omnia tenebris circumfusa esse*, that all things were involved in darkness.[33]

Another contributing factor to nescience both in Greece and Rome and in seventeenth-century England, as Whitby makes clear, was 'the various apprehensions of wise men.' The religious controversy of his era pointed this up with disturbing brilliance, and the seekers after truth had somehow to exorcize this demon who whispered that since equally wise and sincere men came to opposite conclusions, the search for truth was of all expeditions the most futile. It was probably a similar irresponsibility which urged Pilate to his famous question after Jesus, as in his encounter with the 'sons of Abraham,' had declared that 'every one that is of the truth heareth my voice' (John 18: 37).

Dualism and Paradox

Unlike the nescience of the seventeenth century, which is often implied rather than stated and sometimes has to be dug out from beneath expressions of its mysticism and scepticism, the dualism and paradox of the age are everywhere in evidence, even to the most superficial observer. The two foci, in this field, which are most significant for an understanding of seventeenth-century scepticism are the work of the metaphysical poets and the work of the Cambridge Platonists, but there are countless minor manifestations of dualism, contradiction, and paradox—always integral parts of the sceptic pattern. Grierson says,

> The dominant note of the seventeenth century was to be the conflict of the secular and the spiritual, the world, the flesh, and the spirit, a conflict which troubled every sphere of life.[34]

Meissner, in analysing the nature of baroque, sets forth vividly the chief dualism of the age.

> Nie haben Rationalismus und Mystik ähnlich nebeneinander oder richtiger gesagt hintereinander gelagert wie in der Periode zwischen Renaissance und Aufklärung.[35]

Indeed, it is probably this very opposition, indicative as it is of the presence of a deep scepticism, which endows the seventeenth century with a distinctive quality which the eighteenth century lacks—a quality which we have tried to symbolize by 'the knot.'

> Die die damalige Zeit bewegende Frage lautet: Gibt es eine Brücke, welche diese abgrundtiefen Gegensätze verbindet? Fehlt jeder Ausgleich zwischen den entgegengesetzen Polen dieser Zeit? Erst das 18. Jahrhundert hat in der Harmonielehre Shaftesburys die endgültige Lösung dieses Problems bringen können; das 17. hat bis zu seinem Ausgang in den augedeuteten Spannungen gelebt.[36]

As will be apparent later in this discussion, the eighteenth century's bridge-building, necessary for practical purposes, nevertheless minimized the depth of the chasm, an abyss the recognition of whose reality is somehow essential to creative scepticism. Among Protestant apologists, as among poets and philosophers, dualism is consciously maintained.

> With Hooker then we must continue to assert the duality of God and man, the two foci of religion; and yet with him also to assert

that Godhead is the ground of Manhood and that therefore the real Manhood of a Divine Person must be not less but more truly human than any human individual can be.[37]

The constant temptation is that men will lose their hold on a dualism of this sort and cling to one or another of its horns. With the poets, dualism often takes a psychological form as they penetrate the deepest experience of men.

We often find in Vaughan, as we sometimes find in Herbert, an antithesis between nature and man, between the calm, orderly, and obedient behaviour of nature, and the restlessness, self-will, and disobedience of man.[38]

In the realm of philosophy, dualism came to a head in the seventeenth century in the system of Descartes, an attempt to bridge the same gap which we shall see Cudworth and the Cambridge Platonists struggling with. The fundamental dualism of body and soul is the cradle of all scepticism and often is both the seed and the flower of the sceptic's conviction of nescience.

To Pascal's passionately logical mind it seemed that the very source of the human tragedy lay in the fact that we are composed 'de deux natures opposées et de divers genre, d'âme et de corps,' which 's'abuse reciproquement l'un l'autre.' 'Notre âme est jetée dans le corps, où elle trouve nombre, temps, dimensions. Elle raisonne là dessus, et appelle cela nature, necessité et ne peut croire autre chose.' Therefore 'l'homme est à lui-même le plus prodigieux objet de la nature: car il ne peut concevoir ce que c'est que corps, et encore moins ce que c'est qu'ésprit, et moins qu'aucune chose comme un corps peut être uni avec un ésprit.'[39]

Cartesianism was the philosophical form which this insight took, no more striking but perhaps more easily labelled than expressions of the same insight in poetry and theology.

Puis vient l'admirable mouvement cartésien, fécond par lui-même et par les contradictions qu'il suscite, destiné à marquer tout le xviie siécle de sa vigoureuse empreinte.[40]

Willey clearly delineates the nature of the problem and its implications for epistemology.

But there is another aspect of the Cartesian thought which must be emphasised, namely its dualism—that is its division of reality into two substances—thought and extension. Outside, extended throughout infinite space, there is the world of mathematical objects strictly controlled by mechanical law; and that this is real we have seen. Within, there is the thinking substance which is the true 'I,' unextended, distinct from the body, and not subject to mechanical laws; and the reality of this is intuitively certain. Within the human individual, then, these divided and distinguished worlds mysteriously met and blended; soul and body, thought and extension being somehow inexplicably found in union. Descartes is as sure as Plato that 'I' am not my body or any part of it, that my thinking self can be conceived apart altogether from the body, and that thus my soul may be immortal. This fundamental dualism greatly complicated the epistemological problem, for if the soul were totally distinct from the body, how could it have that contact with matter which is implied in knowledge? Whatever theory of sense-perception one adopted, there was always a point at which one arrived at the gulf, which must somehow be bridged, between matter-in-motion and Mind or Soul.[41]

It was in response to this dilemma that Descartes developed his theory of 'animal spirits' to account for the observable fact that body and spirit do somehow constitute a whole, even though one which is not logically explicable.

> our blood labours to beget
> Spirits, as like soules as it can,
> Because such fingers need to knit
> That subtile knot, which makes us man . . .[42]

The refinement of body and the slight coarsening of soul were required in order to effect this awesome combination in the human being. As long as the seventeenth century could hold on to its concept of duality in unity, its scepticism was safe; but once the concept was worn thin and the balance was broken, scepticism was on its way out as a moving intellectual force. As Willey makes clear, even the notion of 'animal-spirits' failed to account, except symbolically, for the reciprocal action of mind and matter.

> In the last analysis there yet remained a point at which matter set in motion that which was not matter, and conversely, at which mind actuated matter.[43]

All of these pronouncements concerning body and soul lose none of their relevance if it is 'discovered' by psychologists or philosophers that, in fact, no such dichotomy exists in the human being. For such dualisms are not so much descriptive as symbolic; and no matter how their definition changes from one generation to another, there has never thus far been eradicated from human experience the sense that man is bifurcated and torn and that in spite of this he must desperately strive toward wholeness. If ever man becomes conditioned, over a period of several generations, to thinking of his life in wholly other terms, then it will be time to revise our conclusions concerning dualism.

Among the Cambridge Platonists, Cudworth provides a good example of how dualism operated in philosophical opposition to the encroaching monism.

> Cudworth thus controverted the monism of Hobbes, the doctrine that all mutation is motion, thought included, and that motion can have no cause except motion. To this, he opposed the philosophical dualism of his *Intellectual System*.[44]

Even though superficially it would seem that Cudworth is merely opposing the reality of spirit to Hobbes' conviction of the primary reality of matter, closer scrutiny will discover that he is really trying to conserve the reality of both and to show their interpenetration.

> And so he returns to the primary and essential strain of all his thought, that 'cogitation is in order of nature before' what he calls 'local motion,' and '*incorporeal* before *corporeal* substance,

the former having a natural imperium upon the latter'—in other words, that Mind is before Matter, and superior to it.[45]

Here, of course, in opposition to Descartes, Cudworth is showing himself to be a consistent Platonist, and the depth of his philosophy is sounded by the fact that the dilemma from which it issues is inescapable and cannot be exorcized by any mere epistemological sleight of hand.

He has shown—no one has ever shown better—how we cannot work from below upwards; and that if we begin with matter and a philosophy of sense, we can never reach conscience and a philosophy of reason. He has exhibited the co-ordination of the different planes of thought, and made it clear how we must stand on the one side or the other. It is not possible perhaps to do more, or to fathom the depths of that dualism that meets us everywhere in the last stages of our inquiry.[46]

The paradox in which such a position always lands a thinker is exemplified by this paraphrase of Cudworth:

We must, as the Greek epigram speaks, *ascend downward* and *descend upward*, if we would indeed come to heaven, or get any true persuasion of our title to it.[47]

This has the ring of genuine scepticism, and it perfectly exemplifies what we mean by 'the subtle knot,' with all its tortuosity and experimental complexity. Behind these words of Cudworth lay his revival of not only the physiological hypothesis but also the moral paradoxes of Democritus and Epicurus.[48]

Henry More was another of the Cambridge Platonists who, like Cudworth, tried his hand at the problem of mind *v.* matter.

More's arguments can perhaps best be viewed, from our present point of view, as an endeavour to reunite matter and spirit, which the rigid logic of Descartes had left in unbridgeable opposition, and to give greater 'body,' or actuality, to both conceptions, which in Cartesianism were too nakedly abstract. More wants his 'spirit' to be more than abstract 'cogitation'; he will have it to be activity, and the activity must be *there where* it is at work, penetrating and moving matter.[49]

Donne would have agreed with More that unless matter is acted upon, 'a great Prince in prison lies.' *Activity* is the key word here, for it presages another important phase of seventeenth-century scepticism, the belief that the good life, whether in terms of philosophy or theology, is the only ultimate answer to the epistemological question, even though the answer may not be given in the same language in which the question was asked.

Metaphysical Poetry

The structure of metaphysical poetry is perhaps the most striking illustration of the way in which dualism and paradox operated, and behind this structure lay the fundamental philosophic dilemma of the age, exacerbated by the Renaissance's new learning, the complexity of which was just beginning to be appreciated. Bush says the metaphysical sensibility represented

> the survival, into an age of critical and realistic scepticism, of the medieval philosophic and allegorical conception of the unity of all things physical and spiritual in the universe, a conception partly supported and partly disturbed by the new science.[50]

Criticism of Donne is full of illustrations of this clash of *Weltanschauungen*. Grierson refers to

> the sceptical sense he reveals of the contradictions inherent in theology and science—of which no man in his day was more acutely aware, . . . conflict of soul, of faith and hope snatched and held desperately, of harmony evoked from harsh combinations.[51]

In Donne, as both poet and priest, the philosophical, poetic, and religious attempts at a unification of a disjointed world came to a focus. The perennial appeal of his poetry and sermons is to generations who likewise are trying to heal their own *Zerissenheit*. The central spiritual problems of the mid-twentieth century are essentially those of the seventeenth, translated into another dialect—the dialect of science rather than that of religion.

The religious revival of the seventeenth century, with its Puritans, Quakers, Neoplatonists, and countless sects, was an attempt to combat the spiritual despair caused by the disintegration. The religiously inclined were seeking a new authority; and whatever theological systems were separately developed, the spiritual urge was much the same.[52]

It constitutes no wrenching, therefore, of spiritual affinities to consider the metaphysicals and the Cambridge Platonists together as fellow-travellers on the road toward a recovered unity. Specifically, in Donne we get the poetic technique which underlies 'the subtle knot' and which tends to perpetuate it. Eliot says of Donne,

> There is a manifest fissure between thought and sensibility, a chasm which in his poetry he bridged in his own way, which was not the way of mediaeval poetry.[53]

Sharp refers to the fact that Donne's mind was an alembic, rather than a mirror.

> This process was both psychological and passionate; thought and feeling were analyzed, introspectively, and then synthesized. The combination was startling and extravagant because both ingredients were far from simple. Especially the thought. For Donne's way of writing included an intense and perverse individualism, fond of cynicism and paradox. This was the very opposite of conventional belief and practice.[54]

Some critics have gone so far as to assert that for the metaphysical poet there is no such operation as the putting of his ideas into verse since his thought 'is in its very process poetical.'[55] Reference is often made to Donne's line, '. . . one might almost say, her body thought,'[56] in itself as brave an attempt as that of Descartes or of Cudworth to bridge the body-soul gap.

As examples of the kinds of paradoxes elaborated by the minor metaphysical poets, who reflect the spirit of the age, let us look first at some lines of Chidiock Tichborne which show the movement from the flippancy of paradox toward its deep wisdom.

My prime of youth is but a frost of cares;
   My feast of joy is but a dish of pain;
My crop of corn is but a field of tares;
   And all my good is but vain hope of gain;
The day is fled, and yet I saw no sun;
And now I live, and now my life is done.

The spring is past, and yet it hath not sprung;
   The fruit is dead, and yet the leaves are green;
My youth is gone, and yet I am but young;
   I saw the world, and yet I was not seen;
My thread is cut, and yet it is not spun;
And now I live, and now my life is done.

I sought my death, and found it in my womb;
   I looked for life, and saw it was a shade;
I trod the earth, and knew it was my tomb;
   And now I die, and now I am but made;
The glass is full, and now my glass is run;
And now I live, and now my life is done.[57]

There is scarcely any profundity here but rather the intellectual fascination of playing with opposites; yet thousands of lines of such verse must have preceded the achievement by Giles Fletcher of this fusion, on a higher plane, of the theology and the poetry of paradox:

The birth of Him that no beginning knew,
   Yet gives beginning to all that are born;
And how the Infinite far greater grew;
   By growing less, and how the rising Morn
That shot from Heaven, did back to Heaven return;
The obsequies of Him that could not die;
And death of life; and of eternity;
How worthily He died that died unworthily;
How God and Man did both embrace each other;
Met in one Person Heaven and Earth did kiss;
And how a Virgin did become a Mother,
And bore that Son who the world's Father is
And Maker of His Mother; and how bliss

Descended from the bosom of the High,
To clothe Himself in naked misery,
Sailing at length to Heaven and Earth triumphantly;
Is the first flame wherewith my whiter Muse
Doth burn in heavenly love such love to tell.[58]

As is suggested by these contrasting bits of paradox verse, the line between success and failure in metaphysical poetry is invisible but unmistakable.

Johnson, who employed the term 'metaphysical poets,' apparently having Donne, Cleveland, and Cowley chiefly in mind, remarks of them that 'the most heterogeneous ideas are yoked by violence together.' The force of this impeachment lies in the failure of the conjunction, the fact that often the ideas are yoked but not united; and if we are to judge of styles of poetry by their abuse, enough examples may be found in Cleveland to justify Johnson's condemnation. But a degree of heterogeneity of material compelled into unity by the operation of the poet's mind is omnipresent in poetry.[59]

This fact that the metaphysicals pick out and emphasize one phase of the normal poetic process seems connected with the parallel fact that scepticism seems always on the verge of losing its identity because it represents an integral portion of the process by which men fight their way toward truth. Coleridge, in speaking of the esemplastic function of the imagination, draws what might be a sketch of the metaphysical method.

This power . . . reveals itself in the balance or reconcilement of opposite or discordant qualities: of sameness, with difference; of the general, with the concrete; the idea with the image; the individual with the representative; the sense of novelty and freshness with old and familiar objects; a more than usual state of emotion with more than usual order; judgment ever awake and steady self-possession with enthusiasm and feeling profound or vehement.[60]

We are now prepared to understand an analysis of the sheer poetic style of the metaphysicals, for we have seen its *raison d'être*.

The metaphysical style, which was so well adapted to the paradoxes of faith, was a European phenomenon. In England it ran throughout our period but was especially strong in the first half of it. Andrewes and Donne, the greatest Anglo-Catholic preachers of the age, were, though very different, the chief exemplars. In prose as in verse wit involved not merely verbal tricks and surprises but the linking together of dissimilar objects, symbols, and ideas philosophized and fused by intellectual and spiritual perceptions and emotions, weighted by frequently abstruse or scientific learning, and made arresting by pointed expression.[61]

The same conviction of a paradoxical oneness is what holds the parts of the metaphysical style together.

Some peculiar and fundamental characteristics of seventeenth-century literature arise from the simultaneous embracing of different planes of knowledge and experience or the habit of immediate and almost unconscious transition from one to another. That is, in brief, the medieval allegorical instinct. Ultimately it springs from the religious belief in the divine unity of all things physical and spiritual, and it works through both intuition and the formal logic in which all men were trained. But in the seventeenth century that belief operates in an enlarged terrestrial and celestial world, against a developing background of philosophic and scientific scepticism, so that the allegorical mode of thought and feeling now appears less instinctive and normal, more eccentric and 'quaint,' than it did when its basic assumptions were universal and unquestioned, when the realm of knowledge had not been separated from the realm of faith. The result is 'metaphysical' poetry and prose. As one of the greatest metaphysical writers [Browne] said, 'thus is man that great and true *Amphibium*, whose nature is disposed to live not onely like other creatures in divers elements, but in divided and distinguished worlds: for though there be but one to sense, there are two to reason; the one visible, the other invisible.'[62]

The distinguishing characteristic of metaphysical wit is 'an instinct for paradoxical contrasts and, as in the poets, realistic particularity barbs the imaginative and emotional arrow.'[63]

The fact that more than one critic classes Browne with the

metaphysicals and also considers him a true representative of his age reinforces what we have been saying about his paradoxical quality.

> Browne seems to be 'a mass of Antipathies'—love of life and disdain of life, devout piety and innocent scepticism, encyclopaedic thirst and obscurantist 'superstition,' scientific exactness and figurative vagueness, sublime imagination and eccentric fancy, cosmopolitan breadth and English insularity, unambitious modesty and amiable egotism, bookish pedantry and bookish humour. . . . But beneath the surface Browne is a completely harmonious microcosm of his paradoxical age.[64]

It is quite in keeping with his nature that he should find the road toward truth more exciting than his ultimate destination.

> Like the metaphysicals, he seems to us to get his thrill rather out of the actual process of fusing disparates than from any 'truth' that may emerge from the process.[65]

What this means is that the truth Browne and the metaphysicals were concerned with never wandered very far from the fusing of disparates. Likewise Latitudinarians such as Chillingworth never lost sight of the often discouraging process of truth-seeking, lest they should forfeit their intellectual humility.

> Men achieve differing degrees of truth according to their several endowments and reasons, but it is the quality and temper of their effort to find truth rather than the perfection of their attainments which God uses as the measure of a man.[66]

Metaphysicals and Platonists alike suspected any truth which was not continuously aware of the rock whence it was hewn.

But there came a day when metaphysical wit could no longer maintain its balance on the knife-blade, and at that point poetry moved into a new phase, where the emphasis was on something more reliable, called judgment. At the same time, as Sharp observes, religion was undergoing a parallel transformation. He charges science with breaking up the old conventions in both fields.

The causes of a change in religious outlook are closely identifiable with the causes of the literary change. The difference is that through God religion ultimately possessed unity though practically this unity was broken up from the beginning of the century, or even from the Reformation. With some small exceptions literature did not possess a similar center because the fancy of the individual poet dictated what he should say.

But the great alteration in the human attitude was necessarily reflected in religion. If it could not alter God, science could alter the human relationship to the deity. Correspondingly, as we have seen, the result in literature was that the basis shifted from wit to judgment. Thus was the change in temper reflected in religion and literature. Of the forces that were responsible for the change the growth of science is the best single representative.[67]

Faith and Reason

The impact of science threw into relief the outstanding dualism of seventeenth-century thought, that of faith and reason. What the Cambridge Platonists did to come to terms with this dualism parallels (though it did not have equally bizarre results) the efforts of the metaphysical poets. Characteristic of both groups, as sceptics, is the propensity for taking in stride both halves of any dualism, not shrinking from the problem but fearing only to lose some of the factors essential to a solution.

It is the glory of the Cambridge divines that they welcomed this new spirit of speculation—gave it frank entertainment in their halls of learning; and, while enriching it with a culture all their own, sought to fuse it by the spontaneous action of their own thoughtfulness into a philosophy of religion at once free and conservative, in which the rights of faith and the claims of the speculative intellect should each have free scope, and blend together for mutual elevation and strength.[68]

An example of how this fusion of the rational and the religious took place, without detriment to either, is given by Tulloch in this comment on John Smith:

While Smith therefore broadened, and in a sense humanised, the conception of religion, he at the same time, with admirable balance of mind, vindicated it as a distinctive divine power revealed in man —a righteousness not self-evolved, but divinely given 'through the faith of Christ, the righteousness which is of God by faith.' He was one of those rare thinkers in whom largeness of view, and depth, and wealth of poetic and speculative insight, only served to evoke more fully the religious spirit; and while he drew the mould of his thought from Plotinus, he vivified the substance of it from St. Paul.[69]

A similar holding of opposites in solution may be seen in John Norris of Bemerton. Lovejoy says he

> dwells with almost equal fondness upon the thought of the eternal self-containedness and the perpetual self-diffusiveness implicit in the idea of an Absolute and Perfect being.[70]

As in the case of the metaphysicals, this was no mirror trick of clever logicians. Its roots were deep in the philosophical and religious experience of men whose integrity would not allow them to deny whatever they had once known. Whichcote tried to harmonize thus the sometimes dissonant spheres of human experience:

> Man's knowledge does not lie in incommunicable spheres—the secular and the spiritual; but in different planes of elevation, the lower tending towards the higher, and the higher sending down its light to the lower levels of intellectual aspiration.[71]

The Platonists seemed to be following the command to Paul, 'What God hath cleansed, call not thou common' (Acts 10: 15). Their reason was presumably of as divine an origin as their faith, and so its dictates might not be disregarded. They had, moreover, as an ideal an expanding concept of truth and of God, characteristic of the sceptic, who has set no bounds for himself but would sail far beyond the Pillars of Hercules.

> They [the Cambridge Platonists] were characteristically *rational* theologians. They sought to bring every truth or doctrine to the

test of the Christian reason, and to estimate it by a moral standard—in other words, by its tendency to exalt or degrade our conceptions of the divine. It was absurd, argues S. P.,[72] to accuse them 'of hearkening too much to their own reason.' 'For reason,' he adds, 'is that faculty whereby a man must judge of everything; nor can a man believe anything except he have some reason for it, whether that reason be a deduction from the light of nature, and those principles which are the candle of the Lord, set up in the soul of every man that hath not wilfully extinguished it; or a branch of divine revelation in the oracles of Holy Scripture; or the general interpretation of genuine antiquity, or the proposal of our own Church consentaneous thereto; or, lastly, the result of some or all of these; for he that will rightly make use of his reason, must take all that is reasonable into consideration. And it is admirable to consider how the same conclusions do naturally flow from all these several principles. . . . Nor is there any point in divinity where that which is most ancient doth not prove the most rational, and the most rational the ancientest; for there is an eternal consanguinity between all verity; and nothing is true in divinity which is false in philosophy, or on the contrary; and therefore what God hath joined together, let no man put asunder.'[73]

This, from another point of view, supports our symbol of the knot. The Platonists not merely admitted reason as a kind of poor relation at the intellectual table. Their hospitality went beyond that and they insisted upon the mutual aid which reason and religion could provide each other. To have denied either would have been to halve man's chances of arriving at the truth. Michael Roberts quotes Culverwel to substantiate this position.

'One light does not oppose another; Lumen fidei & Lumen rationis may shine both together though with farre different brightnesse; *the Candle of the Lord,* 'tis not impatient of a superiour light. . . . The light of Reason doth no more prejudice the light of faith, then the light of a Candle doth extinguish the light of a Star.'[74]

As Smith says,

'It is a fond imagination that religion should extinguish reason, whereas religion makes it more illustrious and vigorous; and they that live most in the exercise of religion shall find their reason most enlarged.'[75]

Culverwel devoted his *Discourse of the Light of Nature* to extolling the function of reason in the search for truth.

> The conciliation of reason and faith in refutation of the Socinians, and all who disparaged the mysteries of the Gospel, was to form the second and more important part of the treatise, which the author did not live to complete.[76]

As Tulloch paraphrases the words of Whichcote, we can see to what extent the sting had been removed from the rational attack upon religion.

> Reason is not only not opposed to faith, but there can be no faith without reason; nor yet any higher reason without faith. In other words, the spiritual life of our race is a unity; all our aspirations are alike divine, whether they are kindled within us by the 'candle of the Lord' set up in our hearts, or by the light of the Divine Word communicated to us from without.[77]

In all the literature of deism, there is hardly a more moving expression of the oneness of truth and of the coincidence of natural and revealed religion. As for the distinction between natural and supernatural, Whichcote illuminates it by the substitution of one verb for another.

> 'Reason discovers what is natural, and reason receives what is supernatural.'[78]

This is an echo of Browne's famous statement, 'And so I teach my haggard and unreclaimed reason to stoop unto the lure of faith.'

> A faith which is real, and a reason which is right, support and do not displace one another.
> This was the confident idea of the Cambridge divines.[79]

One means by which this support was effected relates back to historical scepticism and its *epoché*. Jordan says of Chillingworth,

> He had been guided solely by reason fortified by suspension of judgment.[80]

Reason alone might easily have gotten out of hand (witness the pride of intellect), but suspension of judgment constitutes a reliable brake. The way in which Chillingworth, with this safeguard, utilizes reason is set forth by Jordan thus:

> Chillingworth placed almost complete reliance in the power of reason. In his discussions of the highly controversial topics of his own day his appeal was ever to its judgment. No man should or can be compelled to believe a doctrine repugnant to his reason, nor can faith wholly supplant it. For it is reason that gives us knowledge and faith that gives us belief. Reasonable convictions must undergird all saving faith, since it is by reason alone that we are able to distinguish between truth and error. Above all, we must not so prostitute reason as to believe in a dogmatic system with an infallible faith which we cannot sustain by infallible arguments. In Chillingworth 'authority entirely disappears, and the whole fabric of religion is made to rest upon the way in which the unaided reason of man shall interpret the decrees of an omnipotent God.'[81]

The implications of this method for freedom of inquiry and for progressive revelation are not far to seek.

Looking back through almost three centuries, it is easy enough to be cynical about the results achieved by those who used reason to support faith, but it would seem more to the point to milk this method for all we can get out of it and then scrutinize its results to see how and why it failed.

> Edward Davenant, Fuller's cousin, could not endure, says Aubrey, to hear of the new philosophy, for if that was brought in, a new divinity would shortly follow. Davenant spoke more wisely than he knew. But More, like his fellow Platonists, believed with Whichcote that 'To go against Reason, is to go against God.' It is one of the ironies frequent in the age-old controversy that the defender of liberal religion began by seizing upon the two-edged sword of Cartesianism.[82]

It may even be that this irony in itself contains the germ of a new truth. Whatever was cut out of religion by the two-edged sword may have been only an excrescence and not the heart.

Bush is nearer to grasping what is significant in the Platonists' manipulation of reason and faith when he traces it to a double-vision which they inherited from the Christian humanists, whose very name implies their anti-dogmatism and their determination to embrace what is best in both traditions, lest they miss the truth.

The acceptance of both man's grandeur and his misery, the double vision of a god and a beast, had been a central fact in religious humanism ever since Plato and Cicero, and a temperate faith in the human reason and will was far too strong to be quickly overthrown. . . . Many of the best minds were striving, in the tradition of Christian humanism, to uphold a religious view of man and the world by reasserting the divinity of reason.[83]

It is 'the divinity of reason' which mirrors both the paradox which the Platonists and the metaphysicals would not relinquish and the courage of men whose religious perceptions were too real to be undermined by or relinquished to an enemy who in his blindness could see only one half of a dualism. They refused to recognize reason as a threat to faith, and so they disarmed it by showing its divinity.

The Irenic of Deism

The positive contribution of seventeenth-century sceptics toward settling the reason-faith controversy consists in neutralizing any evil effects of reason by emphasizing its role in support of faith. There followed logically from this procedure the conviction that by means of reason, which is God-given, man may arrive at the central truth of all religion, which is divinely implanted in the human heart. Deism or natural religion had a long and varied career from Lord Herbert of Cherbury through the Cambridge Platonists and on to its full flowering in the eighteenth century. Although among seventeenth-century thinkers there were varying degrees of tolerance, the most far-seeing hope was that an irenic might be devised which would bring into one spiritual community increasing numbers of men—all Nonconformists, then all Protestants, then all Christians, and finally all religious men of whatever creed.

Lord Herbert differs from such men as Baxter, Cromwell or Jeremy Taylor mainly in that, not content with reducing the creed to the minimum possible number of fundamentals, he goes behind Christianity itself, and tries to formulate a belief which shall command the universal assent of all men as men. It must be remembered that the old simple situation, in which Christendom pictured itself as the world, with only the foul paynim outside and the semi-tolerated Jews within the gates, had passed away for ever. Exploration and commerce had widened the horizon, and in many writers of the century one can see that the religions of the East, however imperfectly known, were beginning to press upon the European consciousness. It was a pioneer-interest in these religions, together with the customary preoccupation of Renaissance scholars with the mythologies of classical antiquity, which led Lord Herbert to seek a common denominator for all religions, and thus to provide, as he hoped, the much-needed eirenicon for seventeenth-century disputes.[84]

If truth were one and equally available to all men, it seemed unreasonable to make a serious issue of credal differences. Bush rightly points to the 'sectarian chaos' as breeding both scepticism and deism, emphasizing here the purely negative aspects of scepticism. According to our definition of the word, it would be more accurate to say that the wars of the sects led to scepticism, which in its turn, through an emphasis on reason as the propaedeutic of faith, produced deism as one of its results.

Deism of a kind may be said to have been alive since thought began. Although its modern origins were as various as its manifestations, it was on the negative side the child of scepticism, on the positive of Stoicism, that very malleable Stoicism which could also be fused with Arminianism and Puritanism.[85]

Again it seems wiser, instead of using *scepticism* in this loose way, to recognize how much it partakes of Stoicism, Arminianism, and Puritanism.

Bush calls attention to a Platonic strain in Lord Herbert and thus accounts for 'his conception of the universe as a harmonious organism and . . . the correspondences between it and man.'[86] The fusing of theology and philosophy, of Christian faith and humanistic reason, seems to us more adequately accounted for by the presence of scepticism than by saying that 'the eclectic Platonic tradition' mediated between scepticism and enthusiasm, empiricism and dogmatism. For it would seem to be the sceptic element in Platonism itself which is the mediating and irenic factor. So, too, Bush credits Lord Herbert with steering between two excesses—irreligious scepticism on the one hand and irrational fideism on the other.[87] We should view Lord Herbert rather as in the best tradition of genuine scepticism, which is opposed to both dogmatic disbelief and dogmatic belief. We can find in the seventeenth century few more succinct statements of the central sceptic openness to all kinds of truths than in Jordan's paraphrase of Lord Herbert's position.

In his *De Religione Gentilium* he advanced the radical opinion that all institutional religions were only relatively true and, he added, relatively false. No religion is entirely devoid of truth. Every faith that man has confessed has contained some elements of reason, and it is the task of the critic to examine religious systems dispassionately and comparatively in order to detect which elements are true and which false, and more especially to ascertain those great truths common to all religious communions. Every faith has within it a 'kernel' of truth, which, however, has usually been more or less concealed by the accretions foisted upon religion by the clergy. True faith, then, can be detected by a comparative study of the various historical religions. For the foundations of religion rest upon these universal laws and instincts which man cannot pervert or change without doing violence to his own nature. History reveals no religion or philosophy so barbaric that it did not contain the essential kernel of religious truth. These truths pervade the universe and all men are endowed with knowledge of them.[88]

Here is contained the sceptic *isosothenia*, the use of reason to prepare the ground for faith (the century's distinctive contribution to sceptic dualism), and the sceptic tendency to judge a statement of belief by its intention instead of taking it literally. For scepticism recognizes that each credal statement is but an attempt to mark the spot where an insight has been perceived by its author and his fellows, and that to mistake geography for history is a fatal error.

One specific result of using reason to work out the implications of faith was the elaboration of doctrines which were man-centred and whose justification lay in their promotion of righteousness.

> Thus God's willingness to be a partner with His creatures proved His essential rationality, benevolence, mercy, and forethought for the progressive capacity of man. The covenant helped to resolve the terrible uncertainties of election and reprobation and gave a reasonable basis and incentive for virtuous effort. Such a doctrine, in reinterpreting Calvinism (while trying to shun Arminianism), in enlarging man's powers and reducing the element of arbitrary grace, has affinities with the more liberal and amiable principles of the mainly Puritan group of Cambridge Platonists, with those of the Oxford Latitudinarians, and even with the natural religion of Lord Herbert of Cherbury.[89]

The normal concomitant of such a free launching out into the sea of faith under the aegis of reason was to be harsh criticism from men of a less sturdy spiritual build.

> Chillingworth, said the horrified Cheynell, 'was not ashamed to print and publish this destructive tenet, That there is no necessity of Church or Scripture to make men faithfull men'; and Chillingworth admitted that Scripture could not prove that there is a God or that it is the word of God. When good Christians could go so far, the natural light of reason might take others still farther. The current of rationalism had been rising for centuries, fed by many Christian writers and many ancient and modern sceptics. Chillingworth, for instance, knew Montaigne and, according to Aubrey, was devoted to Sextus Empiricus.[90]

What seems clear from this reaction is that scepticism was fulfilling its highest potentialities. Chillingworth's statements which so disturbed Cheynell were illustrative of the sceptic's ability to relinquish without fear all partial and direct statements of his faith (like saying to all of them, 'I do not know') in favour of what is more comprehensive and oblique and so partakes of the nature of 'the subtle knot.' In so far as the sceptic could admit, 'My religion does not depend upon this, or this,' he was more likely to come upon its essence, perhaps hidden, like all truth, in a dark well. Far from this situation's spelling danger, as Bush implies, it spelled the liberation of true religion from bondage to the non-essentials of faith. When he judges by the history of modern liberal Protestantism that Latitudinarianism was merely the opening wedge in the eventual destruction of religion, he is losing sight of the fact that what really went wrong, somewhere in the eighteenth century, was, as we shall try to show, the untying of 'the subtle knot.' If the lesson of the latitude-men and the Cambridge Platonists had been thoroughly learned, we should today be much farther along on the road toward a religion geared to our human needs, the needs of all sides of our being. Witness for instance how Falkland demonstrates what we have seen to be the characteristic sceptic ability to mediate between opposites, notably reason and grace:

But save Reason herself, he can imagine no ultimate guide to the Truth. Every intelligence in the end must incline to the side of the greater reason. 'For to be persuaded by reason, that to such an authority I ought to submit, is still to follow reason, and not to quit her. And by what else is it that you examine what the apostles taught, when you examine that by ancient tradition, and ancient tradition by a present testimony? Yet when I speak thus of finding the Truth by Reason, I intend not to exclude the Grace of God, which I doubt not (for as much as is necessary to salvation) is ready to concur to our instruction; as the sun is to our sight, if we by a wilful winking chuse not to make, not it, but our selves guilty of our blindness. . . . Yet when I speak of God's Grace, I mean not that it infuseth a knowledge without reason, but works by it, as by its minister, and dispels those mists of passions which do wrap up Truth from our understandings. For if you speak of its instructing any other way, you leave visible arguments to fly to invisible; and your adversary, when he hath found your play, will be soon at the same locke; and I believe in this sense, infused Faith is but the same thing, otherwise apparelled, which you have so often laught at in the Puritans under the title of private spirit.'⁹¹

Falkland must have been quite aware of the spiritual peril represented by the quicksands of antinomianism. In the case of these men of latitude, a necessary distinction must be drawn between responsible and irresponsible mysticism. The one, closely allied with reason yet not coincident with it, might project men toward the truth. The other, by its very lack of inclusiveness, bore the seeds of its own destruction. On the basis of one, men were drawn together in the unity of truth. As a result of the other, they approached spiritual anarchy as a limit.

On both sides of the Channel during the seventeenth century there were attempts other than those specifically deistic to bring together Jew and Christian, Jew and Gentile, and even to understand the intention behind classical mythology, on the theory that one God would not have left the world irreconcilable pictures of himself. This procedure is somewhat reminiscent of Paul's interpreting to the Athenians their unknown God. Early in the seventeenth century Philip Sidney and Arthur Golding translated from French the work of Phillippe de Mornay entitled *Traité de la Verité de la religion Chrétienne*, in which he was seeking a common ground for religious agreement on the theory that 'Divinity' and nature are not incompatible. Of God, Mornay says,

The rules thereof, and the principles of Nature which he hath made, cannot be contrary vnto himselfe: And he is also the very reason and truth it selfe. All other reason then, and all other truth dependeth vpon him, and relieth vpon him, neither is there or can there be any reason or truth but in him: So far off is it, that the thing which is true and reasonable in nature, is or can be false in Diuinity, which (to speake properly) is not against nature, but against the corruption of nature, and in very deed above nature.⁹²

But when there is involved the question of man's knowing either

Divinity or nature by means of his reason, Mornay reverts to a characteristically sceptic position. As for reason's being adequate to understand faith, it is not even adequate to understand nature, as all the sceptics from Pyrrho to Montaigne have argued. Concerning the men who say faith is not to be supported by reason, Mornay comments,

> Surely I will say more for them then they require: namely, that mans reason is so farre off from being the measure of faith, which very farre exceedeth nature, that it is not so much as the measure of nature, and of the least creatures which lye farre vnderneath man, because of the ignorance and vntowardnesse which is in vs and reigneth in vs. But in this way they deceive themselves, that they imagine vs to vphold, that we should beleeue no further than reason can measure and comprehend. For what a great way doth the truth of things extend further than mans reason? But we say that mans reason is able to lead vs to that poynt, namely, that we ought to beleeue even beyond reason, I meane, the things whereunto all the capacitie of man cannot attaine.[93]

It is as if earth-bound and often faulty reason propelled man, like a rocket, out into a spiritual stratosphere. But the intellectual operation which must precede this, like the compression of a spring, is that nescience which prepares man for whatever he may find beyond the atmosphere of this earth.

So, too, on the assumption of truth's unity, Cudworth sought to account for what seemed to him superficial discrepancies in theology.

> He entered into the whole subject of Pagan theology, and sought to trace the hidden Monotheism underlying its polytheistic modes of expression.[94]

None but the sceptic will have the flexibility which is a prerequisite for this operation.

Within the bounds of Christianity itself, there was a succession of writers throughout the century who were emphasizing what men had in common and trying to minimize their differences. It was the differences, long and loudly wrangled over, which had impressed onlookers with the irresponsibility of religious thinkers and had often cast the first doubt on man's ability to arrive at the truth—

> the unedifying spectacle of rival ecclesiastical groups making mutually contradictory, unreasonable, and, at times absurd claims with an air of absolute certainty and assurance.[95]

Hooker, early in the century, was willing to conceive of the Church, representing Christianity, as broad enough to comprehend all Christian activity and therefore to stand as a bulwark of tolerance.

> The Church was to Hooker, in fine, no dogmatic or exclusive institution—as the Puritans would have made it—partitioning by formal lines and boundaries the cosmos of spiritual thought and experience which had sprung from the divine ideal in Christ, and in Him recreated and transformed humanity. It was a spiritual order, capable of diverse forms, and tolerantly comprehensive of all Christian gifts and activities.[96]

Behind this statement of policy lay Hooker's personal religious experience which was of a piece with that of many outstanding religionists of his century.

> When Richard Hooker said at the beginning of the century that 'faith is more certain than any science,' he was voicing more than the spirit of his age, for religion, science, and the conflict between the two are timeless. Yet his words may conveniently be taken as a point of departure. The gentle and learned churchman had found security in God, and, like him, other men, learned and unlearned, continued to do so throughout the century. Donne, Baxter, and Fox were alike in turning to God. But the last two unexpectedly show traces of doubt. Baxter confessed in his *Autobiography* that he had 'lost much of that zeal which I had to propagate any truths to others, save the mere fundamentals.' One recognizes the impatience of a man who finds truth so clearly evident that he has no sympathy with the slow comprehension of others. But in addition, there is a

strain of the toleration and wise doubt of this part of the century: 'I am lately much prone . . . to be too indifferent what men hold and to keep my judgment to myself, and never to mention anything wherein I differ from another.'[97]

Two things are noteworthy here. One is that scepticism in the seventeenth century, where it was usually 'integrated into faith,' often meant a laying hold upon a dimly but certainly grasped reality and then slowly pulling oneself up to it. The other, a corollary of this, is that in the process, since men may necessarily have different methods of reaching the truth which they hold in common, it ill behooves any individual to separate himself from his fellows because they cannot agree on non-essentials. The claim is often made that such men, particularly the Latitudinarians and the Cambridge Platonists, in making a place for tolerance in their religious structure, destroyed organized religion.[98] From our point of view, it can only be countered that perhaps the kind of organized religion which hinders instead of promotes the truth had better be relinquished, just as the larger insight includes and transcends the more limited.

Something of the peculiar faith of the seventeenth century, in its highest manifestations, enabled men to exhibit a certain nonchalance toward the truth. We should account for this as a combination of sceptic nescience plus the certainty that there is a far-off terminus for man's truth-seeking, a conviction that a man is headed right, even though he cannot draw a detailed map of either his route or his destination. The resulting confidence in the power of truth is matched only by the seventeenth century's drive, in all fields, to recover it.

Vaughan seems to hold that the power of truth and reason must be relied upon to bring men to a common faith. Truth will in time be self-evident, for it is armed with sufficient power to overthrow all error. Although it may for a time 'be darkened by a cloude, yet at last it prevailes and gettes a victory; and the heretickes themselves are by Gods speciall judgments confounded, and their contagious opinions in a moment abated.'[99]

Milton echoes the same confidence in *Areopagitica* and couples with it a theory of progressive revelation. Thus there was a positive quality about seventeenth-century tolerance. It represented not merely a balancing of forces which otherwise would have been at each other's throats, but a broad foundation of syncretism.

> His [Taylor's] aim is not only reconciliation, but reconstruction on a wider basis. His position is near to that of a sceptical eclectic.[100]

By 1675 this kind of activity in the century was heading up into natural religion as a dynamic blending of reason and faith which should conserve the virtues of both. Tillotson says in his preface to Wilkins' *Of the Principles and Duties of Natural Religion*,

> The *Design* is threefold.
> *First*, To establish the great Principles of Religion, the *Being of God*, and a *Future State*; by shewing how firm and solid a Foundation they have in the Nature and Reason of Mankind.[101]

Action and Knowledge

An emphasis upon action has always been prominent in sceptical thought, ever since Carneades' assertion that, far from requiring absolute certainty, men may act even on the basis of probability. Seventeenth-century scepticism, too, retraced this phase of the pattern, with characteristic variations. The attempt of men throughout the century to discover in what kind and degree truth is available culminated in the latter half in what some might have called an abandonment of the problem. It seems wiser, however, to describe this as the gradual abandonment of the narrowly intellectualist approach with which the century opened. The purgative effect of a civil war had been to convince men that pure speculation was more futile in seeking out truth than was the action into which men were forced without adequate premises. In the field of religious thought, years of controversy had wrung from many of its participants the conclusion that what men do is of vastly more importance than what they are intellectually certain of. All the criteria for truth which were developed toward the end of the century partake of a certain anti-intellectualism—the appeal to universally acceptable notions, to what is in harmony with nature and reason, and most important for our purpose, to what is inwardly approved by a moral sense forged in the fires of practical living. What makes the seventeenth-century struggles in this respect so relevant in our own day is that we are perennially carrying on in one field after another the same kind of exploration for the establishment of new bases. As Willey says,

> The 'inner light' of the Quakers ranks with the 'Reason' of the Platonists, the 'clear and distinct ideas' of Descartes, or the 'common notions' of Lord Herbert of Cherbury, as another of the inward certitudes by means of which the century was testing the legacies of antiquity and declaring its spiritual independence.[102]

The next step after the Renaissance inheritance of classical wisdom was to scrutinize that with an eye on imitation, in the spirit of Emerson, who reminded his Phi Beta Kappa audience that 'Cicero, Locke, and Bacon were only young men in libraries when they wrote these books.'[103] The century was gradually substituting varieties of inward certitude for the authoritarianism of either a Church or of a philosophical system based on the infallibility of sense-impressions and of reason.

The Platonists, remembering still that the century had opened with the cry, 'How can we know?' reduced their formula for certitude to an attempt to purify the means of knowing.

> They would have less faithfully interpreted their master had they not gone on to insist, as they did, that the pursuit of 'Truth' involved the purification of the heart and the disciplining of the will; only the pure in heart could see God. 'Nothing is the true improvement of our rational faculties,' said Whichcote, 'but the exercise of the several virtues of sobriety, modesty, gentleness, humility, obedience to God and charity to men.' Thus as philosophers the Platonists found in the metaphysics of Plato a defence against Hobbesian materialism, while as moralists and preachers they found in him authority for their characteristic message, that conduct mattered more than creed.[104]

Similarly, the emphasis of Herbert of Cherbury had been on conduct as central to worship, in the spirit of Carlyle's *'Laborare est orare.'* Willey thus glosses a text from Lord Herbert:

> 'That the good ordering or disposition of the faculties of man constitutes the principal or best part of divine worship, and that this has always been believed.'
>
> About ceremonies men have disputed, but about the necessity for good conduct there has been a universal consensus. Piety and holiness of life are forms of worship, for they naturally produce love towards God and faith in him. We have, it is true, our bodily nature; but nature has implanted in us a taste for virtue, so that our souls may be gradually detached from earthly delights, and dwell in the constant enjoyment of inner tranquillity.[105]

There seems sufficient evidence to maintain the thesis that this tranquillity is connected with sceptic *ataraxia* by the ties of nescience, dualism, and paradox, as we have seen demonstrated.

We should perhaps digress briefly at this point to note the Platonic and mystical quality of the instrument by which these men would achieve, if not knowledge, wisdom. As Anderson paraphrases Henry More,

> The element that could unite religious people was not discursive analysis of the Scriptures, not rational thought on nature or morality, not acceptance of historic ideas, but rather an inward working spirit which found its source in the realm of eternal truth behind the world of material objects and which could be apprehended through the purification of the soul for a receptive grasp of divine knowledge.[106]

Here the road to truth is thought passable only by a soul which through right action has been rendered pure. Emerson was to approach the same end through his concept of the Oversoul.

Cudworth recognized that by the very nature of the soul thus purified, the often disregarded solipsism of the human spirit is thrown into bold relief. We may grasp a truth, he holds, in the midst of a welter of words and phrases; but there is no evidence that the words and phrases are the conductors of truth. They may be the innocent bystanders while truth is being conveyed from a higher to a lower potential. As Tulloch says, paraphrasing Cudworth,

> Words and syllables, which are but dead things, cannot possibly convey the living notions of heavenly truths to us. The secret mysteries of a divine life, of a new nature, of Christ formed in our hearts, they cannot be written or spoken, language and expressions cannot reach them; neither can they be ever truly understood, except the soul itself be kindled from within, and awakened into the life of them.[107]

It is obvious that men who felt thus about the transcendent power of truth could not have been very impressed by the claims of Sprat for the plain style. But they did understand the rationale of paradox, that perhaps the striking together of opposites may generate a spark to kindle the flame of truth. George Rust, in discoursing of the *Use of Reason In . . . Religion,* is one with the Platonists in recommending a holy life to the man who would come at the truth.

> I add moreover, that to render ourselves obedient to the will of our Heavenly Father, is the only plain and easie way to the attaining a true Knowledge and Vital Sense of Divine Revelations.
>
> For heavenly things are not otherwise to be known but by such an inward rellish and affecting light as Divine Grace usually imparts to defecate & humble Minds.[108]

The concept of grace, as far as we can see, bears no obvious relationship to scepticism except in so far as the sceptic is prepared by his nescience and his struggles with dualisms and paradoxes to admit truth, even from an unfamiliar direction. Not that he will abandon reason to embrace faith, but that his intellectual humility will have been the best preparation for a truth which continually breaks out of logical and verbal fetters.

John Norris of Bemerton, just after the century closed, showed himself as aware as Renaissance men were of his sceptical heritage but also aware, as only a seventeenth-century man could be, of scepticism's religious counterpart.

This latter part of Tranquility of Mind, was that which was so much both the Talk and Boast of some of the Heathen Philosophers, and concerning which one of them has written a particular Treatise. But the Philosophy of it is one thing, and the Possession of it is another. And though there is no doubt, but that Reason and Philosophy may go very far in composing the Mind into this sort of Tranquility, yet after all that Philosophy can do, the best and most effectual Remedy to lay the fury of the Passions, is the same that remedies the corruption of our Nature from whence it Springs, *viz*. the Grace of God.[109]

Suffice it to say here that 'the Grace of God' was an x to mark the spot at which a scepticism aware of its classic origins moved out into a greater creativity. Perhaps Baxter was talking of the same phenomenon in different terms.

In one of the interesting passages of self-analysis to be found in his *Autobiography*, he tells us that as he grew older he became more and more convinced of the supreme need for the 'witness of the indwelling Spirit.' Whereas in youth all his concern had been for the correctness of his doctrinal position, now it was centred upon 'internal experience.' In spite of the excesses of Ranters and Illuminists who find their 'witness' in 'a certain internal assertion or enthusiastic inspiration,' he feels that in another manner 'the Holy Ghost is the witness of Christ . . . the Spirit by renovation, sanctification, illumination and consolation, assimilating the soul to Christ and to heaven.'[110]

Every student of the seventeenth century recognizes that *scepticism* is only one of the words whose definition is essential to an understanding of the period. *Reason* is another important word whose meanings will throw considerable light on our own spiritual origins. The Platonists found themselves, like true sceptics, objecting to narrow definitions for terms which might have wider and more illuminating meanings. Hence they were dissatisfied with Descartes because reason seemed to them to include something more than logic. It was intimately bound up, for them, with right action. Michael Roberts, in analysing the origins of the modern mind, names 'fundamental honesty' as another ingredient of their 'reason.'

> This fundamental honesty, which the Platonists believed to be implanted in every man, was what they meant most often when they spoke of 'reason'; and this idea of reason led at once to their conception of God.[111]

Bush further elaborates this conception and makes clear its humanistic origins.

> The candle of the Lord is the *recta ratio* of the humanistic tradition, and *recta ratio* is found, Whichcote says to Tuckney, where *vera fides* is found. There is no conflict between reason and faith, because God is perfect reason and goodness and because reason and goodness are natural to man, whatever his unnatural lapses. Nothing truly religious is irrational and nothing truly rational is irreligious. The meanings of 'reason' in seventeenth-century thought 'admit a wide solution,' but for Whichcote, as for Taylor and Milton and others, reason signifies not the mere logical and critical faculty but the Platonic capacity for attaining divine truth, the whole unified personality of the well-disposed man.[112]

This last phrase, 'the whole unified personality of the well-disposed man,' is most significant for its relation to 'the subtle knot,' which from its origin means the inexplicable and fundamental binding together of body and soul into the human entity. It was fidelity to this knot which brought the Platonists into conflict with the intellectualism of Hobbes. They insisted upon the truths which seemed to them the result of their own religious experience, regardless of whether those could be made logically intelligible. Man, to them, was something more than his mind. Similarly, they were faced with the choice of making God a 'remote and unconvincing abstraction' or sacrificing logical coherence.

> English churchmen on the whole preferred to sacrifice consistency, and they asserted a duality of truth which made them ridiculous in the eyes of those who valued logical coherence more highly than practical morality.[113]

Here again is the sceptic alliance of dualism and practical morality.

The Platonists also felt the impact of the scientific thought which was coming to a focus in the Royal Society and of the related wariness of any language but the most clipped and precise. But they had been nurtured on the poetry of Plato and the English Bible, and like true sceptics, they refused to deny its insights and thus to narrow their conception of truth. Their importance in the history of the science-religion controversy, as Roberts says, was

> their typically English empiricism, their Protestant insistence on the capacity of the individual man to make right judgments for himself and above all, on their fundamental honesty.[114]

It was this honesty which prevented the Platonists from disregarding one-half of any dualism. For this reason, Henry More clung to both rationalism and enthusiasm.

> A cool, intellectual, mechanical and dualistic system could not satisfy the soul of a man like More, whose religious and ethical faith was a vital flame, who with all his rationalism had, as he confessed, a strain of 'enthusiasm' and whose profound intuition of the divine, coupled with a philosophic belief in the 'extension' of spirit, led him to find the omnipresence of God in infinite and indwelling space.[115]

Let us now look at the words of Smith and of Whichcote in order to substantiate the thesis that the Platonists were representative of men in the late seventeenth century who followed the sceptic way until it came full circle, from nescience to its answer (though perhaps not a logically explicable one) in the highest living of which men are capable. These are from John Smith:

> 'Were I indeed to define *Divinity*, I should rather call it a *Divine life* than a *Divine science*; it being something rather to be understood by a *Spiritual sensation* than by any *Verbal description*.'[116]
>
> 'They cannot be good at Theorie that are bad at Practice.'[117]

Whichcote applies the same principle to the theological point of Heaven's location. 'Heaven is *first* a temper, and *then* a place.'[118] Tulloch subsumes thus the contribution of Whichcote and in doing so makes evident the Platonists' conformity to the sceptic pattern in their refusal to be diverted from the concept of wholeness:

> Religion is not a mere section of knowledge supernaturally communicated, nor a side of life supernaturally imparted, but a culture and discipline of the whole man—an education and consecration of all his higher activities. And so religion is not only not independent of morality, but its necessary complement—not only not an enemy of philosophy, but its highest fulfilment. Christianity binds the broken lines of human aspiration into a well-orbed power, which embraces and completes them all.[119]

Other men than the Platonists demonstrated the pragmatic basis upon which much religious conviction came to rest. It was not so much that action would provide men with logically formulable truths but that it would bring a tranquillity and satisfaction which by-passed the need for absolute certainty. Richard Baxter, as we shall discover later, was a shining example of the way in which this process worked.

> For many years he had acted as if Christianity were true without once supposing the contrary; and the result had been a deepening conviction of its truth because of the light, strength and peace it had brought to him. So he had this to fall back upon as something sure when reason was baffled; and for this he thanked God, who had spared him the Temptation of searching doubt until he was able to bear it.[120]

It is for such reasons as this that those who have a sceptic approach to religion are for ever undaunted by the threat of doubts.

Fruits of Creative Scepticism

What then can we say, now that we have traced the pattern of scepticism in seventeenth-century thought, were the fruits of this scepticism, and with what justification can it be called creative? As it was the sorry picture of warring sects which often caused men to doubt the very existence of truth, so it was in the field of religious controversy that scepticism bore its most luxuriant fruit. From there we shall not find it difficult to translate the results into other terms which have a more immediate relevance for our day.

It is to religious controversy that we are indebted for having made explicit the otherwise undeveloped film of Richard Baxter's scepticism. In the contrast between his irenicism and the vindictive dogmatisms of other men we can see clearly the creative role of scepticism.

> In Baxter's day parties and sects were strongly marked and fiercely divided. The peacemaker, who desired to do what S. T. Coleridge and F. D. Maurice aimed at in their attempts, to show how portions of truth had been appropriated by minds differing widely, had no place of honour in the seventeenth century.[121]

But Baxter was not a man to be ignored, and his forthright attempts at mediation only involved him more deeply in the controversy which all his life he was trying to prevent.

> In fact, the middle way turned out for him, as for many another, a *via dolorosa*. It exposed him to rebuffs from extremists on both sides. But holding, as he did, that the middle way is the golden way of truth and peace, he set himself to find and follow it, in scorn of personal consequence.[122]

In analysing the self-destructive methods of the controversialists, William Haller pulls together a number of the phases of scepticism which we have hitherto treated. He paraphrases the arguments of those who, like Baxter, were striving for an intellectually respectable basis for unity.

> If in the field of reason no man can hope to attain perfect knowledge of truth, it does not follow that truth cannot exist or cannot be known. Truth is absolute, knowledge relative. Truth, in itself one and entire, is reflected diversely in a myriad of facets in the reasons of men. . . . Consequently, every man must be free to let

whatever ray of light may be vouchsafed him shine forth and to search the scriptures for more light. . . . Pride then stops the process of search and discovery, of distinguishing the true from the false, by which knowledge grows, while we go about extirpating not error, which is always with us, but our opponents, who may be wiser than we.[123]

Here is nescience, implied paradox, and an openness to the promptings of truth from whatever direction they may come. It is so much easier to attack personalities than to grapple with issues that a constant threat lies in wait for travellers along the sceptic way.

Where the presence of scepticism was recognized by the controversialists themselves, the recognition often resulted in a clarifying and sharpening of issues, all of which contributed to a more self-conscious and effective use of scepticism.

The notions that every man must be ruled by his own conscience and that no man is so free from error that he may dictate what others must believe obviously meant that no power existed in human form that could absolutely declare what is truth. This, as the critics of Acontius and men of similar opinions objected, calling them generally Socinians, was to come close to downright scepticism. The humanist reformers had, however, their own considered reply to such attack. They attempted to draw a clear line between the field of faith and that of reason. The things to be believed were few; they were revealed directly to the heart of man, and they alone were essential to salvation. The things to be discovered and determined by reason were well-nigh infinite in number, attainable only at the end of something like infinite inquiry and discourse but inessential to salvation.[124]

It is interesting to note here the point at which there was the risk of abandoning scepticism, as indeed the fideists did. The genuine sceptic, however, does not take the direct and easy way of jumping from one half of a dualism to another—from reason to faith—but attempts to salvage the insights of both. Faith gives him general truths, like the five common notions of Lord Herbert, and reason is occupied in working out their implications, *ad infinitum.* This distinction between fundamental and non-fundamental doctrines was the contribution of Arminianism toward destroying both Protestant and Catholic dogmatism.[125] The position of Episcopius, the great Dutch systematizer of Arminianism, was that

> Christians should be content so long as the fundamentals of faith are maintained. The goal of an exact uniformity is quite impossible of attainment and perhaps undesirable, and any effort to secure it by harshness and rigour can find no support in Christianity.[126]

What Jordan is referring to here is undoubtedly the pure spirit of Christianity rather than its all too human exemplifications.

There can be seen in the writings of Francis Quarles the kind of thinking, essentially sceptical, out of which toleration was to grow. That it was later to lose some of its richness is attributable, as we shall show, to the untying of 'the subtle knot.'

> The writer [Quarles] pleaded that Christians should rid themselves of dogmatic zeal and that they should endeavour to gain perspective and objectivity in their estimate of the problems created by religious differences. When a man succeeds in establishing this sceptical yet charitable attitude, the errors and intolerance of both sides become immediately apparent. He will see that most of the harshness and bigotry proceeds from a concern with matters of faith which are not essential.[127]

Only the sceptic has the ground on which he can stand to make this analysis, for he does not allow himself to become involved in half-truths.

Willey picks up this sceptic virtue from the seventeenth century and applies it with percipience to the science-religion controversy, against whatever backdrop it may be enacted.

> Perhaps there may be in truth more than one kind of humility; a humility of religion, and a humility of science. The man of religion humbles himself before Being; the man of science, before Becoming. And as long as religion is whispering results, as long as science is whispering results, so long each is showing its own proper humility. The greatest results in each sphere have been won through

humility. But as 'results' accumulate, both begin to dispute and assert; religion ceases to be *scientifically* humble, and science ceases to be *metaphysically* humble. The humility of each consists largely in keeping to its own sphere, and recognizing the independent validity of the other.[128]

It was in the spirit of this kind of far-sighted and creative tolerance that Peter Sterry exhorted his brethren to make the most of every faint glimmer of truth instead of extinguishing it by the fury of controversy.

'O that I had a hundred mouths,' he writes, 'an hundred tongues, a Voice like the Voice of God that rends Rocks, to cry to all sorts of Persons and Spirits in this Land and in all the Christian World through the whole creation: "Let all that differ in Principles, Professions, Opinions and Forms see the good there is in each other!" '[129]

The Cambridge Platonists were one of the answers to Sterry's prayer, but they could not single-handed stem the tide of dogmatism although they did somewhat divert it and left for all future generations an eternally burning beacon of hope.

These latitudinarian Platonists shared with Lord Falkland's Oxonian group the desire to find a peaceful *via media*, but the Cambridge men tried to lay a broader philosophic foundation in ground which was more and more dangerously undermined. Illuminated by belief in the unity of truth, the ordered harmony of God's universe, the active reality of spirit, and the 'deiform' nature and freedom of man, they found in these conceptions a fullness, strength, and inwardness of rational faith which raised them above bitter contention, above both enthusiasm and ritualism, above the hard determinism first of Calvin and later of Hobbes.[130]

This general statement is implemented by the performance of Hales, who stressed both the unity of men and the superior value of a life to a creed.

Hales had little more trust than Selden in church councils and the Holy Ghost's attendance upon majorities. In his sermons and tracts he is always pleading for 'the unity of the Spirit in the Bond of Peace,' the true unity of individual men who follow the plain guidance of Scripture and avoid vain speculation and debate about things not fundamental in the warfare of life. 'It was never the Intent of the Holy Ghost, to make it a matter of Wit and Subtilty, to know how to be saved.' 'Christ is our Aristotle.' The natural reason of the 'Ethnick Philosophers' brought them close to Christianity, and a Fabricius or a Regulus belongs as much to the Church of Christ as a Christian whose life falls short of his beliefs.[131]

Falkland, of the Oxford Group, considered scepticism self-regulatory since those who are seriously searching for truth will have no time or energy to go heresy-hunting among their neighbours.

Falkland recommended a sceptical humility, a searching for truth which would absorb every man and leave him disposed to permit to every other man the same freedom.[132]

From Whichcote comes the most psychologically powerful deterrent to dogmatism ever devised.

'It becomes the modesty of particular persons when their sentiments are singular to ask themselves this sober question, How went the Spirit of God from the generality of His worshippers, and determined itself to me?'[133]

If a man could remain a dogmatist after honestly asking himself this question, he would be hopelessly entangled in the lunatic fringe. Stillingfleet felt that the mere diversity of an opinion did not constitute it as heresy but that what was damnable was the kind of persecution to which that diversity often led.

It is only the 'endeavour, by difference of opinion, to alienate men's spirits one from another, and thereby to break the society into fractions and divisions, which makes men liable to restraint and punishment.'[134]

That men like Whichcote understood the kind of opposition they would meet and with sceptic flexibility adapted themselves to it is a tribute to the method of truth-seeking which they were employing.

To men of the class of the Westminster Divines, in whom the spirit of dogmatic affirmation is strong, and the spirit of speculative insight weak, if not utterly wanting, few things are more difficult to understand than a theological standpoint different from their own, and, indeed, not only different, but incommensurate—stretching widely beyond their doctrinal particularism, and taking it up into a higher synthesis as of little or no account. They are out of their reckoning before the advance of a new line of thought, which overlooks rather than crosses or opposes their favourite dogmas, and starts on a fresh career. On the other hand, a mind like Whichcote's, meditative rather than polemical, speculative rather than dogmatic, does not court notice for its growing light, but adapts itself as far as possible to the theological atmosphere and associations surrounding it. He was far too wise and broad-minded to be intent merely on the assertion of his own views, and not to feel that all changes of opinion which are really worth promoting must be gradual, and spring organically from the natural decay of pre-existing modes of thought.[135]

Tillotson's funeral sermon for Whichcote contains a passage which shows that Whichcote's scepticism, far from being a relatively objective method, permeated all his experience.

'And although he had a most profound and well-poised judgment, yet he was of all men I ever knew the most patient to hear others differ from him, and the most easy to be convinced when good reason was offered; and, which is seldom seen, more apt to be favourable to another man's reason than his own. Studious and inquisitive men,' he [Tillotson] adds, 'at such an age (at forty or fifty, at the utmost) have fixed and settled their judgments on most points, and, as it were, made their last understanding—supposing that they have thought or read or heard what can be said on all sides of things; and after that they grow positive and impatient of contradiction. But our deceased friend was so wise as to be willing to learn to the last, knowing that no man can grow wise without some change of his mind—without gaining some knowledge which he had not, or correcting some error which he had before.'[136]

This is both the essence of the sceptic method and the evidence that it has borne abundant fruit.

George Rust puts into the characteristic sceptic form of a paradox his belief that there are worse sins than heresy, and that perhaps the method of attaining truth is more important than the end result.

> Nay certain it is, that he who after an humble, pious, and attentive weighing of Things shall yet fall into Error, is upon better grounds to be judged if not worthy of Praise, yet at least of Pardon, then he that shall blindly and fortuitously assent, though to Truth itself.[137]

One is reminded of the admonition, 'He that entereth not by the door into the sheepfold, but climbeth up some other way, the same is a thief and a robber' (John 10: 1). Perhaps we cannot with impunity rest in a shallow pragmatism which holds that the end is more important than the means.

Even natural genius, according to Phillippe de Mornay, can become the slave of dogmatism, but he has the greatest likelihood of finding the truth who will maintain a sceptic hospitality to all ideas, by which ultimately his will may be guided.

> For foredeemings & foresetled opinions do bring in bondage the reason of them that have best wits, whereas notwithstanding it belongeth not to the will to overrule the wit, but to the wit to guide the will.[138]

Whitlock was as aware as other sceptics that the mind's tran quillity and independence lies in its power to forgo the fatal intellectual luxury of dogmatism.

> To be of *Truths Jury*, not *Knight of the Post* to any *Opinion* or *Interest*: this temper *Serenes* the *Soule* from *Passion*, cleareth its *Intellectualls, and* restoreth it (in part) to its first, and best Independency.[139]

To achieve this combination of *ataraxia*, purgation of the mind, and intellectual freedom—all in the service of truth—was the goal of the seventeenth-century sceptic. To what degree he achieved this goal may be estimated by examining the writing produced by five of such sceptics.

CHAPTER IV

JOHN DONNE AND THE POETRY OF SCEPTICISM

✂

TO those who equate scepticism with dogmatic disbelief the phrase 'the poetry of scepticism' will seem anomalous. But since the rich and flexible scepticism which made its appearance in seventeenth-century England was true to its Greek origins, it has many points of contact with poetry, just as did Greek scepticism, no matter how the boundaries of poetry are drawn. To observe scepticism being forged from the poetic experience of John Donne is perhaps to arrive at a clearer understanding of its nature than can result from a logical analysis in terms of abstractions.

Both by temperament and by the accident of his position in history, Donne was placed advantageously to demonstrate the poetic possibilities of scepticism—some of which both Sir Thomas Browne and Richard Baxter inadvertently touched with the wings of their prose. All Donne's critics have been aware of his 'cautious, sceptical temperament.'[1] Courthope notes the 'mixture of strong religious instinct and philosophical scepticism,'[2] and T. S. Eliot talks about 'a manifest fissure between thought and sensibility.'[3] Such dichotomies are the stuff of scepticism; and no matter into what divergent patterns the formal philosophy of sceptics may finally settle, the essential experience which makes them sceptics will be found to be that embodied in the poetry of Donne.

> By his fidelity to deep and sullen learning, to the demands of flesh and the promptings of a sensitive conscience, all presenting truths appearing to contradict one another, he was led into a troubled state of mind from which he never realized complete freedom.[4]

It is only from his momentary glimpses of such freedom that we may project what might have been his path toward complete release.

The late Renaissance in England provided both a reflection and a reinforcement of the troubled spiritual state in which Donne found himself. Although diverse elements had contributed to the intellectual unsettling which was to give the period its distinctive character, the Copernican revolution has long stood as a convenient symbol and focus of this dilemma. As a result of scientific experimentation and discovery, faith and knowledge, passion and reason struggled for supremacy, and there no longer existed, either in the scientific world or in the soul of man, an infallible authority which should silence all controversy. The Renaissance man, once the first fine enthusiasm for the new learning had subsided, discovered that the very axis of his universe had slipped, and his minor uncertainties were overlaid by the doubt that there was any sure foundation for human knowledge, whether in science or in the more immediate and pressing areas of ethics and religion.

The fact that in Donne's work we have predominantly the reactions of a poet to this situation, rather than those of a prose writer, means that we have two advantages in tracing the emergence of his scepticism. One is that his experience is thus transmitted to the reader with greater immediacy than if the medium were prose, and the other is that whatever insights the poet achieves as a sceptic are clothed with metaphor, the traditional language of poetry, and so will lend significance to a wider area of experience than would rigorous philosophical conclusions. Moreover, we, who are sufficiently congenial with the temper of the Renaissance to share Donne's emotional perturbation over the fact of crumbling spiritual foundations, may take courage from his illuminating metaphors. As Robert Hillyer says of him, 'He is the subtle spokesman for the darker margins of consciousness; . . . [he] accompanies us down the labyrinth of melancholy with promise of the light to come.'[5] Whatever solace Donne can give us is essentially that of the poet rather than of the philosopher or theologian (although he can be said to have played all three roles), for he 'silences the sceptical and destructive wit by the power of vision rather than of intellectual conviction.'[6] Perhaps sharing the immediacy of Donne's experience as a sceptic, as well as his resulting vision, will enable us to understand the complexity and profundity of the scepticism which flourished among his contemporaries of the late Renaissance and throughout the seventeenth century.

Nescience

In the poetry of the English Renaissance there are few more poignant lines than those in which Donne expresses for his generation the shattering effect of the new learning. Amid the *tour de force* of 'The First Anniversary,' when he is led from sorrow at the death of Elizabeth Drury to the conclusion that man himself is a 'trifling thing,' he puts the ultimate blame for man's corruption upon the Fall—the fact that the world was 'almost created lame'; but he puts an almost equal responsibility upon the 'new Philosophy.'

> And new Philosophy calls all in doubt,
> The Element of fire is quite put out;
> The Sun is lost, and th'earth, and no mans wit
> Can well direct him where to looke for it.
> And freely men confesse that this world's spent,
> When in the Planets, and the Firmament
> They seeke so many new; then see that this
> Is crumbled out againe to his Atomies.
> 'Tis all in peeces, all cohaerence gone;
> All just supply, and all Relation:
> Prince, Subject, Father, Sonne, are things forgot,
> For every man alone thinkes he hath got
> To be a Phoenix, and that then can bee
> None of that kinde, of which he is, but hee.[7]

Not only does the new philosophy take away one of the four elements, but not content with this world it ranges over the universe seeking new planets. The organization of the one world which men formerly knew has been dissolved; relation and coherence exist no longer, either in the physical realm or in the social. And once man slips his social ties, his individualism leads on to anarchy.

Proceeding to the 'Second Anniversary,' Donne diagnoses this intellectual confusion as symptomatic of man's fundamental ignorance. 'Poore soule, in this thy flesh what dost thou know?'[8] Quite apart from the mysteries of birth and death, man does not even know how to explain his own bodily functions— how blood circulates and how nails and hair grow. Here Donne expresses a fundamental insight of scepticism when he says,

> And one Soule thinkes one, and another way
> Another thinker, and 'tis an even lay.[9]

In order for a truth to satisfy the sceptic completely it must lie on a plane above that on which either of two propositions could be true. Its inclusiveness must not admit of an opposite. Because the arrival at such a truth is practically impossible on this earth, Donne, like other sceptics whose background is religious, sets the goal of perfect knowledge in an after-life.

> Thou shalt not peepe through lattices of eyes,
> Nor heare through Labyrinths of eares, nor learne
> By circuit, or collections to discerne.
> In heaven thou straight know'st all, concerning it,
> And what concernes it not, shalt straight forget.[10]

Like Sir Thomas Browne, Donne scorns the desperate search on this earth for a knowledge 'which Death gives every fool gratis, and is an accessory of our glorification.'[11] This does not mean that the sceptic abandons the search for truths, tentative and partial though they may be. It means only that because he has seen the extreme difficulty of arriving at any knowledge, he maintains a more casual attitude than other thinkers toward the problem of knowing, especially in view of the contrast between 'man's nothing perfect and God's all complete.'

In one of his sermons (many of which contain as much poetry as any of his verses) Donne makes use of a striking simile to express the quality of death which hangs about all human knowledge.

And how imperfect is all our knowledge? What one thing doe
we know perfectly? Almost all knowledge is rather like a child that
is embalmed to make Mummy, then that is nursed to make a Man;
rather conserved in the stature of the first age, then growne to be
greater; And if there be any addition to knowledge it is rather a
singularity in a desire of proposing something that was not known
at all before, then an emproving, an advancing, a multiplying of
former inceptions; and by that means, no knowledge comes to be
perfect.[12]

Donne seems to imply here that a proper nurture of any specific
bit of human knowledge might succeed in turning it into perfect knowledge, that it is not our material but our technique
which is at fault.

What, then, is the outcome of this fundamental despair concerning the possibility of man's knowing anything with certainty?
For one thing, it gives Donne a certain lightness of touch in
dealing with the imperfections of human knowledge.

In such things as are problematicall, if thou love the peace of
Sion, be not too inquisitive to know, not too vehement, when
thou thinkest thou dost know it.[13]

This is not a proscription against investigation nor a condemnation of the *libido sciendi*. Rather is it a caution against dogmatizing
on the basis of partial truths.

Again, Donne recognized and apparently had considerable
sympathy with the Pyrrhonism of his day. In the passage quoted
above in which he uses the mummy figure, he says apropos of the
deadly kind of learning which only adds fact to fact,

One Philosopher thinks he is dived to the bottome, when he sayes,
he knows nothing but this, That he knows nothing; and yet another
thinks, that he hath expressed more knowledge then he, in saying,
That he knows not so much as that, That he knows nothing.[14]

Justifiable as such conclusions are, Donne feels the essential
futility of this *reductio ad absurdum*. In another sermon he demonstrates the creative use which he can make of his scepticism, how

instead of adding fact to fact, he can allow a single fact to grow and blossom and so fulfil itself.

> To know how near nothing, how meer nothing, all the glory of this world is, is a good, a great degree of learning. . . . I shall know . . . that a flower that lives but a day, is an abridgment of that King, that lives out his threescore and ten years; but I shall know, too, that all these Ants and Bees, and Flowers, and Kings, and Kingdoms, howsoever they may be Examples, and Comparisons to one another, yet they are all as nothing, altogether nothing, less than nothing, infinitely less than nothing, to that which shall then be the subject of my knowledge, for, *it is the knowledge of the glory of God.*[15]

In the swing between man's nothingness and God's completeness, Donne transmutes his nescience into an arc of poetry. The continual focussing upon the perfection of knowledge in another life accounts for both Donne's despair of human knowledge and his warning not to treat it as final and complete.

The Function of Doubt

In the light of his attitude toward knowledge it is fruitful to investigate the use which he makes of doubt. It is easily seen how a man with his set of mind would be completely fearless in the face of doubts. With knowledge so confused and uncertain and partial, there is no closed and dogmatically defended system for doubts to attack; therefore Donne is able to use them constructively and creatively in his search for truth. With a single analogy he removes their sting.

> Oft from new proofes, and new phrase, new doubts grow,
> As strange attire aliens the men wee know.[16]

There is perfect confidence, on Donne's part, that 'the men we know' constitute a solid and unchanging base, no matter what the variations may be. Here again is the sceptic emphasis on the human element symbolized by 'the subtle knot.' Donne combines a keen perception of his own mental processes with an uncanny sense for the precise metaphor when he describes thus the process

of approaching truth through the devious ways made necessary
by man's essential ignorance:

> To adore or scorne an image, or protest,
> May all be bad; doubt wisely; in strange way
> To stand inquiring right, is not to stray;
> To sleepe, or runne wrong, is. On a huge hill
> Cragged, and steep, Truth stands, and hee that will
> Reach her, about must, and about must goe;
> And what the hills suddennes resists, winne so;
> Yet strive so, that before age, deaths twilight,
> Thy Soule rest, for none can worke in that night.[17]

This one figure sets forth vividly the sceptic despair of knowledge, the belief in doubt as a valuable technique, the inevitability
of dualism and paradox ('about must, and about must goe'),
and the conviction that truth will finally be found at the top of a
huge and cragged hill. Donne's chief fear was that men should
come to rest in dogmatisms part-way down the mountain-side,
and so should cease struggling. He is not merely making a virtue
of necessity when he cries up the value of arguing constructively
about religion.

> And who can deny but *Controversies in Religion* are growne
> greater by *discord*, and not the *Controversie*, but *Religion* it selfe:
> For in a *troubled misery* Men are alwaies more *Religious* than in a
> *secure peace.* .... Wee are ascertained of all *Disputable* doubts onely
> by *arguing* and differing in *opinion*, and if formall *disputation* (which
> is but a painted, conterfeit, and dissembled *discord*) can worke us
> this benefit, what shall not a full and maine *discord* accomplish?[18]

Donne's scepticism is nowhere more apparent than in his suspicion of a 'secure peace' and his maintenance that 'a troubled
misery' accords better with the nature of man. For is not 'a
troubled misery' another name for 'the subtle knot which makes
us man'? The doubts which his experience wrung from him and
which he saw reflected in the men about him had a catalytic
influence upon the thought of this period.

That doubt, leading even to disillusionment, may be one of the ways of getting toward the truth can hardly be denied. In fact, such a questioning attitude was one of the freshest impulses released by the Renaissance. When exerted against the shame of antiquity it strengthened the grounds for a true 'advancement of learning'; when put to use in the search for philosophical truth, it led to the evolution of a *Discourse on Method* whereby the truth might be found; again, when it infected the poet's imagination it threw into their right perspective the obvious, and therefore easily neglected or conventionalized, experiences of flesh and spirit.[19]

Paradox

The most superficial reader of Donne's poetry cannot fail to be struck by its paradoxes, sometimes flippant and sometimes grave. His 'By tomorrow I may think so too' might argue an irresponsible carelessness where truth is concerned. But we take one step nearer the essential seriousness which underlies his use of paradox when we hear him say,

> So though some things are not together true,
> As, that another is worthiest, and, that you:
> Yet, to say so, doth not condemne a man,
> If when he spoke them, they were both true than.[20]

What these two passages demonstrate is Donne's intellectual honesty, which prevents him from setting consistency above truth. The guiding principle which underlies such easy paradoxes is to be found far beneath the surface of ordinary controversy. It is a conviction born out of the most elemental experience of man, a conviction that there can be no ultimate peace between flesh and spirit, that their knotted oneness is at once his glory and his tragedy. This primary dualism breeds others whose halves are equally unreconcilable, until any conclusion which is formed must inevitably take on the nature of paradox. Donne's insistence upon the eternal war between flesh and spirit is reminiscent of his warning against a deceptive peace in the field of religious controversy.

Woe be to that man that is so at peace, as that the spirit fights not against the flesh in him; and woe to them too, who would make them friends, or reconcile them, betweene whom, God hath perpetuated an everlasting war.[21]

Perhaps it takes a statement like this, centuries after the event, to gloss effectively Jesus' words, 'I came not to send peace but a sword.'

Dualism

For Donne the dualism of flesh and spirit underlies the complexity of human experience, and all other dualisms take on the rhythm of this one.

To find the One behind the Many, to trace the permanent throughout the ever-changing, to ask the riddle of the universe, this was the quest on which Donne set forth early, and continued late till death overtook him.[22]

The outcome in terms of answers was not pat and puerile. Donne's great contribution was his insistence that the answer, when it came, must partake of the nature of the question. It must not by-pass the essential dualism of man's experience. It must not cut or untie 'the subtle knot.' Characteristically, the nearest he ever came to an answer was to propose a striking and fecund metaphor to light up the area of his deepest perplexity. Here is the prose version:

Take a flat Map, a Globe *in plano*, and here is East, and there is West, as far asunder as two points can be put: but reduce this Map to roundnesse, which is the true form, and then East and West touch one another, and are all one: So consider mans life aright, to be a Circle.[23]

And in the 'Hymn to God, my God in my sicknesse,' we get the same figure expanded and applied to the experience of death.

As West and East
In all flatt Maps (and I am one) are one,
So death doth touch the Resurrection. . . .
Therefore that he may raise the Lord throws down.[24]

In both these passages there is the implication that if the world
which is seen dualistically could be viewed as it really is, with
another dimension added, all dualisms would be resolved in oneness. Thus when man moves into the orbit of God, he has an
analogous experience to that of human love, which always adds
other dimensions to what was previously a flat world. But
because such beatific vision is the exception rather than the rule,
Donne must rely upon the use of paradox to express his quotidian
perception of truth. His poems are full of such paradoxes, ranging
from the easy and the flippant to the profoundly moving. One
of them echoes his prose lament that the most trivial distractions
keep him from his devotions—'a light in mine eye, a straw under
my knee.'

> Oh, to vex me, contraryes meet in one:
> Inconstancy unnaturally hath begott
> A constant habit; that when I would not
> I change in vowes, and in devotione. . . .
> So my devout fitts come and go away
> Like a fantastique Ague: save that here
> These are my best dayes, when I shake with feare.[25]

For Donne the mystery of the incarnation represents only a
heightening of the mystery which inheres in every human birth
and which, before that, has hung about the act of love itself, which
inexplicably unites flesh and spirit in 'the subtle knot.' To Mary
in the 'Annunciation,' he says,

> That All, which alwayes is All every where,
> Which cannot sinne, and yet all sinnes must bear,
> Which cannot die, yet cannot chuse but die . . . yea thou art now
> Thy Makers maker, and thy Fathers mother.[26]

In the 'Nativitie' Donne asks,

> Seest thou, my Soule, with thy faithes eyes,
> how he
> Which fils all place, yet none holds him,
> doth lye?[27]

Proceeding to the practice of the Christian way of life, he puts
his deepest insights into paradoxical form.

> Churches are best for Prayer, that have least light:
> To see God only, I goe out of sight:
> And to scape stormy dayes, I chuse
> An Everlasting night.[28]

>   for, the losse
> Of this Crosse, were to mee another Crosse;
> Better were worse, for, no affliction,
> No Crosse is so extreme, as to have none.[29]

> Take mee to you, imprison mee, for I
> Except you'enthrall mee, never shall be free,
> Nor ever chast, except you ravish mee.[30]

There is an echo here of the smart young courtier who fathered
Paradoxes and Problems for the amusement of his witty friends.
But whether he was gay or sober, the set of Donne's mind was
the same, and he never lost sight either of dualisms or of the
paradoxes in which they issue.

Reason and Faith

When Donne attempted to objectify his personal experience
of dualisms and set it alongside the experience of other men,
he found both centred in the most serious and deep-seated
spiritual dilemma of the age—the relationship between reason
and faith. Not only had the new philosophy made all knowledge
suspect. It had also weakened the comfortable mediaeval conviction that reason and faith are interdependent and that one
reinforces the other. Too often the Renaissance man saw the
two in conflict, and he was perpetually abandoning himself now
to one and now to the other, since he was without any hope of
their *rapprochement*. As a sceptic, Donne does not allow himself
any *ex cathedra* pronouncements on the subject. Rather does he
express his insights by means of metaphors whose beauty and
variety recall his warning,

> On a huge hill,
> Cragged, and steep, Truth stands and hee that will
> Reach her, about must, and about must goe.[31]

In both its origins and its effect his method is similar to that used in the parables of Jesus. It is as if both teachers made a concession to the fact that abstract discourse often breaks down and must be superseded by something more imaginative and more akin to the complex oneness of the human personality, to 'the subtle knot.'

The first of these metaphors occurs in a poem praising Mrs. Magdalen Herbert, where Donne is drawing an analogy between knowing her and knowing divine truths.

> Reason is our Soules left hand, Faith her right,
> By these we reach divinity, that's you. . . .
> But soone, the reasons why you'are lov'd by all,
> Grow infinite, and so passe reasons reach,
> Then backe againe to'implicite faith I fall,
> And rest on what the Catholique voice doth teach; . . .
> For rockes, which high top'd and deep rooted sticke,
> Waves wash, not undermine, nor overthrow.[32]

Here Donne sees the necessary co-operation of reason and faith, the way in which faith supports those who have pushed reason to its farthest limits, and the solidity of convictions which are at once 'high top'd and deep rooted,' which thrust in two directions.

For the second metaphor Donne goes to the new astronomy and exorcizes its disruptive quality by making it a symbol. In the following lines he elaborates the 'left hand, right hand' figure to make reason and faith co-regnant over realms which cannot interfere with each other, and which seen from above almost coincide.

> Looke to mee faith, and looke to my faith, God;
> For both my centers feele this period.
> Of waight one center, one of greatnesse is;
> And Reason is that center, Faith is this;

For into'our reason flow, and there do end
All that this naturall world doth comprehend:
Quotidian things, and equidistant hence,
Shut in, for man, in one circumference.
But for th'enormous greatnesses, which are
So disproportion'd, and so angulare,
As is Gods essence, place and providence,
Where, how, when, what soules do, departed hence,
These things (eccentrique else) on faith do strike;
Yet neither all, nor upon all alike.
For reason, put to'her best extension,
Almost meetes faith, and makes both centers one.33

The 'enormous greatnesses . . . so disproportion'd, and so angulare' dwarf reason and all its realm; and in their light all petty and
earth-born rivalries disappear.

For reason, put to'her best extension,
Almost meetes faith, and makes both centers one.

The third figure is a favourite one with Donne. He uses it at
least three times, once in a poem and twice in sermons. It is not
difficult to account for his popularity as a preacher when we listen
to the roll of his moving and illuminating periods. Triumphant
as were the metaphors quoted above and confident as Donne was
of the ultimate reconciliation of reason and faith, he was equally
aware of the dangers involved when the two should conflict. He
picks up from archaeology a metaphor which stresses the care and
tact necessary in handling the two kinds of light.

They had a precious composition for *lamps*, amongst the *ancients*,
reserved especially for *Tombes*, which kept light for many hundreds
of yeares; we have had *in our age* experience, in some casuall open-
ings of ancient vaults, of finding such lights, as were kindled (as
appeared by their inscriptions), *fifteen* or *sixteen hundred* yeares
before; but, as soon as that light comes to our light, it vanishes.
So this *eternall*, and this *supernaturall light*, *Christ* and *faith* en-
lightens, warmes, purges, and does all the profitable offices of *fire*
and *light*, if we keep it in the right spheare, in the proper place (that
is, if we consist in *points necessary* to salvation, and *revealed* in the

Scripture) but when wee bring this light to the common light of *reason*, to our inferences, and consequencies, it may be in danger to vanish it selfe, and perchance extinguish our reason too; we may search so far, and reason so long of *faith* and grace, as that we may lose not onely *them*, but even our reason too, and sooner become *mad* then *good*. Not that we are bound to believe anything *against reason*, that is, to believe, we know not why.34

By this last sentence Donne saves himself from the charge that he would renounce reason. Having moved around to the other side of the steep and cragged hill of truth, he sees both the pitfalls of reason and the impossibility of abandoning it. Again he condenses the same idea into two succinct lines:

> Let not my minde be blinder by more light
> Nor Faith, by Reason added, lose her sight.35

The paradoxical quality of these lines, if nothing else, would identify them as Donne's. By an interesting shift of this metaphor, the Cambridge Platonists, later in the century, conceived of 'the candle of the Lord' as merely an earthly reflection of an eternal sun in whose effulgence all lesser beams would be swallowed up. Those who argue against Donne's mysticism might take this as a starting point.

In another sermon he turns a theological conundrum into a striking symbol when he compares reason's light with the light which existed before the creation of the sun.

Before the sunne was made, there was *a light* which did that office of distinguishing night and day; but when the sunne was created, that did all the offices of the former light, and more. *Reason* is that first, and primogeniall light, and goes no farther in a naturall man; but in a man regenerate by faith, that light does all that reason did, *and more*; and all his *Morall*, and *Civill*, and *Domestique*, and indifferent actions, (though they be never done *without Reason*) yet their principall scope, and marke is the glory of God, and though they seeme but *Morall*, or *Civill*, or *domestique*, yet they have a deeper tincture, a heavenly nature in relation *to God*, in them.36

133

It is not that man abandons reason at her limits and takes up faith, but rather that one touch of faith transforms his reason and gives it an almost divine discernment.

The fourth metaphor which Donne uses is an outgrowth of the third. In it he tries to express the difference between the vision of the ordinary man guided by the light of natural reason and that of the regenerate Christian whose reason has been touched by faith.

> Divers men may walk by the Sea side, and the same beames of the Sunne giving light to them all, one gathereth by the benefit of that light pebles, or speckled shells, for curious vanitie, and another gathers precious Pearle, or medicinall Ambar, by the same light. So the common light of reason illumins us all; but one imployes this light upon the searching of impertinent vanities, another by a better use of the same light, finds out the mysteries of Religion; and when he hath found them, loves them, not for the lights sake, but for the naturall and true worth of the thing it self.[37]

The man who has added faith to his reason has his eyes fixed upon the mysteries which he is trying to penetrate and not upon the instruments he is using.

In a magnificent passage from the sermon preached at St. Paul's on Christmas Day, 1621, Donne uses the same metaphor to crown his persuasive argument.

> But if thou canst take this light of reason that is in thee, this poore snuffe, that is almost out in thee, thy faint and dimme knowledge of God, that riseth out of this light of nature, if thou canst in those embers, those cold ashes, finde out one small coale, and wilt take the paines to kneel downe, and blow that coale with thy devout *Prayers*, and light thee a *little candle*, (a *desire* to reade that Booke, which they call the Scriptures, and the Gospell, and the word of God;) If with that little candle thou canst creep humbly into low and poore places, if thou canst finde thy Saviour in a *Manger*, . . . (all this is, That if thou attend the light of naturall reason, and cherish that, and exalt that, so that that bring thee to a *love of the Scriptures*, and the *love to a beleefe* of the truth thereof, and that *historicall faith* to a *faith of application*, of *appropriation*, that as

all those things were certainly done for thee) thou shalt never envy
the lustre and glory of the great lights of worldly men, which are
great by the infirmity of others, or by their own opinion, great
because others think them great, or because they think themselves
so, but thou shalt finde, that howsoever they magnifie their lights,
their wit, their learning, their industry, their fortune, their favour,
and *sacrifice to their owne nets*, yet thou shalt see, that thou by thy
small light hast gathered *Pearle* and Amber, and they by their great
lights nothing but shels and pebles; they have determined the light
of nature, upon the booke of nature, this world, and thou hast
carried the light of nature higher, thy naturall reason, and even
humane arguments, have brought thee to reade the scriptures, and
to that *love*, God hath set to the seale of *faith*.[38]

The last metaphor which we shall cite is one which Donne
uses to emphasize the spiritual daring of the man who goes on
from reason to faith and so launches out into the uncharted
depths in which he may find truth, if he is to find it at all.

Men which seek God by reason, and naturall strength, (though
we do not deny common notions and generall impressions of a
soveraign power) are like Mariners which voyaged before the
invention of the Compass, which were but Costers, and unwillingly
left the sight of the land. Such are they which would arrive at God
by this world, and contemplate him onely in his *Creatures* and
seeming Demonstration.[39]

The whole range of Donne's scepticism, from the first glimmering
of his doubt, had prepared him to move out beyond the confines
of mere coastwise travel. Only the sceptic, who has finally
emancipated himself from dogmas, is capable of this rewarding
flexibility. Even as Donne has set forth what seems to him the
road to the highest truth man can know, he reminds himself that
there may be other ways and that finally only God can know by
what devious paths men come to Him.

The wayes of the Lord are past my finding out; And therefore
to those, who doe open their eyes to that light of Nature, in the
best exaltation thereof, God does not hide himselfe, though he have
not manifested to me, by what way he manifests himselfe to them.[40]

This is the apotheosis of that awareness of human ignorance with which Donne began, and it contains the living germ of tolerance.

Action and Knowledge

In the end, the poet asks himself, what is the purpose of man's knowing? Does he want knowledge for the mere sake of knowledge, and is that why he must turn away empty-handed? Returning from his speculative flights, often with a sense of their futility, Donne concludes,

> As it is in *Agendis*, in all things which wee are bound to doe; As it is in *Petendis*, in all things which we may pray for, so it is in *Credendis*, all things that all men are bound to beleeve, all men have meanes to know.[41]

Whether or not this links Donne with the proponents of a natural religion, it does show the direction in which, if anywhere, he was to find certainty. Not only are the minimum essentials for action known to all men, but it is only through action, Donne believes, that speculative dilemmas may be resolved.

> Arguing is heretiques game, and Exercise
> As wrastlers, perfects them; Not liberties
> Of speech, but silence; hands, not tongues, end heresies.[42]

This comes very close to the words of Jesus, 'If any man will do his will, he shall know of the doctrine.' Thus the conclusion of Donne, worked out on one of those plateaus on which he so rarely came to rest, was that although man's knowledge cannot equal God's, he knows enough for the conduct of his own life, and in living worthily he approximates as nearly as possible the divine pattern.

> Joy is peace for having done that which we ought to have done. . . . To have something to doe, to doe it, and then to Rejoyce in having done it, to embrace a calling, to performe the Duties of that calling, to joy and rest in the peaceful testimony of having done so; this is Christianly done, Christ did it; Angelically done, Angels doe it; Godly done, God does it.[43]

CHAPTER V

SIR THOMAS BROWNE AND THE
GENESIS OF PARADOX

WHENEVER a man has fought his way to some reasonably adequate conception of the truth, his first impulse has been to describe to others the stages of his progression. While the world would be infinitely poorer without such accounts, it is only at rare moments that they can be effective; for they will make contact with but one class of men—those who have accepted the fundamental human obligation to do their own seeking. Such responsive readers do not appear save in periods of spiritual crisis. When life flows smoothly, men are carried along with it and perhaps swept up in its creativity. A striking example is that two of the most troubled and creative English thinkers of the nineteenth century, Coleridge and Newman, were consistent readers of the minor seventeenth-century poets, divines, and lay philosophers. There was an affinity operative which leapt across centuries and united men in a single quest for the certainty they could live by. Whatever it was in the seventeenth century which attracted both men and which both were able to make use of seems worth ferreting out as a possible source of our own illumination in the twentieth century. For it may be that contemporary intellectuals, having wandered so long in the wilderness, have now the requisite background for understanding and using the wisdom of their forebears.

We choose Sir Thomas Browne from among these seventeenth-century English thinkers because his very 'quaintness' has provided a protective colouring and has kept him from being mauled by every scholar with a thesis to prove. When we push on beyond the cadences of his Latinity, we find ourselves caught up in an exciting search for truth and one which, if we can comprehend it, may serve to bring a pattern out of our own chaos.

The Enjoyment of Truth

Browne's experience parallels our own just often enough so that the divergences become significant. One of the most striking of these is indicated by what he says about the enjoyment of truth. Of all the attitudes toward truth through which we have moved in the past fifty years, surely enjoyment has not been included. We have debated truth's existence endlessly; and we have honestly sought the meaning behind the word, even to the point of declaring a temporary moratorium upon it in deference to those of our fellows who could no longer use the word and maintain their intellectual self-respect. In so far as we have admitted aiming at the truth or a truth, we have gone about our task so grimly that to suggest enjoyment would have been to pose an absurdity. As well ask us whether the quantum theory is sweet or sour.

We find, however, that Sir Thomas Browne, Norwich physician living in seventeenth-century Puritan England, speaks casually of enjoying truth as if he saw nothing anomalous therein. Early in his *Religio Medici* Browne says:

> A man may be in as just possession of Truth as of a city and yet be forced to surrender; 'tis therefore far better to enjoy her with peace than to hazzard her on a battle.[1]

Beyond the extraordinary tact which this statement implies there is what might be called the humility of a man who will not engage in religious disputes 'when the cause of Truth might suffer in the weakness of my patronage.'[2] And yet this is no ordinary humility which cries, 'Oh, Lord, who am I, to defend Thee?' Rather is it the kind which explains, 'My contact with truth has been so fleeting and my comprehension of its mystery is so incomplete that to rush forth to its defence thus ill-prepared would be a great disservice.' Not all men, Browne felt, have an equal right to set themselves up as defenders of the truth. It is not that he is timorous or afraid to take chances with the truth.

We shall see him climbing to the dizziest heights and risking all for the integrity of his own spiritual experience. It is only that Browne does not want the splendour of truth in any way diminished by insisting too strongly upon his own necessarily partial vision of it. He is content rather to enjoy whatever insight he can achieve than to run unthinkingly to its defence. He has seen too many men who thought they had seized all of truth and who, as a result, not only missed the rightful enjoyment of a partial truth but mistook that part for the whole.

> Those have not only depraved understandings, but diseased affections, which cannot enjoy a singularity without an Heresy, or be the Author of an Opinion without they be of a Sect also.[3]

Opinions, even odd opinions, Browne does not condemn, so long as they are recognized for what they are. He recommends that they be held lightly, used to give direction to one's thinking and then easily discarded when they have issued in more comprehensive views of the truth. Browne warns his reader against clinging to these first insights beyond their normal life-span merely for the sake of simplicity and a narrow consistency. For example, a man may discover that once having exercised blind faith, he moves on an appreciable distance toward truth, and he is tempted to exalt this technique into an absolute prescription. Such a man will find that as a result he consistently makes the wrong guesses, but another man, deciding that the true way is rather to disbelieve, will lack the capacity for enjoyment.

> As Credulity is the cause of Error, so Incredulity oftentimes of not enjoying truth.[4]

Thus Browne warns against the idolatry of techniques.

If these statements about enjoying truth differed only on the surface from what we can say, the whole matter might be dismissed as an interesting but unimportant example of historical divergence. But we keep wondering as we read Browne what kind of person one needs to be in order to come to such conclusions. What is it at the very centre of his being which enables a man to refrain when he knows he is ill-equipped to defend the truth, which allows him to savour to the full the quality of what truth he has perceived, and which keeps him from taking the part for the whole? Those of us whose lives have been passed in the unquiet atmosphere of the twentieth century can appreciate, even if we cannot at once imitate, the pervasive calm and confidence of Browne's thinking—a calm and a confidence which we cannot dismiss as merely the common equipment of his age. Consistent as this was with the Puritan heritage, it was desperately and discriminatingly re-won by Browne, as by every thinker of integrity, and made his own.

Nescience

We get a clue to what it is that determines his poise when we see how unconcerned he is about what he cannot yet explain. When we, on the other hand, discover that we lack a ready explanation for some fact, we beat our heads against the wall of truth and torture ourselves with our own finiteness. Sir Thomas, however, knows how circumscribed is the sphere that belongs to man, and without the slightest loss of dignity he can publicly acknowledge his own ignorance.

In *Pseudodoxia Epidemica,* where he exposes the 'vulgar errors' of men, Browne strikes out against the inane quibbling over the Adam and Eve story.

> We leave it unto GOD. For he alone can truly determine these, and all things else; Who as he hath proposed the World unto our disputation, so hath he reserved many things unto his own resolution; whose determination we cannot hope from flesh, but must with reverence suspend unto that great Day, whose justice shall either condemn our curiosities, or resolve our disquisitions.[5]

Here is certainly an original gloss on God's omniscience. He is not the super-wisdom which looks down from its heights and mocks man with the question, 'What can you know?' Rather is he a thoroughly congenial spirit who has divided the field with man and whose greatest joy is to watch his creature approximating the eternal wisdom. From the standpoint of man, however, wrestling with the unknown, there is to be a clear-eyed recognition that he cannot at once know all, and as a consequence, not supine resignation but a reverent suspension of judgment until some final illumination, whose date is hid among the secrets of God. It is difficult for us to put ourselves imaginatively at the heart of such an attitude toward truth because we are in the habit of being much more absolute, of swinging between the pride of knowledge and the despair of ignorance. From the maturity of his adulthood Browne calls to us that in order to pass over from our position to his we must forgo our absolutism and accept the mixed human portion of wisdom and ignorance.

If we have sufficient imagination we shall not be disturbed by Browne's reference to 'that great Day.' Because our world no longer takes for granted a future moment in time as the terminus of all human activity, we are somewhat poorer than the seventeenth century for having lost also the imaginative aura of such a concept. To see what Browne makes of it is to see the folly of arguing on the level of chronology. For him it becomes the convenient locus of all perfect wisdom, which must never be supposed to inhabit flesh; therefore the reverent suspension of judgment which he recommends may not end simply with God's revealing which of our opposed theories is true. Browne looks beyond that to the possibility that all of them may be swept aside as irrelevant. But so poised and flexible is his imaginative conception of the truth that he is certain only of the rightness of what the 'great Day' will reveal and not at all of its form or content. An appreciation of this fact makes understandable the central thesis of *Pseudodoxia Epidemica*.

> Thus have I declared some private and probable conceptions in the enquiry of this truth; but the certainty hereof let the Arithmetick of the last day determine; and therefore expect no further belief than probability and reason induce. Only desire men would not swallow dubiosities for certainties, and receive as Principles points mainly controvertible; for we are to adhere unto things doubtful in a dubious and opinative way; it being reasonable for

every man to vary his opinion according to the variance of his reason, and to affirm one day what he denied another. Wherein although at last we miss of truth; we die notwithstanding in inoffensive errors; because we adhere unto that whereunto the examen of our reasons and honest enquiries induce us.[6]

To appreciate Browne's renunciation to God of the ultimate responsibility for truth is to understand what would otherwise appear as trifling inconsistency. Once he has found anchorage in the conception that 'the Arithmetick of the last day' is fixed and certain, though unrevealed, he is free to vary his opinions endlessly in accordance with each new perception of truth. Considerable intellectual courage is required to concede that perhaps at last we shall 'miss of truth.' If our contemporaries have allowed that conception at all, it has led them to a wringing of the hands and a crying, 'We shall never know! We shall never know!' Browne walks directly up to the idea and accepts all its implications as incident to his being man and not God. 'The best we can do,' Browne would say, 'in view of the gulf fixed between our partial wisdom and the wholeness of the "last Day," is to exercise manfully our reason, preserve the honesty of our enquiry, and so fulfil our human obligation even though at last we "miss of truth."' This is not at all the anti-intellectualism which holds that one opinion is as good as another, since none can achieve perfect truth. Browne holds man as responsible for the quality of his thinking as for the quality of his action. The man who is faithless to his own latest vision of the truth because he fears being labelled vacillating and inconsistent repudiates his essentially human prerogative. Thus the underlying calm which we feel in Browne is a function of the eternal perspective in which he sets human thought. Just because the final outcome, truth, is the responsibility not of man but of God, there is possible a certain human poise and grace which could be achieved on no other basis.

Once Browne has revealed this underpinning of his thought, he overcomes the temptation to linger among the ultimates and concerns himself rather with the practical problems of thinking.

It is not his audacity but his insight which allows him to draw parallels between Plato's teaching of Aristotle and Aristotle's teaching of Browne's generation. In both cases the success of the teaching is gauged by the student's ability to confront opposed points of view with equanimity.

> We do but learn to-day what our better advanced judgments will unteach us to-morrow; and Aristotle doth but instruct us, as Plato did him; that is, to confute himself. I have run through all sorts, yet find no rest in any: though our first studies and *junior* endeavours may style us Peripateticks, Stoicks, or Academicks; yet I perceive the wisest heads prove, at last, almost all Scepticks, and stand like Janus in the field of knowledge.[7]

But lest the figure of Janus be confused with Mr. Facing-Both-Ways, Browne hastens to offer a practical expedient whereby one can retain his intellectual integrity and at the same time guard against the interference of heretic-baiters. He throws together the framework of a respectable defence to serve as his official philosophy. Behind that he is safe to follow the promptings of his deepest experience, to add and subtract and keep whittling away at his private conception of truth, unembarrassed by a critic at his elbow.

> I have therefore one common and authentick Philosophy I learned in the Schools, whereby I discourse and satisfy the reason of other men; another more reserved, and drawn from experience, whereby I content my own.[8]

Keats, with less regard for a 'common and authentick Philosophy,' was employing a similar method when he insisted that truths must be 'proved upon the pulses.' Browne, however, had the resources for a certain detachment which were unavailable in Keats' day. The seventeenth century, if it knew the sources of a deeper despair than the Romantics, was also capable of relaxing the intellectual effort to know, without throwing reason to the winds. This ability is a close corollary of Browne's confidence in the revelation of 'the last Day.'

Solomon, that complained of ignorance in the height of knowledge, hath not only humbled my conceits, but discouraged my
endeavours. There is yet another conceit that hath sometimes made
me shut my books, which tells me it is but vanity to waste our days
in the blind pursuit of knowledge; it is but attending a little longer,
and we shall enjoy that by instinct and infusion, which we endeavour at here by labour and inquisition. It is better to sit down in
a modest ignorance, and rest contented with the natural blessing of
our own reasons, than buy the uncertain knowledge of this life
with sweat and vexation, which Death gives every fool *gratis*, and
is an accessory of our glorification.[9]

The advocacy of a 'modest ignorance' is not intellectual treason
but rather the end term in a progression which had begun bravely
but unseeingly with the *libido sciendi*.

The Knot

To have been present at such an intimate revelation of Browne's
thought-processes is the best preparation for understanding
Coleridge's judgment upon *Religio Medici*. He says the book
should be considered 'in a dramatic, and not in a metaphysical,
view, as the sweet exhibition of character and passion, and not
as an expression or investigation of positive truth.'[10] The seventeenth century, before modern specialization had raised barriers
between the fields of speculation, was prolific in writers who,
without being professional philosophers, saw no incongruity in
handling the deepest of philosophical problems. Herbert of
Cherbury writing his *De Veritate* is an outstanding example.
Among these Browne's uniqueness lay in his decision to present
himself, a man seeking the truth, instead of presenting merely
the conclusions at which he had arrived. This 'dramatic' approach
determines to some extent the kind of criticism which will be
relevant. Edward Dowden, one of the most penetrating of
Browne's critics, has said that *Religio Medici* is 'not moulded on
the articles of a creed, but is far more the exposition of a religious
temper; it concerns itself with the Christian graces.'[11] A man
who calls forth such critical judgments will have an approach

to truth characterized first of all by its wholeness, reflecting the wholeness of the seeker, and secondly by its obliqueness, in contrast to the direct approach of the creed-maker.

For seven years, from 1635 to 1642, *Religio Medici* circulated among Browne's friends in manuscript form and enjoyed the immunity of that private philosophy whereby he 'contented' his own reason. But the publication of a pirated edition in 1642 brought the author face to face with a public which expected of him a 'common and authentick Philosophy.' Once the issue had been forced, Browne could only make a gallant effort to educate the reader and at the same time preserve his own intellectual integrity. Some of the keenest commentaries upon early seventeenth-century English writers have pointed out that what they say on the fundamental issues which they took it upon themselves to discuss is more important as indicating the direction of their thought than for its objective truth. Browne anticipated this criticism when he wrote the following words in a preface to *Religio Medici*:

> There are many things delivered rhetorically, many expressions therein merely tropical, and as they best illustrate my intention; and therefore also there are many things to be taken in a soft and flexible sense, and not to be called unto the rigid test of reason. Lastly, all that is contained therein is in submission unto maturer discernments; and, as I have declared I shall no further father them than the best and most learned judgements shall authorize them: under favour of which considerations, I have made its secrecy publick, and committed the truth thereof to every ingenuous reader.[12]

This is not to be a book in which the author interrupts his process of truth-finding to present certain definite conclusions which he will defend against all comers. The process will continue while Thomas Browne has breath, and each 'maturer discernment' will cancel a certain portion of what he had thought was truth. The onlookers must take their chances at understanding. Browne will think of them—yes. But he will not toady to them. They must be prepared to take certain things in a 'soft and flexible sense' and to emulate the author's tact and fine balance. The developing insights to be presented in the book would demand of its readers a corresponding flexibility. Did ever author devise a better insurance that if he were understood at all, it would be by those who had followed the very road he was describing? Here is 'reader participation' at its vigorous best.

At the end of the book, far from trailing off into inconclusiveness, Browne focusses all his powers in a prayer which reflects the line his speculations have been taking. He shows that it is possible to have convictions without dogmatism, and that as he could envision finally missing the truth and yet being justified, so he can trust the ultimate disposition of his life to the God who knows, as he can never hope to know on this earth.

> Bless me in this life with but peace of my Conscience, command of my affections, the love of thy self and of my dearest friends, and I shall be happy enough to pity Caesar. These are, O Lord, the humble desires of my most reasonable ambition, and all I dare call happiness on earth; wherein I set no rule or limit to thy Hand or Providence. Dispose of me according to the wisdom of thy pleasure: they will be done, though in my own undoing.[13]

The man whose mind we must scrutinize is one whose most famous book was swung between the two poles of such a preface and such a conclusion. We must watch him react to the faintest glimmerings of truth, often in unsuspected places. We must see what estimate he put upon human nature and how this determined his treatment of men who opposed him. Finally, we must investigate the kind of trial working arrangement which he set up between faith and reason as the dualism which most persistently troubled seventeenth-century thinkers. The very nature of his thought requires all this delving and probing before we can evaluate any metaphysical truths in which it issues.

'The Fellowship of the Saints'

Browne shows throughout his work that keen spiritual sensitivity which is born of an independent mind. Those who have not bothered to do their own thinking will necessarily rely arbitrarily upon authorities, but a man with Browne's hardly-won perceptions will seek out unerringly all that substantiates them and so collect his own authorities. He will greet fellow-travellers of remote ages and conditions, once he perceives the badge of their fraternity. Leaping across superficial human judgments, Browne makes for the deep correspondences which determine whether a man is spiritually saved or spiritually lost. His words are clear and incisive:

> There are many, questionless, canonized on earth that shall never be saints in heaven; and have their names in histories and martyrologies, who, in the eyes of God, are not so perfect martyrs as was the wise heathen, Socrates, that suffered on a fundamental point of religion, the unity of God.[14]

Browne does not measure the doctrines of other men by an arbitrary set of values. He considers them as sympathetically as if they were his own, and looks first of all for their origins in human experience. What must have happened to this man, he asks, to make him draw such conclusions? What area of his own experience was he trying to illuminate when he formulated this doctrine? Thus Browne holds that the direction of a man's thought is more significant than its bare conclusions.

> That doctrine of Epicurus, that denied the Providence of God, was no Atheism but a magnificent and high strained conceit of his Majesty, which he deemed too sublime to mind the trivial actions of those inferior Creatures. That *fatal necessity* of the Stoics is nothing but the immutable Law of his Will. Those that have heretofore denied the Divinity of the Holy Ghost, have been condemned but as Hereticks; and those that now deny our Saviour, (though more than Hereticks) are not so much as Atheists; for though they deny two persons in the Trinity, they hold, as we do, there is but one God.[15]

Browne's own far-ranging thought had so often skirted these same doctrines that he could not carelessly label other men atheists, as many of his contemporaries were quick to do. He was eager to give full credit for the most tenuous insight into the nature of God. Coleridge shared the same kind of intellectual humility when he said, 'Man may perchance determine what is a heresy; but God only can know who is a heretic.'[16]

Browne's caution in applying the term *atheist* does not mean that he found no use for it. Once he was convinced that genuine atheism was present, no sectarian could be more scathing in his denunciation (of the idea, not of the individual).

> For Atheism is the greatest falsity, and to affirm there is no God, the highest lie in Nature.[17]

Here it was spiritual obtuseness rather than theological nonconformity which disturbed Browne. To the man who could feel the presence of no God and who was driven by no inner compulsion toward the concept of immortality, Browne held out little spiritual hope. A man need not be able to draw a ground-plan of Heaven; but to deny that this life is, by its nature, a prelude is to insult the deepest human potentialities. 'How the dead shall arise,' says Browne, 'is no question of my Faith.'[18] As with the Adam and Eve story, the explanation can safely be postponed until 'the last Day,' but man cannot with impunity play fast and loose with the fact.

Characteristically, Browne does not isolate the concept of immortality and treat it as if in a test tube. He reiterates that the idea must stand or fall by its origins and its effect within a human *milieu*.

> It is the heaviest stone that melancholy can throw at a man, to tell him he is at the end of his nature; or that there is no further state to come, unto which this seems progressional, and otherwise made in vain; Without this accomplishment the natural expectation and desire of such a state, were but a fallacy in nature. . . . But the superior ingredient and obscured part of our selves, whereunto all present felicities afford no resting contentment, will be able at last to tell us we are more then our present selves; and evacuate such hopes in the fruition of their own accomplishments.[19]

It is a tribute to the insight of many seventeenth-century thinkers that they found it necessary to provide a place in their thinking for what Browne here calls 'the superior ingredient and obscured part of ourselves.' Herbert of Cherbury's 'right reason' guided by natural instinct, is another example of this unwillingness to delimit man and oversimplify the complexities of human nature, this carefulness to preserve 'the subtle knot.' Both thinkers were trying to describe an element which they considered central to their systems of thought. Browne held that if the findings of this 'superior ingredient' were to be proved false, then all was lost.

> The life therefore, and spirit of all our actions is the resurrection, and a stable apprehension that our ashes shall enjoy the fruit of our pious endeavours: without this, all Religion is a Fallacy, and those impieties of Lucian, Euripides, and Julian, are no blasphemies, but subtle verities, and Atheists have been the onely Philosophers.[20]

Browne's system is not like a pyramid, built solidly from the foundation up (and housing a dead body) but rather like an ocean voyage which is guided throughout by the unapproachable stars.

The Presence of God

Behind Browne's charity toward heretics and his discrimination among atheists lay the experience of a man who found God everywhere.

> All that is truly amiable is God, or as it were a divided piece of him, that retains a reflex or shadow of himself.[21]

Theologians might not wholly have agreed with Browne's glossing of God's immanence, but in at least one gloss posterity has been left richer by a confession both piquant and profound.

> Whoever is harmonically composed delights in harmony; which makes me much distrust the symmetry of those heads which declaim against all Church-Musick. For my self, not only from my obedience, but my particular Genius, I do embrace it: for even that vulgar and Tavern-Musick, which makes one man merry, another mad, strikes in me a deep fit of devotion, and a profound contemplation

of the first Composer. There is something in it of Divinity more than the ear discovers; it is an Hieroglyphical and shadowed lesson of the whole World, and creatures of God; such a melody to the ear, as the whole World, well understood, would afford the understanding. In brief, it is a sensible fit of that harmony which intellectually sounds in the ears of God.[22]

The swing between the premise of immanence and such a conclusion measures the expanse of Browne's thought and footnotes his extreme abhorrence of atheism. To such a man atheism would appear not as unorthodox but as unthinkable.

Let us look farther into this back-shop of Browne's mind for other clues which may help us to understand the psychology of the man. He speaks directly to a familiar yet rarely discussed experience in this sentence from *Religio Medici*:

> Surely there are in every man's Life certain rubs, doublings, and wrenches which pass a while under the effects of chance, but at the last, well examined, prove the meer hand of GOD.[23]

From tavern music to intellectual harmony, from chance to the hand of God! Has any thinker a keener sense of the unsuspected richness and power of human living? That some men, suddenly perceiving the pattern of their lives, have worshipped fortune is understandable to Browne, as understandable as Socrates suffering for his belief in the unity of God.

> The Romans, that erected a Temple to Fortune, acknowledged therein, though in a blinder way, somewhat of Divinity; for in a wise supputation, all things begin and end in the Almighty.[24]

Browne is here commending not the theology of the Romans but their sensitivity to one important phase of experience. He recognizes that superstition and insight lie very close to each other and that he must cut by the fine thread which separates them. There are those who deny or try to explain away all coincidences because some men have drawn superstitious conclusions from them. Says Browne, 'To be sagacious in such intercurrences is not Superstition, but wary and pious Discretion.'[25]

We shall do well to remember this phrase of Browne's—'wary and pious Discretion.' As it describes his habitual method of discrimination, it introduces an arresting paradox. 'Pious' is not a word we ordinarily use with 'discretion'; and whether we consider 'pious' with its Virgilian or its Christian connotations, it strengthens and gives metaphysical implications to 'discretion,' which is otherwise only 'wary.'

Dualism

In a world shot through with truth, where around the next corner a pious discretion might come face to face with it, what of the nature—the limitations and the possibilities—of man? Browne follows in the footsteps of Montaigne by using his self-knowledge to illumine the deep mysteries of human nature. As in the microcosm of his own life, so in the macrocosm of the life of man, the predominant pattern is duality.

> I find there are many pieces in this one fabrick of man; this frame is raised upon a mass of Antipathies. I am one methinks, but as the World; wherein notwithstanding there are a swarm of distinct essences, and in them another World of Contrarieties; we carry private and domestic enemies within, publick and more hostile adversaries without. The Devil, that did but buffet St. Paul, plays methinks at sharp with me. Let me be nothing, if within the compass of my self I do not find the battail of Lepanto, Passion against Reason, Reason against Faith, Faith against the Devil, and my Conscience against all. There is another man within me, that's angry with me, rebukes, commands and dastards me.[26]

A congregation of all the thinkers who have set out from similar premises might take for its motto Browne's description of man as 'that great and true Amphibium, whose nature is disposed to live, not onely like other creatures in divers elements, but in divided and distinguished worlds.'[27]

The direction in which Browne moves from this central thesis is worth charting. He proceeds from the consequent impossibility of perfectly knowing oneself or others to the assurance that man's ignorance finds its necessary complement in the wisdom of God—all this in answer to the practical problem of whether men shall pass judgment upon their fellows.

> No man can justly censure or condemn another, because indeed no man truly knows another. This I perceive in my self; for I am in the dark to all the world, and my nearest friends behold me but in a cloud. Those that know me but superficially, think less of me than I do of my self; those of my neer acquaintance think more; God, who truly knows me, knows that I am nothing. . . . Further no man can judge another, because no man knows himself; for we censure others but as they disagree from that humour which we fancy laudable in our selves, and commend others but for that wherein they seem to quadrate and consent with us.[28]

Man's solitude, like every other fact about him, becomes one term of a dualism; and therefore instead of leading to intellectual despair, it is made tolerable by the perfection of divine knowledge which continually haunts him.

> But the superior ingredient and obscured part of our selves, whereunto all present felicities afford no resting contentment, will be able at last to tell us we are more than our present selves.[29]

Only because 'we are more' is Browne encouraged to press on beyond man's natural obtuseness and inadequacy.

> However, I am sure there is a common Spirit that plays within us, yet makes no part of us; and that is, the Spirit of God. . . . This is that gentle heat that brooded on the waters, and in six days hatched the World; this is that irradiation that dispels the mists of Hell, the clouds of horror, fear, sorrow, despair; and preserves the region of the mind in serenity.[30]

Here is the Christian counterpart of Pyrrhonian *ataraxia* and the prototype of Emerson's Oversoul.

From what we have seen of Browne's nonchalance toward his own truth-seeking and of his burning confidence in the judgments of God, we can posit the two poles of his attitude toward controversy. On the one hand he rejects consistency where it inhibits intellectual growth, and on the other he reminds himself that

God is not bound to defend his own creature's partial vision of the truth.

> I could never divide my self from any man upon the difference of an opinion, or be angry with his judgment for not agreeing with me in that from which perhaps within a few days I should dissent myself.[31]

As if human considerations would not deter him from dogmatism, there are always the ways and the thoughts of God, which are not the ways and the thoughts of man.

> The Divine Eye looks upon high and low differently from that of Man. They who seem to stand upon Olympus, and high mounted unto our eyes, may be but in the Valleys and low Ground unto his; for he looks upon those as highest who nearest approach his Divinity, and upon those as lowest who are farthest from it.[32]

Amind the violent controversies of his day, Browne could afford to be moderate and reasonable, for he felt that 'a good cause needs not to be patron'd by passion, but can sustain itself upon a temperate dispute.'[33] Heresies had no terror for this man, who continued to exercise 'a wary and pious Discretion.' He would not be disturbed by winds of doctrine in which he could discover 'nothing that may startle a discreet belief.' The men he held to be most inimical to truth were not those who disagreed with him but 'those vulgar heads that look asquint on the face of Truth, and those unstable Judgments that cannot consist in the narrow point and centre of Virtue without a reel or stagger to the Circumference.'[34] But even as he condemns, he brings succour. He too has known the intellectual difficulties common to men, and here is how he has met them:

> If, therefore, there rise any doubts in my way, I do forget them, or at least defer them till my better settled judgment and more manly reason be able to resolve them; for I perceive every man's own reason is his best Oedipus, and will, upon a reasonable truce, find a way to loose those bonds wherewith the subtleties of error have enchained our more flexible and tender judgments.[35]

A confidence in the ultimate triumph of truth, quite apart from his advocacy, makes it possible for him to face with patient insight his own and other men's errors.

Reason and Faith

Although Browne extols the power of reason to serve as a man's 'best Oedipus,' he would be untrue to his own dualism if he did not present the obverse side of the medal. Not all difficulties will vanish at the approach of reason. Some are more persistent, and for these there is required another technique.

> There are, as in philosophy, so in divinity, sturdy doubts, and boisterous objections, wherewith the unhappiness of our knowledge too nearly acquainteth us. More of these no man hath known than myself; which I confess I conquered, not in a martial posture, but on my knees.[36]

Had we not seen how Browne arrives at this point, we might conclude that in despair of knowing, he had abandoned the quest. The truth of the matter is that he has achieved sufficient flexibility to be able to employ diverse methods as they are needed. Just as there are facts of nature which must be demonstrated to the senses rather than reasoned about, so there are facts on a third level which also will not yield to reason. Browne's problem is to vary his technique to meet changing situations. The difficulties of epistemology, he feels, are too profound to be rationally resolved. Hence he turns to myth.

> For questionless, in Knowledg there is no slender difficulty; and Truth, which wise men say doth lye in a Well, is not recoverable but by exantlation. It were some extenuation of the Curse, if *In sudore vultus tui* were confinable unto corporal exercitations, and there still remained a Paradise, or unthorny place of knowledg. But now our understandings being eclipsed, as well as our tempers infirmed, we must betake ourselves to the wayes of reparation, and depend upon the illumination of our endeavours. For, thus we may in some measure repair our primary ruines, and build ourselves Men again.[37]

Here we see what guides the oscillations between reason and submission. It is the over-all aim to retrieve man's pristine wholeness and integrity—'to build ourselves Men again,' to preserve 'the subtle knot.'

The persistence with which Browne kept this aim in view liberated him from the fears known to men who could not achieve such breadth. They would have lacked the assurance to cry, 'I love to lose myself in a mystery, to pursue my reason to an *O altitudo*!'[38] For Browne, as we have seen, this was not a manifesto of obscurantism but a badge of intellectual maturity. There are frequent opportunities to observe in his writings the kind of mystery in which he so willingly lost himself, and to such purpose. He would, for example, pursue his reasoning about the knowledge of God to a point at which it turned back upon itself and the glow of a mystery was generated.

> No man knows the end of the world, nor assuredly anything in it: God sees it because unto his Eternity it is present; he knoweth the ends of us, but not of himself: and because he knows not this, he knoweth all things, and his knowledge is endless, even in the object of himself.[39]

This is typical of the process which came to characterize Browne's search for truth. He perfected it through trial and error, guided always by the principle of 'man's nothing perfect' and 'God's all-complete.' One passage in *Religio Medici* points up the poetry inherent in Browne's method of truth-seeking.

> Where there is an obscurity too deep for our Reason, 'tis good to sit down with a description, periphrasis, or adumbration; for by acquainting our Reason how unable it is to display the visible and obvious effects of Nature, it becomes more humble and submissive unto the subtleties of Faith; and thus I teach my haggard and unreclaimed Reason to stoop unto the lure of Faith.[40]

Browne had struggled long and desperately with the angel of reason, and there was to be no relinquishment without a blessing. That he should have spoken of 'the lure of Faith' signifies his awareness that faith and reason operate according to separate techniques. How much of the history of human controversy would become irrelevant were this insight to be adequately established. The man who teaches his 'haggard and unreclaimed Reason to stoop unto the lure of Faith' is the same man, you will remember, who preferred to 'enjoy Truth with peace' rather than 'to hazzard her on a battle.' The two operations—the teaching and the enjoyment—are both vulnerable to attacks from narrowly consistent and inflexible thinkers. Seldom is the triumph of these two outwardly acknowledged, yet somehow their frail and quiet persistence is of a kind that slowly cracks more pretentious intellectual structures and sends up through their ruins the flowering of organic life.

Paradoxes

But what of the end results of the process we have traced through all its meanderings? Did the man really leave the world richer by a series of truths thus wrought out? The answer is that Browne will always be more valued for his illuminating method than for any body of systematic truths. Whether in co-operation with the Zeitgeist or because any other formulation would have broken down, the conclusions at which he did arrive are all paradoxes—deep and sometimes tortured. No one can quite explain why at this stage in man's intellectual history he should have been so intrigued by paradoxes, but it is nevertheless true, as Louis Bredvold observes, that 'the age loved paradoxes better than either philosophical systems or devotional treatises.'[41] Perhaps we can today feel our way back to their position and there pick up a significant broken thread.

Undergirding all Browne's paradoxes, which must be understood against a background of their origins, is his conviction of man's essential duality. Indeed, the obverse side of dualism is always paradox. Thus apparent harmony is always an unstable equilibrium needing constantly to be reachieved.

We do but imitate our great selves, the world, whose divided Antipathies and contrary faces do yet carry a charitable regard unto the whole, by their particular discords preserving the common harmony, keeping in fetters those powers, whose rebellions, once Masters, might be the ruine of all.[42]

One of Browne's most striking paradoxes follows naturally from his sympathetic insight into the workings of other men's minds. 'Some Truths seem almost Falsehoods; and some Falsehoods almost Truths.'[43] Coming from a shallow thinker or heard by the uninitiated, this statement might be flippant rather than discerning. It epitomizes for Browne the insight that the highest human truths contain the seeds of decay and that even the deepest errors carry the promise of a truth not yet revealed.

Again, Browne puts into the necessary form of paradox his conviction that man, a curious combination of the human and the bestial, finds it almost impossible to win through to any salvation, although the impossibilities are other than we had supposed.

> There is a depraved appetite in us, that will with patience hear the learned instructions of Reason, but yet perform no farther than agrees to its own irregular humour. In brief, we are all monsters, that is, a composition of Man and Beast, wherein we must endeavour to be as the Poets fancy that wise man Chiron, that is, to have the Region of Man above that of Beast, and Sense to sit but at the feet of Reason. Lastly, I do desire with God that all, but yet affirm with men that few, shall know Salvation; that the bridge is narrow, the passage strait, unto life: yet those who do confine the Church of God, either to particular Nations, Churches, or Families, have made it far narrower than our Saviour ever meant it.[44]

Narrow is the way, says Browne, but not narrow with the narrowness of men. There is more mystery to its narrowness than that, a mystery which some religious thinkers have labelled 'grace.' Within a few pages we catch the pendulum swing of Browne's thought on the downbeat and follow it until it issues in this blasting of an over-arrogant reason:

> It is an insolent part of reason to controvert the Works of God, or question the Justice of his proceedings. Could Humility teach

others, as it hath instructed me, to contemplate the infinite and incomprehensible distance betwixt the Creator and the Creature; or did we seriously perpend that one simile of St. Paul, *Shall the Vessel say to the Potter, Why hast thou made me thus?* it would prevent these arrogant disputes of reason.[45]

Because of what we have seen to be the experimental nature of Browne's thought, and consequently of his writing, it is often possible to be present at the gestation and birth of a paradox. What is then apparent is that behind the paradox lies the characteristic response of Browne to the complex and contradictory aspects of his experience, all of which are conserved and focussed in the resultant formulation. Here, for example, is the way his thought moves from intense inner experience to concluding paradox.

And, whether out of the prejudice of my affection, or an inverting and partial conceit of his mercies, I know not; but those which others term crosses, afflictions, judgments, misfortunes, to me, who inquire farther into them then their visible effects, they both appear, and in event have ever proved, the secret and dissembled favours of his affection. It is a singular piece of Wisdom to apprehend truly, and without passion, the Works of God, and so well to distinguish his Justice from his Mercy, as not to miscall those noble Attributes: yet it is likewise an honest piece of Logick, so to dispute and argue the proceedings of God, as to distinguish even his judgments into mercies. For God is merciful unto all, because better to the worst than the best deserve; and to say he punisheth none in this World, though it be a Paradox, is no absurdity.[46]

Again Browne recognizes how close to each other are the true and the absurd. Such recognition must always characterize the masterful handler of paradoxes, else he cannot be trusted with these potentially fissionable materials.

Union of Contraries

When we turn from the mind of Sir Thomas Browne to the comments of his critics, we discover that what from within showed the pattern of paradox, from without appears as a uniting of contraries. Perhaps what the critics give us is the schematism of Browne's poetry. The one characteristic upon which all his critics agree is the faculty which Paul Elmer More sees him sharing with Coleridge, 'the faculty, that is, by which we unite the broken and dispersed images of the world into an harmonious poetic symbol, . . . the power of subjecting the less to the greater reality, of associating the outer with the inner, and thus of finding through the many that return to the one, which was, as Coleridge interpreted the phrase, the *esemplastic* function of the imagination.'[47] To Wilbur Jordan, writing of the *Development of Religious Toleration*, Browne 'represents the finest union of the strands of humanism and of rationalism in the seventeenth century.'[48] C. H. Herford, introducing the *Religio Medici* in its Everyman edition, says,

> Two great intellectual traditions which had for the most part run counter met in his mind in a curious, unexpected harmony—a harmony obtained without apparent commotion or forced division of either from its course; as if the contending streams which in other intellects jostled each other aside or settled their differences by compromise and subterfuge had in his been transmuted into a warp and woof of differently-coloured threads, whose crossing only evolved a brilliant pattern.[49]

Going behind the mere observation of unity in order to account for its presence there, William P. Dunn voices a judgment which coincides with our previous analysis. 'Browne was a natural believer, who really knew that the intellect is not the only road to truth, and who by virtue of that instinct managed to unify his world.'[50] Men who were content with the intellect alone landed in untenable half-truths and despair, but Browne's essential wholeness made him shy of backing reason against faith or faith against reason. What may have looked to the world like inconsistency or even the balancing of dualisms was really the flowering of a 'natural' belief, a conscientious maintenance of 'the subtle knot.'

All these testimonials to the unifying character of Browne's thought are but attempts to define from without the peculiar quality of his paradoxes, whose growth we have traced in the farthest recesses of his thought. Having thereby cast some light upon what seemed at first his strange and unaccountable enjoyment of the truth and having explored the devious processes which lay behind that, we set ourselves to reap the perennial reward of such an investigation, a fuller appreciation of the mind of man, in its frailty and its magnificence, and a confidence that these our groanings and travailings may yet find their justification and their redemption.

CHAPTER VI

RICHARD BAXTER AND THE PROBLEM
OF CERTAINTY

HAD Richard Baxter chosen any other profession than the ministry, he might, like Sir Thomas Browne, have been able to elaborate his religious philosophy far from the disturbing clash of controversy. The Norwich physician could set down calmly and with conscious attention to literary style the principles governing his religious thinking. Even when the manuscript of *Religio Medici*, having circulated among his friends, was eventually published without his consent, Browne was not thereby directly involved in the desperate controversy of his day. Baxter, although he was, like Browne, essentially a man of the study, found himself as a Nonconformist divine catapulted into the midst of one of the most violent ideological struggles England has ever known, the struggle between Puritan and Anglican. The immediate issue was uniformity of worship, but this branched out and became part of a larger movement headed toward toleration and freedom of thought. Between the publication of *The Saints' Everlasting Rest* in 1650 and Baxter's death in 1691, he produced more than one hundred and forty controversial tracts, whose purpose was either to answer attacks of Conformist clergymen or to bolster the faith and practice of Church members who were felt to be in danger of missing the central truths of their religion. Pastor first and writer afterward, Baxter was mainly concerned with the essential and catholic core of Christianity which could serve as the sure ground of unity. Because this outpouring came from the pen of one who 'spoke as a dying man to dying men,' little thought could be given to its literary form, which is now careless and now inspired, as the urgency of Baxter's message falls and rises. Yet, what inevitably links the physician and the divine in any study of seventeenth-century thought is the fact that in spite of the disparate circumstances under which they wrote, the thought of both coincides in broad outline with what may be described as the sceptic pattern. There is the same sense of man's ignorance and a conviction that he may win his way through doubts to a certitude which is human and not absolute, which partakes of the nature of the knot, and which is therefore perpetually aware of dualisms and frames its conclusions in the form of paradoxes.

It is ironic that Baxter's professional life should have been so hedged about by controversy, for he believed controversialists to have been responsible for most of the religious ills of his day, foremost of which was *prefidence*.[1] This disease of the religionists he diagnoses with the familiarity of a man who has once been its victim. He recalls that in his early writings he had seized too eagerly upon each new truth and had ridden it too hard, not realizing how many differences are purely verbal and how unwilling men are to relinquish an intellectual position, once they have taken it. Since those early days, he had learned also

> that nothing so much hindreth the Reception of the Truth, as urging it on Men with too harsh Importunity, and falling too heavily on their Errors: For hereby you engage their Honour in the business and they defend their Errors as themselves, and stir up all their Wit and Ability to oppose you: In controversies it is fierce Opposition which is the Bellows to kindle a resisting Zeal.[2]

The psychological climate of controversy, he discovered, is not at all conducive to the nurture of truth. The 'prefident, hasty judgers,' Baxter says, have so many bastards of their own brains to maintain because they think it necessary to defend all the opinions they have ever embraced.[3]

He thinks that the ideal progression is from the position of men who know little and think they know much, through the stage in which men know more and think nothing is certain, to that in which they 'find a certainty in the great and necessary things, but confess their ignorance in abundance of things which the presumptuous are confident in.'4 So carping were his opponents that even in making such a simple statement as this, he found it necessary to protect himself from the charge of intellectual pride by quoting Augustine:

> *Adversus eos qui sibi videntur scire quod nesciunt, hoc tutiores sumus, quod hanc ignorantiam nostram non ignoramus.*5

Therefore, were it only for the sake of increasing the world's knowledge, Baxter would oppose 'a disputing way, . . . believing that it tempteth men to bend their wits, to defend their errors and oppose the truth, and hindereth usually their information.'6 He proposes, rather, 'a learning or a teaching way of converse' and asserts,

> In all companies I will be glad either to hear those speak that can teach me, or to be heard of those that have need to learn.7

In contrast to the prefident, Baxter presents the hypothetical minister who, confronted with questions of free will, reprobation, and predetermination, should say:

> These things are above my understanding; I cannot reach to know what Freewill is, nor whether all causes natural and free be predetermined by Divine premotion, &c. I cannot say neither it is so, nor it is not; they are above my reach.8

Would such a man, asks the author, be forbidden to preach the gospel? And the answer is that if he were, he would at least have won a moral victory over his silencers.

> He that fixeth not till he feel firm ground, nor buildeth till he feel a rock, need not pull down, and repent so oft as rash presumers.9

Baxter is careful to point out that differences and disputations are not in themselves evil.

> He that wonders to see wise men differ, doth but wonder that they are yet Imperfect, and know but in part. . . . And indeed were Pride and Passion laid aside in our Disputes, and men could gently

suffer contradiction, and heartily love and correspond with those that in lower matters do gainsay them, I see not but such friendly debates might edifie.[10]

Unfortunately, neither Baxter's good example nor his exhortation was sufficient to accomplish this transformation in his day.

The specific evils which Baxter laid at the door of religious controversy serve to define the boundaries of his own intellectual system. Over against prefidence he set man's essential ignorance and his necessary wrestling with his own doubts. Against what his opponents presented as simple and direct truths, he offered the dualistic nature of man and his world and therefore the paradoxical and oblique quality of truth. In place of their initial confidence, which was soon dissipated, he proposed a terminal confidence built up gradually on the principle that 'if any man will do his will, he shall know of the doctrine.'

Baxter and Scepticism

In view of our attempts to define scepticism, it is enlightening to come upon Baxter's use of the term. At least twice in *A Treatise of Knowledge and Love Compared* he uses *sceptic* in the sense of one who thinks nothing is certain. The sceptic is, for him, the man who stops half-way on the road from prefidence to 'certainty in the great and necessary things.' Elaborating upon a statement of Paul's, he says,

> It is none of the apostle's meaning that men should be mere sceptics: nor am I seconding Sanchez's 'nihil scitur,' unless you take science for adequate science, or in a transcendent notion, as it signifieth that which is proper to another world, and therefore may be denied of this. He can neither play the part of a Christian or of of a man, who doubts of all things, and is assuredly confident of nothing.[11]

Baxter goes on to implement this statement by distinguishing between objective and subjective certainty and by listing a number of truths in the order of their progressive certainty (cf. *infra*, p. 171). As a practical man of affairs, he could not admit Sanchez's *nihil scitur* and so remain in a state of complete *ataraxia*. He must of necessity move on to the truths by which men can live; therefore, he renounces scepticism as inadequate.

But at least one of his biographers, Sir James Stephen, notes a large proportion of the sceptical in Baxter's make-up. He points out, however, that the scepticism toward which Baxter was drawn by his physical and intellectual temper was counterbalanced by his ardent piety and devotion.

> The radiance from above gradually dispersed the vapours from beneath, and through half a century of pain, and strife, and agitation, he enjoyed that settled tranquillity which no efforts merely intellectual can attain, nor any speculative doubts destroy—the peace of which it is said, that it passes understanding.[12]

Indeed, this curious and fecund combination of scepticism and faith characterizes many seventeenth-century writers and determines our use of the term *scepticism* in a somewhat broader sense than that in which either Baxter or Stephen uses it. There simply is no other convenient English word, as we have seen, to designate a process, particularly prominent in seventeenth-century England, whereby men used the more limited kind of scepticism to help them toward a practical Christian philosophy. Baxter thus appears as an outstanding exponent of the sceptical method put to the use of Christian apologetics.

Nescience

Let us see first of all what observations he has to make on the ignorance of man, for the way in which a thinker presents this phase of scepticism sets the tone of his whole intellectual position. Baxter's attitude is far removed from an irresponsible *Que sais-je?* What impresses him in the controversies of Protestants with each other and with their Catholic and heathen opponents is that pride of intellect rules everywhere. Bringing men to a recognition of their own ignorance, then, is a first step toward reconciling their differences, most of which are concerned with non-essentials.

In a word, almost all the contentions of divines, the sects, the factions, the unreconciled feuds, the differences in religion, which have been the taunt of the devil and his emissaries in the world, have come from pretended knowledge and taking uncertain for certain truths.[13]

From several directions Baxter brings proof of the impotence of that intellect upon which man leans most heavily in disputes. First of all, there is the disproportionate amount of time and labour which must be spent to acquire knowledge. And after 'long, hard, patient studies, . . . how little do we obtain!' says Baxter. 'Is this an intellect to be proud of?'[14]

In the second place, consider the paltry sum of man's knowledge. After more than five thousand years, he has amassed very little which is methodically and uncontrovertibly known. (We are reminded of Carneades' gradations: the probable; the probable and undisputed; the probable, undisputed, and tested.) Even among philosophers, whose vocation is wisdom, Baxter finds so little real knowledge that he becomes suspicious of their authority.

> I find the wisest of them so conscious of their ignorance, that they take most for uncertain which they say themselves; and confess they talk but in the dark: which made the Pyrrhonians and Arcesilaus have so many followers.[15]

This is not the only evidence that Pyrrhonism had its attractions for Baxter, even though he often uses the word *sceptic* in the loose manner of some of his contemporaries.

If man required further proof of his essential ignorance, it would be necessary only for him to observe the controversies of his fellows—men of differing faiths wrangling over points of doctrine—papists, according to Baxter, debasing man further than even the infidels do.[16]

> And yet shall men be proud of wit? O what is man! How dark, how sottish and mad a thing! All these great princes, doctors, cardinals, universities and kingdoms, are born with natures as capacious as ours. They are in other things as wise: they pity us as

heretics, because we will not cease to be men: The infidel that denieth man's reason and immortality, would but level us with the brutes, and allow us the pre-eminence among them in subtlety: but all these Papists forswear or renounce that sense which is common to brutes with us, and sentence us either below the brutes, or unto hell. Pretend no more, poor man, to great knowledge. As the sight of a grave and a rotten carcase may humble the fool that is proud of beauty, so the thought of the Popish, Mahometan and Heathen world, may humble him that is proud of his understanding.[17]

If there were no other arguments, this one would surely suffice to destroy man's inordinate intellectual pride. Yet with a gesture which is reminiscent of his contemporary, Pascal, Baxter turns to retrieve human self-respect.

Let no pretence of humility tempt you to debase human nature below its proper excellence; lest thence you be tempted to think it uncapable of the everlasting sight and fruition of God.[18]

It is this same inadequate and unregenerate intellect which must nevertheless be depended upon in the endless search for truth.

The principle which Baxter adopts as his guide is admirably contrived to accommodate both the feebleness of the human intellect and its infinite possibilities: 'Nothing is so *certainly* known as God and yet nothing so imperfectly.'[19] Thus while holding steadily to what is incontrovertible the certainty of God—he makes a place for the characteristic ambivalence of human knowledge, which now approaches and now withdraws from its true centre. In the specific application of this principle, Baxter gets within hailing distance of the *credo quia absurdum*, or perhaps it would be more accurate to say that he reveals what we may conjecture to have been the experience crystallized in Tertullian's pronouncement.

I will believe anything in the World which I know certainly that God speaks or revealeth; Though the thing in it self seem never so unreasonable. For I have reason to believe (or rather to know) that all is true which God revealed, how improbable so ever to flesh and blood.[20]

The crucial unknown for which we need to solve this formula is the sign of God's revelation. How shall men know what it is that God reveals? As we proceed with an analysis of Baxter's method, we shall get some clues to the answer, but they are not clues to satisfy the most literal-minded investigator. In his struggle toward truth, Baxter often took an imaginative leap in a direction pointed to by his deepest experience, and when he had landed, he made room on his intellectual map for the inclusion of this spot, even though to do so necessitated a new scale or the representation of another hemisphere. Indeed, this is the means by which he kept his conception of truth flexible and adaptable to new insights. Though nothing was so certainly known as God, nothing was so imperfectly known; and therefore he found little difficulty in abandoning one intellectual position in favour of another which more closely approached the certainty which is God.

Baxter's use of this guiding principle is glimpsed on the title page of *A Treatise of Knowledge and Love Compared*, which he published in 1689, near the end of his career.

> By Richard Baxter, who, by God's blessing on long and hard studies, hath learned to know that he knoweth but little, to suspend his judgment of uncertainties, and to take great, necessary, certain things for the food of his faith and comforts, and the measure of his church communion.

Here is the intellectual humility of the man, his practical use of *ataraxia*—suspension of judgment on what is uncertain—and his reaffirmation of the 'great, necessary, certain things.'

Just as all the truths of which men are certain may be graded according to their degree of certainty, so Christians range from the most ignorant, who should avoid controversy, to the least ignorant, who shall hardly succeed in presenting an intellectually adequate defence of their faith. Baxter would not prevent the unlearned from trying and judging, but he would warn them to check their results against the great certainties and to maintain the humility which will look for flaws first of all in themselves.

'There is a great deal of difference between searching as a Learner, and disputing as a Caviller, or boldly Determining as a Competent Judge.'[21] A distinction must be made between the spirit of holiness which reveals the truths necessary to salvation and the ability to defend and explain and teach these truths when confronted with an adversary.

> Alas, it is but few of the multitudes of Christians that have a clear knowledge of the true grounds of the Christian Belief! And then when they hear the contradiction of Seducers, and are put to give a reason of their hopes, they are presently at a loss: And when they find themselves non-plust, they have not the reason of humility, to lay the blame on themselves where it is due, and to lament their own negligence and unprofitableness, that by so much means have attained to no better understanding; but they presently suspect the truth of God, as if it were not possible that there should be light, and they not see it; or as if there could be no answer given to the cavils of the adversary, because they themselves are unable to answer them; and as if *others* could not untye the difficulties, or reconcile the seeming contradictions of the word, because *They* cannot do it![22]

Here is the way Baxter uses the principle that nothing is so certainly known as God. To this centre man must return, whether his ignorance be that of the newly converted or that of a Church Father. The truths of God are not obscure and contradictory although they may seem so to man's imperfect comprehension. His progress as a Christian may be gauged by the consistency which he has achieved in his religious philosophy.

The Function of Doubt

It is understandable that in the progression from prefidence through *ataraxia* to authentic certainty, the honest man will continually be assailed by doubts. They are implicit in the very instrument which he uses. One of Baxter's most effective methods of undercutting the arrogance of his opponents was not only to admit his own doubts, past and present, but to affirm that there is no unpenalized by-passing such doubts on the road to truth.

He several times refers to the fact that early in his Christian experience he was troubled more about his own sincerity than about the objective validity of his religion. Indeed, in these early days he saw no intellectual difficulties whatsoever in Christianity. His blind faith was sufficient. But once he entered the ministry and shouldered the responsibility for other men's faith, he began to question the truth of the scriptures and the immortality of the soul. With characteristic insight into the subtleties of his own experience, Baxter admits,

> These temptations assaulted me not as they do the Melancholy, with horrid vexing Importunity; but by pretence of sober Reason, they would have drawn me to a settled doubting of Christianity.[23]

Only a very stupid Devil would have failed to see that ingress to the soul of Richard Baxter could be obtained most easily by 'pretence of sober Reason.' The reader of these autobiographical passages, whether in the seventeenth or in the twentieth century, is in no danger of considering them merely a part of the argument. They have the ring of authenticity, and the reader feels the same tension as in the rising action of a drama. The outcome is never for one moment a foregone conclusion. Says Baxter,

> Had I been void of internal experience and the adhesion of love, and the special help of God, and had not discerned more reason for my religion than I did when I was younger, I had certainly apostatised to infidelity.[24]

Here again the great and certain things came to his rescue, and as a result he advocates the 'well-grounding' of men in these essentials to insure against their ultimate defection.

Once this grounding has been accomplished, what resolution may the doubting Christian hope for? On the basis of his own experience, Baxter cannot promise the disappearance of all difficulties.

> Though I am not so unmolested as at the first, yet is my Faith I hope much stronger, and far better able to repel the Temptations of Satan, and the Sophisms of Infidels than before: But yet it is my

daily Prayer that God would increase my Faith, and give my Soul a clear sight of the evidences of his Truth, and of himself, and of the invisible World.[25]

Two aspects of this position are important for our understanding of the kind of certainty which Baxter, as a sceptic, considers defensible. First, there is the conviction that 'nothing is so firmly believed as that which hath been sometime doubted of.'[26] The Christian is 'not forbidden, but encouraged to try the spirits, and not to believe every spirit nor pretended prophet.'[27] It is a central tenet of Baxter's faith that as the result of such testing the truth will emerge.

Second, there is the recognition that he has not yet arrived and perhaps never will arrive at the final answers to all his questions. Hence, the prayer that God would give him progressively clearer insights into truth. From time to time, the Christian who has risen on the stepping stones of his doubts will stop to assess his gains, and when he does so, it will be in terms of comparative certainties, as in the famous passage from the *Reliquiae* beginning,

> My certainty that I am a man is before my certainty that there is a God. My certainty that there is a God is greater than my certainty that he requireth love and holiness of his creature. My certainty of *this* is greater than my certainty of the life of reward and punishment hereafter. My certainty of that is greater than my certainty of the endless duration of it, and of the immortality of individual souls.[28]

This is not unrelated to the five common notions upon which Lord Herbert set the foundation of deism, although his formulation appears more static than Baxter's and less expandable.

There is great significance in the regularity with which Baxter affirms his certainty that he is a man before he is a Christian. He thereby insures that his Christianity will draw a wide enough circle to include the traditional richness and complexity of humanism, at whose very heart is a recognition of man's dual nature. Thus, like a true sceptic, he will not repudiate 'the subtle knot.' The force of personal experience rather than the speculation of a theologian lies behind this admission:

I feel and see the Scripture verified, which describeth all the temptations of Satan, and the secret war within us between the spirit and the flesh.[29]

This dualism developed into the opposition between 'the Heavenly and the Earthly Mind,' and at the end of *A Treatise on Self-Denial* Baxter threw into verse form a dialogue between flesh and spirit to illustrate principles set forth in the prose portion of the book.

Faith and Reason

What this recognition of fundamental dualism means is seen most clearly when Baxter tries to explain the relationship of faith to reason. As we should expect, he sees no opposition between natural and revealed religion since a man's Christianity is necessarily built upon the foundation of his humanity.

I find in general, that there is an admirable concord between Natural Verity, and the Gospel of Christ; and that Grace is medicinal to Nature; and that where Natural light endeth, Supernatural beginneth; and that the superstructure which Christ hath built upon Nature is wonderfully adapted to its foundation. . . . Reason, which is our Nature, is not destroyed, but repaired, illuminated, elevated and improved, by the Christian faith. . . . The Natural part of Religion is so far from being abrogated by Christianity, that the latter doth but subserve the former.[30]

Thus Baxter conceives of reason as a necessary propaedeutic to faith.

He that hath the best and rightest Reason, and by consideration makes the most use of it, is the best Christian, and doth God best service: And . . . all sin is on the contrary, for want of Right reason, and the using of it by consideration.[31]

As we have seen previously in Baxter's writing, he leaves the casual reader speculating on the lengths to which he is to go in 'the using of it by consideration.' A part of this mystery may be cleared up if we look in detail at his prescriptions regarding faith.

Having postulated that 'there is no faith, but on supposition of sense and understanding,'[32] he asserts,

> You must believe nothing but what you have sufficient reason to believe. But then you must know what is sufficient reason for Belief. Prove but the thing to be the Testimony of God, and then you have sufficient reason to believe it, whatsoever it be.[33]

At first glance it would seem that this advice merely replaces a simple obscurity with a more complicated variety. Even Baxter's staunchest defender must admit that the passage just quoted does not give precise and unmistakable directions for the considered use of reason where faith is involved. But it shows at least the direction in which the author is moving, and no more can be expected from any sceptic. What Baxter advocates is that the Christian should make use of reason to determine what is 'the testimony of God' (and thus to be believed), and then that he should have the courage not to flinch if he is unable by reason to justify the details of such testimony. Beyond that, the way is open to every honest, inquiring Christian who remembers that he is first of all a human being. The farther he pushes his reason, the less opposition he finds between reason and faith. Only at their extreme boundaries may they be contrasted. Baxter might very well have joined John Donne in asserting that reason

> put to her best extension
> Almost touches faith, and makes both centers one.[34]

Like Dante, Baxter sees the intellectually curious Christian being guided by the hand of reason until he has reached reason's bounds and then making a graceful transition to the guidance of faith. Virgil and Beatrice are not, therefore, opposed forces. Each plays his own unique role in the education of the Christian.

> Faith is an act, or species of knowledge: it is so far from being contrary to reason that it is but an act of clear elevated reason. ... They that wrangle against us for giving reason for our religion, seem to tell us that they have none of their own, or else reprehend us for being men.[35]

The fulcrum by which Baxter moves his world is the fact that he and his fellows are men, with all the paradoxical complexity involved therein.

Theological Dualisms

When the opposition is not between the fundamental tools, reason and faith, but between theological points of view, Baxter varies his basic pattern. With deep insight into the religious aspirations of men, he proceeds through pamphlet after pamphlet to seek out the reasonable truth in each position, on the theory that every dogma represents a partial insight into truth. Sometimes he graphically represents the two extremes and his *via media* by the use of three parallel columns. This practice could not have made him acceptable as a party man, but it does serve to clarify many of the theological issues of his day (for instance, the Calvinism-Arminianism controversy) and illustrates the complex nature of the truths toward which Baxter was aiming, truths which mirror the dualistic nature of man. A mind with a greater bent toward the curious—for example, the mind of a Sir Thomas Browne or of a Donne—would at this point begin to elaborate paradoxes; but Baxter was hurried along in the rush of controversy and could allow himself no such luxury. Paradox is implicit, however, in all the conclusions he draws, for the set of his mind is essentially the same as that of the paradox-makers.

The Joy of Religion

One of the most striking indices of this similarity is the genuine enjoyment which both Browne and Baxter found in their experience of religious truth. If it was Baxter's temperament which predisposed him to joy, it was his penetrating mind which made the most of that predisposition in order to reinforce his faith. He is sorry that so many Christians do not lay hold on 'the solid comforts which their religion doth afford.'

> Indeed it is to be lamented that few of the heirs of life do live according to the happiness and dignity of their calling; nor are the great things that God hath done for them so apparent in the cheer-

fulness and comforts of their lives as they should be: But some that are addicted to dejectedness, do in a greater measure wrong Christ and themselves, being always feeding upon secret griefs, and torturing themselves with doubts and fears, and acquainted with almost no other language but lamentations, self-accusations and complainings.[36]

This is reminiscent of Montaigne's shrewd observation that if men were once touched by Christianity, it would irradiate all their lives. The passage also recalls Baxter's admission that his early doubts, in spite of their persistence, were not those of a melancholy man. It makes understandable, too, the rare appearance, amid the arid controversial wastes, of religious insights which are of the essence of poetry. Often the very intensity and beauty of Baxter's perceptions moulds his words and gives them song and wings.

> Think but of Gods *Love*, and *Goodness*, and *Fidelity*, as you do of his Power, and then you will find that there are *rivers of pleasure in his presence, and fulness of joy at his right hand*, the fore-tastes whereof are the only delights that can quiet the troubled thirsty soul.[37]

Here, strangely enough, is a partial answer to that tantalizing riddle of Baxter's thought: how are men to know 'what God revealed'? Certainty, for him, stems directly from religious experience—not from the transports of the mystic but from the reasonable flowering of man's humanistic search for truth. Individuals will assume their stations along the road toward truth in accordance with the faith they have been able to achieve, and thus no uniformity can be expected. (Dogmatists and bigots take note.) There is, nevertheless, one touchstone of certainty.

> When doubting is so far overcome, as that the mind doth find rest and satisfaction in the truth, it may be called certainty. But when doubting is either prevalent, and so troublesome as to leave us wavering, it is not called certainty.[38]

'Satisfaction with the truth,' for Baxter as for Browne, is the outward and visible sign of an inward grace.

'The Witness of the Spirit'

Baxter rehabilitates the phrase, 'witness of the spirit,' to mark out this area of certainty; but he warns his reader against understanding thereby a kind of mystical and anarchic approach to Christianity.

> The Spirit is the great witness of Christ and Christianity to the world. And though the folly of fanatics tempted me long to overlook the strength of this testimony of the Spirit, while they placed it in a certain internal assertion or enthusiastic inspiration, yet now I see that the Holy Ghost in another manner is the witness of Christ and his agent in the world.[39]

Baxter's respect for the reason of man, reed-like though it be, saves him from the pitfalls of enthusiasm. Orme illuminates the foundations of Baxter's position when he explains that 'witness of the spirit'

> is founded on 'He that believeth hath the witness in himself,' a text which has been variously expounded, and which Baxter thinks signifies that those enlightened and holy impressions formed on the soul by the Spirit, become in us a standing testimony or witness for the truth within us. 'For none but the sacred Redeemer of the world, approved by the Father, and working by his Spirit, could do such works as are done on the souls of all that are truly sanctified.'[40]

To make a detour here into sanctification and predestination would defeat our purpose, which is to avoid the subtleties and technicalities of Baxter's theology in order to follow the larger drift of his thought. He himself provides material for the working out of this purpose and at the same time answers the modern reader's request for a guiding thread through the maze of pseudo-authenticated 'Words of God.' Hunt has paraphrased Baxter's words thus:

> There may be no testimony as to Joram's descendants, nor clear proof that Paul left his cloak and parchments at Troas, but there is a witness to the fact of men being reclaimed from selfishness and sensuality, and re-made in the image of God. Christianity is a life.

Let men live it, and they will feel its truth. The greater progress we make in righteousness, the clearer will be our view of its everlasting foundations.[41]

Action and Knowledge

Baxter's prescription for certainty, then, leans in the direction of the practical and the moral. It goes back and picks up a psychologically penetrating technique which Jesus made use of when his followers wanted proof of the gospel's truth before they would live by it. Behind the darkness of the understanding, according to Baxter, lies 'an alienation of the life from God,' and this can be remedied only by action. He who wishes ultimately to know must work out the terms of that knowledge in the interaction between his life and the life of the world. With all the rhythm and beauty which his style takes on at high moments, Baxter explains simply the operation that lies behind the 'witness of the Spirit':

> Lastly it is hence apparent also, That the way to have the firmest belief of the Christian Faith, is to draw neer and taste, and try it, and lay bare the heart to receive the impression of it, and then by the sense of its admirable effects, we shall know that which bare speculation could not discover. Though there must be a belief on other grounds first, so much as to let in the Word into our Soul, and to cause us to submit our hearts to its operations, yet it is this experience that must strengthen it, and confirm it. *If any man do the will of Christ, he shall know that his doctrine is of God.* John 7. 17. The melody of Musick is better known by hearing it, then by reports of it; and the sweetness of meat is known better by tasting, then by hear-say; though upon report we may be drawn to taste and try. So there is a *Spiritual sense* in us, of the effects of the Gospel on our own hearts, which will cause men to love it, and hold it fast, against the Cavils of Deceivers, or the Temptations of the great Deceiver.[42]

Who else but the sceptic can allow himself to explore unreservedly a way of life in order to garner there the fruits of truth? By the use of an image, in the manner of a poet, Baxter has said perhaps the last word on the question of certainty. Before he tastes, the

Christian need not have ultimate proof of the sweetness of the meat; it is enough if he be drawn by whatever report to 'taste and try.' This procedure stands, indeed, as a symbol for Baxter's whole approach to the problem of discovering religious truth.

Baxter's Legacy

Perhaps the farthest reaching and the least predictable result of England's attempt to enforce religious conformity was that the more active spirits among the dispossessed clergy were forced thereby to give reasons for the faith within them. Certainly this was true in Baxter's case, for had he not been, along with other Nonconformists, the victim of a kind of Protestant Inquisition, deprived of his living and hounded from place to place, he would undoubtedly have continued to minister quietly and unobtrusively to his own congregation, and, content to practise his faith instead of accounting for it, would have left no written testimonials of its riches. The lives of countless men and women would have absorbed and reflected truths which because of the exigencies of controversy have come down to later generations in a form in which they may be grasped intellectually. We thus have the basis for an insight into the Nonconformist mind at the point at which it had stripped away all the spiritual luxuries of peace and was seeking to propagate only what was essential to the continuance of its faith. In addition, Baxter, because of his fundamental hatred of controversy, was continually waging a war to end war, and thus to an even greater extent than his colleagues he was laying emphasis upon 'the great and essential things.' The fact that the techniques which he employs ally him with the great stream of historic scepticism lends additional interest to the legacy which he has left. Because we of the twentieth century are dealing with comparable problems, though not couched in theological language, Baxter and his kind can be the source of abundant courage, and if not the bearers of final wisdom, they can at least illuminate our path toward certainty.

CHAPTER VII

JEREMY TAYLOR, THE SCEPTIC AS
CHURCHMAN

※

AMONG seventeenth-century English thinkers in whom can be traced the pattern of classical scepticism, Jeremy Taylor is distinguished by the comparative regularity and conventionality of his religious position. Donne had travelled from an inherited Catholicism to an uneasy Anglicanism; Browne, a nominal Anglican, felt the necessity of defending himself, as a physician, against the charge of atheism; Baxter, the Puritan, waged a life-long struggle to grasp and transmit the core of Christianity in spite of persecution for his Nonconformity; and Glanvill tried to reconcile his Anglicanism with his deep scientific faith. That similar ways of thought, however, should be found in such diverse settings establishes scepticism as an important phase of the seventeenth-century climate of opinion. In the case of Taylor we can examine the scepticism of a man who, although his latitudinarianism often disturbed his more orthodox brethren, maintained a relatively untroubled theological position, founded upon the minimum essentials of faith and a holy life. Perhaps it is because he has left no account of how he won his way through to such a position that Taylor proceeds along what seems relatively solid ground toward his ultimate goal, the elaboration of a Christian irenic.

Nescience

Like all sceptics, Taylor was keenly aware of human ignorance and of its compensating pride and dogmatism. But the fact that man never knows as much as he thinks he knows, instead of leading Taylor to despair of human knowledge, persuaded him to caution. The inconclusiveness and dubiousness of man's knowledge at any moment should, he felt, keep man continuously humble and critical and therefore willing to understand and co-operate with his fellows. In his Epistle Dedicatory to *The Real Presence* Taylor gives evidence of an approach to truth which has characterized all sceptics.

> But I see it is possible for a man to believe any thing he hath a mind to; and this, to me, seems to have been permitted to reprove the vanity of man's imagination, and the confidence of opinion, to make us humble, apt to learn, inquisitive and charitable; for if it be possible, for so great a company of men, of all sorts and capacities, to believe such impossible things, and to wonder that others do not 'eandem insaniam insanire,' it will concern the wisest man alive to be inquisitive in the articles of his first persuasion, to be diligent in his search, modest in his sentences, to prejudge no man, to reprove the adversaries with meekness, and a spirit conscious of human weakness, and aptness to be abused.[1]

The intellectual gullibility and even perverseness of men has for Taylor two advantages. First of all, no matter how far the ways of God transcend and contradict those of men, so long as man maintains his capacity for flexible belief, the door to truth can never be finally closed to him. And secondly, by his very 'human weakness, and aptness to be abused,' he has no excuse for ever settling into the rut of dogmatism. Yet Taylor was aware that the obverse of these advantages was man's susceptibility to unscrupulous dogmatists who should offer a haven from his uncertainty.

> This pretence of a necessity of humbling the understanding, is none of the meanest arts whereby some persons have invaded, and have usurped a power over men's faith and consciences, and, therefore, we shall examine the pretence afterwards, and try if God hath invested any man, or company of men, with such a power.[2]

As if to illustrate the liberty of the sceptic churchman to range over the fields of both secular and sacred writing in his search for truth, Taylor points up the common humanist and Christian proscription of intellectual pride.

And although I be as desirous to know what I should, and what I should not, as any of my brethren, the sons of Adam; yet I find that the more I search, the further I am from being satisfied, and make but few discoveries, save of my own ignorance: and, therefore, I am desirous to follow the example of a very wise personage, Julius Agricola, of whom Tacitus gave this testimony, 'Retinuitque (quod est difficillimum) ex scientia modum': or, that I may take my precedent from within the pale of the church, it was the saying of St. Austin, 'Mallem quidem eorum, quae a me quaesivisti, habere scientiam quam ignorantiam; sed quia idenondum potui, magis eligo cautam ignorantiam confiteri, quam falsam scientiam profiteri.' And these words do very much express my sense.3

The sceptic is driven from the spectacle of the world's dogmatisms to take *cautam ignorantiam* for his guide toward the only kind of knowledge which he can respect, the knowledge which is relevant to the good life.

It is amusing to note reflections of Taylor's attitude toward women in his insistence that most of what human beings pride themselves upon knowing is of no importance for what matters most in their lives, the doing of their duty. This core of usable truths is equally available to men and to women, and whatever human beings pride themselves on beyond this is shot through with uncertainty and unimportance.

Our learning is then best, when it teaches most humility: but to be proud of learning is the greatest ignorance in the world. For our learning is so long in getting, and so very imperfect, that the greatest clerk knows not the thousandth part of what he is ignorant; and knows so uncertainly what he seems to know, and knows no otherwise than a fool or a child, even what is told him or what he guesses at, that except those things which concern his duty, and which God hath revealed to him, which also every woman knows so far as is necessary, the most learned man hath nothing to be proud of, unless this be a sufficient argument to exalt him, that he uncertainly guesses at some more unnecessary thing than many others, who yet know all that concerns them, and mind other things more necessary for the needs of life and commonwealths.4

The rule for *Holy Living* in which this observation issues calls attention to the two pitfalls of prefidence, the intellectual embarrassment of admitting error and the shamelessness of dogmatism.

> Pretend not to more knowledge than thou hast, but be content to seem ignorant where thou art so, lest thou beest either brought to shame, or retirest into shamelessness.[5]

For Taylor, as for Donne, Baxter, and Browne, there is a divine counterpart of the essential knowledge which is revealed to all men. Once the individual has passed this earthly life and has attained Heaven, he will know the overarching complement of what was here only meagre and hard-won wisdom.

> The knowledge of the greatest wise men and philosophers of the world, even in things natural, is full of ignorance and deceit; because they know not the substances of things, but through the shell of accidents: so as the most simple peasant, arriving at the height of glory, shall be replenished with a knowledge, in respect of which the wisdom of Solomon and Aristotle were but ignorance and barbarism.[6]

For the sake, then, of what Sir Thomas Browne calls this 'accessory of our glorification,' man can afford to abide in patience and humility and a cautious ignorance because he looks forward to the day beyond this life when he will outstrip Solomon and Aristotle.

'The Fellowship of the Saints'

Had Taylor been concerned with human ignorance and its resultant dogmatism merely as a background for his own epistemology, he could never have left us such stirring indictments of men who are bent on separation rather than on 'conjunction.' Such men constitute for him the chief obstacles in his pathway toward a comprehensive truth on which not only all Christians but all humanists as well can come together. Here, for example, is his endorsement of Homer, Euripides, Pindar, Aeschylus, Plutarch, Plato, Aristotle, and Porphyry as more profitable reading for Christians than are hair-splitting theologians:

> But I consider, that the wisest persons, and those who know how to value and entertain the more noble faculties of their soul, and their precious hours, take more pleasure in reading the production of those old wise spirits, who preserved natural reason and religion in the midst of heathen darkness . . . than the triflings of many of the latter schoolmen, who promoted a petty interest of a family, or an unlearned opinion, with great earnestness; but added nothing to Christianity but trouble, scruple, and vexation.[7]

Taylor believes that God has left accessible to men whatever truths they need to know for the conduct of their lives and that these will become available if men will only proceed by cautious ignorance. What he deplores is the insistence that one's own opinions are really the axioms of religion and that whoever does not conform to them is lost. The following vivid description mirrors in its authenticity countless debates in which Taylor must have participated:

> While all strive for truth, they hug their own opinions dressed up in her imagery, and they dispute for ever; and either the question is indeterminable, or, which is worse, men will never be convinced. For such is the nature of disputings, that they begin commonly in mistakes, they proceed with zeal and fancy, and end not at all but in schisms and uncharitable names, and too often dip their feet in blood.[8]

Even the victor in such a contest cannot flatter himself that the ideas he has upheld by force are necessarily true. He may be in the position of the man who gains the whole world and forfeits his own soul. Taylor, like Rust, would have praised the sceptic who falls into error above the dogmatist who accidentally hits the truth.

> In the meantime, he that gets the better of his adversary, oftentimes gets no good to himself; because, although he hath fast hold upon the right side of the problem, he may be an ill man in the midst of his triumphant disputations.[9]

Rather than end as 'an ill man,' it is better to have seized hold of the wrong side in the controversy, that is, if one can maintain a spirit of cautious ignorance.

Semantics as a prescription for settling or easing controversies was known even in Taylor's day, but he felt that the deep forces of human nature were forever working against its success.

> Others, who understand things beyond the common rate, observing that many of our controversies and peevish wranglings are kept up by the ill stating of the question, endeavour to declare things wisely, and make the matter intelligible, and the words clear; hoping, by this means, to cut off all disputes. Indeed this is a very good way, so far as it can go; and would prevail very much, if all men were wise, and would consent to those statings, and would not fall out upon the main inquiry, when it were well stated; but we find, by a sad experience that few questions are well stated; and when they are, they are not consented to; and when they are agreed on by both sides that they are well stated, it is nothing else but a drawing up the armies in battalia with great skill and discipline; the next thing they do is, they thrust their swords into one another's sides.[10]

Thus it is wisdom and the good life, 'piety and practical duties,' which are the gravest casualties in the battle for truth. Much as Taylor takes delight in projecting what seem to him the intellectual boundaries of truth, he realizes that this is not his real vocation.

> My work here is not to please the speculative part of men, but to minister to practice, to preach to the weary, to comfort the sick, to assist the penitent, to reprove the confident, to strengthen weak hands and feeble knees.[11]

Indeed, it was out of this kind of experience that Taylor hoped ultimately to forge eternal truths.

Dualism and Paradox

Once most sceptics have become aware of the difficulties of knowing, they usually pass through a stage in which all the data of their world are presented in the form of dualisms. This represents a slight advance beyond the point of asking, 'What can we know?' even though it may mean only a tidying up and pairing off of the epistemological dilemmas. Usually the third step is the construction of a series of paradoxes which shall conserve both halves of each dualism. Whether because Taylor maintains a fairly impersonal style of writing or because he never knew the struggle with such dualisms as flesh and spirit, we find very little direct evidence of his having taken the second step. Only by the reflected light of what he says about paradoxes are we able to conjecture the missing experience. For example, when Taylor is confronted with the 'faith-works' controversy, where the protagonists are St. Paul and St. James, he treats it in a spirit whose transcendence is reminiscent of Jesus' answers to the pharisaical quibblings.

> St. Paul proves his doctrine by the example of Abraham, to whom faith was imputed for righteousness; and, therefore, not by works. And what can be answered to this? Nothing but this, that St. James uses the very same argument to prove that our justification is by works also; 'For our father Abraham was justified by works, when he offered up his son Isaac.' Now which of these says true? . . . My purpose is not with subtle arts to reconcile them that never disagreed; the two apostles spake by the same Spirit, and to the same last design, though to differing intermedial purposes; but because the great end of faith, the design, the definition, the state, the economy of it, is that all believers should not live according to the flesh, but according to the Spirit.[12]

Thus the larger paradox involving the relation of flesh to spirit swallows up the intellectually troublesome dualism of faith and works. By such methods does Taylor strive to bring together apparently irreconcilable intellectual positions as well as the people who sponsor them.

In considering a different kind of dilemma, the opposition between profaneness and superstition, Taylor reaches back into humanistic wisdom for a solution. His answer is consonant with his conviction that men have means of knowing what is necessary to guide their lives.

There are thousands of scandals, millions of errors, to be avoided, but truth and holiness are in the middle, in a little compass; and happy is he that shuns extremes and falls perpendicularly upon the golden mean. . . . Profaneness neglects the honour of God: superstition falls into needless excesses about it: the true fear of God is in the centre, as far from the one extreme as from the other.[13]

On the far side of dualism, where it merges into paradox, Taylor uses the sacrament of the Lord's Supper to symbolize the resolution of the many into the one.

It is a sacrament to combine, and to knit together, holding us fast into one communion, that there may be no breaking asunder of the parts and members. Many grains of wheat are kneaded into one loaf, many grapes are trodden, that their liquor may be pressed into one cup. We, being many, are one bread, and one body.[14]

No matter what the paradox that Taylor discusses, we have the feeling that, unlike Donne, he is throwing his weight on the side of its unity rather than on that of its diversity. So although he recognizes that contradictions are involved in living the life of a Christian, he keeps pulling toward the centre, where unity can be achieved.

All the actions of religion, though mingled with circumstances of differing, and sometimes of contradictory, relations, are so concentred in God their proper centre, and conducted in such certain and pure channels of reason and rule, that no one duty does contradict another; and it can never be necessary for any man, in any case, to sin.[15]

The test of Taylor's scepticism at this point is that he does not make reconciliation and oneness too easy. The complex knot of paradox cuts deep into the fleshly mind which the Christian is trying to subdue.

The eight beatitudes, which are the duty of a Christian and the rule of our spirit, and the special discipline of Christ, seem like so many paradoxes and impossibilities reduced to reason; and are indeed virtues made excellent by rewards, by the sublimity of grace, and the mercies of God, hallowing and crowning those habits which are despised by the world, and are esteemed the conditions of lower and less considerable people. . . . And they are states of suffering rather than states of life: for the great employment of a Christian being to bear the cross, Christ laid the pedestal so low, that the rewards were like rich mines interred in the deeps and inaccessible retirements, and did choose to build our felicities upon the torrents and violences of affliction and sorrow.[16]

Thus it would appear that paradox is the emergence into thought of a desperately achieved synthesis at the level of a man's deepest living. Now and then Taylor is able to indicate this whole process by simple and beautiful language whose spine is experience.

But, therefore, since we are so miserable, and are in error, and have wandered very far, we must do as wandering travellers use to do, go back just to that place from whence they wandered, and begin upon a new account. Let us go to the truth itself, to Christ; and he will tell us an easy way of ending all our quarrels: for we shall find Christianity to be the easiest and the hardest thing in the world: it is like a secret in arithmetic, infinitely hard till it is found out by a right operation, and then it is so plain, we wonder we did not understand it earlier.[17]

What distinguishes the dogmatist from the sceptic is that the dogmatist can never admit of going back for a new beginning, while the sceptic's whole progress consists of a series of undulating movements which at once conserve past values and make new attacks upon an unexplored future.

Most sceptics, even though they be churchmen, show a remarkable sympathy toward heretics and atheists. In seventeenth-century England this often took the form, as we have seen, of making a place among the ranks of Christian teachers for the Greek and Roman philosophers. Less often it consisted of a penetrating insight into the heretic's mode of thought, with which all sceptics have much in common. Taylor defines heretics as 'erring and mistaken people' and so takes the sting out of the epithet.

Although their doctrines are such, that, if men should live according to their proper and natural consequences, they would live impiously, yet in every one of these there are persons so innocently and invincibly mistaken, and who mean nothing but truth, while in the simplicity of their heart they talk nothing but error, that, in the defiance and contradiction of their own doctrines, they live according to its contradictory.[18]

Here is demonstrated the sceptic ability to make the most of men's intentions and so remain charitable toward their achievements. Taylor is convinced that since man's chief concern should be to know his duty and to do it and since truth founded in action far outweighs mere intellectually formulated truth, it is men's lives rather than their arguments by which they should be judged.

Reason and Faith

Let us look closely at how Taylor resolves the central dualism of his age by transforming it into an illuminating paradox. Ever since the Renaissance had set man adrift without the shelter of an unimpeachable theology, the claims of reason and of faith had been tearing him apart. He wanted, if possible, to retain the values inherent in faith; yet he could not repudiate the gains of reason, which was leading him into a progressively more comprehensible world. Was it necessary, as he sometimes feared, to abandon one or the other if he was to know peace? Taylor encountered this dilemma in a theological setting, and it was his task to give specific directions for satisfying the claims of both reason and faith.

As he phrases his conclusion in *Holy Living* it seems to today's reader to be heavily weighted on the side of faith.

To believe every thing, which God hath revealed to us: and, when once we are convinced, that God hath spoken it, to make no further inquiry, but humbly to submit; ever remembering, that there are some things, which our understanding cannot fathom, nor search out their depth.[19]

A careful scrutiny of this rule reveals that Taylor has left an area open for the exercise of reason. He implies earnest and reasonable inquiry which shall determine whether a particular 'revelation' comes from God or not. Here, as elsewhere, Taylor would not qualify as a sceptic if his reconciliation of opposites were clear and easily grasped. We still wonder, as we do in the case of Baxter, how, short of an authoritarian answer, man is to learn what God reveals; but as we go farther, we shall see that this mystery is somehow related to the sceptic recognition that 'there are some things which our understanding cannot fathom, nor search out their depth.' The submission which Taylor advocates is not a blind submission, for reasoning has prepared the way for it. However, the quality of that reasoning has been such that it could envisage and even welcome its own transcendence.

> When we discourse of mysteries of faith and articles of religion, it is certain that the greatest reason in the world, to which all other reasons must yield, is this—'God hath said it, therefore it is true.'[20]

In so far as we may still be irked by the apparent dogmatism of that statement, let us set it aside until we can explore farther the use which Taylor makes of reason as a handmaid of faith.

One clue to his position is to be found in his fundamental assumption (corollary to the postulate of human ignorance) that God's ways are not man's ways. Therefore over against all human speculation there stands the threat that man may have finally missed the truth of God. This makes necessary his maintaining the kind of flexibility which will enable him at any moment to abandon his own highest reasoning if he is convinced that it does not accord with what God sees as the truth. As a consequence, when Taylor realizes that God has endorsed what his own reason cannot fathom, he capitulates and recognizes the sophistry in which he had been floundering. Yet no one is more keenly aware than Taylor of the dangers of such a procedure.

> But if God hath not plainly declared against that which I call reason, my reason must not be contested, by a pretence of faith, but upon some other account: 'Ratio cum ratione concertet.'[21]

To know when to oppose reason with faith and when to oppose it with other reasons constitutes the rare discrimination which is required of sceptics.

The revelation of God, which for Taylor is contained in the life of Christ, bears the same relation to man's reasoning as a knowledge of substance does to a knowledge of accidents. And who would prefer the lesser to the greater knowledge? Concerning the resurrection, Taylor says,

> And in this, and in all the like cases, faith is a submission of the understanding to the word of God, and is nothing else but a confessing, that God is truth, and that he is omnipotent; that is, he can do what he will, and he will, when he hath once said it. And we are now as ignorant of the essence and nature of forms, and of that, which substantially distinguishes man from man, or an angel from an angel, as we were of the greatest article of our religion, before it was revealed; and we shall remain ignorant for ever of many natural things, unless they be revealed; and unless we knew all the secrets of philosophy, the mysteries of nature, and the rules and propositions of all things and all creatures, we are fools if we say, that what we call an article of faith, I mean, truly such, is against natural reason. It may be indeed as much against our natural reasonings, as those reasonings are against truth.[22]

In such a world, then, where reason cannot be completely trusted, what is the best method for making it yield its maximum return? In answering this question Taylor brings his readers close to the immediate technique of his scepticism. Here in *Doctor Dubitantium*, is a straightforward account of how reason may clear the way for faith:

> That we must submit our understanding to God, is very true, but that is only when God speaks. But because we heard him not, and are only told that God did speak, our reason must examine whether it be fit to believe them that tell us so; for some men have spoken falsely, and we have great reason to believe God, when all the reason in the world commands us to suspect the offsprings of some men; and although we ought, for the greatest reasons, sub-

mit to God, yet we must judge and discern the sayings of God, from the pretences of men; and how that can be done without using our reason in the inquiries of religion, is not yet discovered.[23]

Yet all is not smooth sailing where reason is being employed. We shall often grope uncertainly in the intervals between clear revelations.

> For reason itself is not fallible; but if reason, that is, reasonings, be fallible, so are the pretences of revelation subject to abuse; and what are we now the nearer? Some reasons are but probable, and some are certain and confessed, and so it is in the sense of scriptures, some are plain and need no interpreter, no discourse, no art, no reasonings, to draw out their sense; but many are intricate and obscure, secret and mysterious; and to use a fallible reasoning to draw out an obscure and uncertain sense of Scripture, is sometimes the best way we have, and then we must make the best of it we can: but the use of reasoning is not only to find out truth the best we can, but sometimes we are as sure of it, as of light, but then and always our reason (such as it is) must lead us into such proportions of faith as they can: according as our reason or motives are, so ordinarily is the degree of our faith.[24]

So intimately are reason and faith associated that what strengthens one, strengthens the other, for each gains its relevance from being set in the midst of human action. It is the lives of men which determine the quality of their faith and the extent of their heresy. After exalting the Apostles' Creed as a means to the faith, hope, and charity which will induce men to honour and obey Christ, Taylor undertakes to distinguish between faith and heresy.

> Now, because faith is not only a precept of doctrines, but of manners and holy life, whatsoever is either opposite to an article of creed, or teaches ill life, that is heresy; but all those propositions, which are extrinsical to these two considerations, be they true or be they false, make not heresy, nor the man an heretic; and, therefore, however he may be an erring person, yet he is to be used accordingly, pitied and instructed, not condemned or excommunicated; and this is the result of the first ground, the consideration of the nature of faith and heresy.[25]

It was this same kind of thinking which led Coleridge to observe that however man may define heresy, only God knows who is a heretic.

'The Candle of the Lord'

More than one sceptic in seventeenth-century England attempted to set forth figuratively the relation between reason and faith. One of the most famous and striking metaphors is that of Donne:

> Reason is our Soules left hand, Faith her right,
> By these we reach divinity. . .[26]

Equally illuminating and showing the marks of Taylor's emphasis on unity rather than on duality is the first of his answers, in *Doctor Dubitantium*, to arguments against the use of reason in matters of faith.

> Reason is the eye of the soul in all things, natural, moral, and religious; and faith is the light of that eye, in things pertaining to God; for it is true, that natural reason cannot teach us the things of God: . . . but though natural reason cannot, yet it is false to say that reason cannot; for reason illuminated can perceive the things of God; that is, when reason is taught in that faculty, under that master, and by those rules which are proper for spiritual things, then reason can do all its intentions.[27]

Thus it is an enlightened and spiritually disciplined reason which we must strive for. A God-illumined reason can be trusted to lead man toward the ultimate source of its light.

As for the raw material upon which man operates in this life, it is as neuter as his propensity to believe 'anything he hath a mind to.' Its nature is determined only by what he makes of it.

> 'There are two handles to take hold of every thing,' says a heathen: a dissolute man takes hold of original frailties, and makes them serpents: a holy man declines their serpentine nature, and catcheth them by that part which may conduce to all manner of virtue. This is the comfort of hope against original inquination, that

this great enemy, by the operation of the Spirit, shall be made our friend, or our footstool.[28]

Those who would irresponsibly quibble and consequently would dogmatize about unessential aspects of religion are guilty of exploiting the indeterminate nature of the stuff man works in. Taylor condemns Roman Catholic apologists for making an uncreative use of their scepticism by employing it as a support for dogmatism.

> For uncertain answers make with them no uncertain resolution; for they teach us, that in such cases we may follow either part: and therefore they studiously keep up this academical or rather sceptic theology, 'alii aiunt, alii negant; utrumque probabile.' And upon this account, although with greatest severity they bind on men's persuasions the doctrines of meats and carnal ordinances, yet they have left them loose enough when it comes to the conscience, so loose that the precept is become ridiculous.[29]

The conscience represents for Taylor the focus of man's morality. Like the Cambridge Platonists, he believed that regardless of subsequent revelation, God had implanted within the natural man a 'candle of the Lord' which should guide him into truth and righteousness. Such light was not to be employed frivolously or irresponsibly to solve insignificant riddles, but it was to be conserved for the main business of living.

> Now God, who takes more care for the good of man, than man does for his own, did not only imprint these laws in the hearts and understandings of men, but did also take care to make this light shine clear enough to walk by, by adopting some instances of the natural laws into religion.[30]

Taylor was somewhat consoled for the fact that man could not know everything when he recognized that there was yet allowed him a light 'clear enough to walk by.'

Perhaps because of the very tentativeness of their method, thinkers who follow the sceptic pattern are more likely than others to savour the quality of whatever truths they achieve. Sir Thomas

Browne is continually assuming that truth is something to be enjoyed, and Taylor takes cheerfulness to be the badge of successful Christian living.

> And beside, cheerfulness is not only an adjunct, or companion with all the works of grace, in that time they are bringing forth; but being done and finished, that which is 'post nate,' the after-birth, as I may call it, comes with such a gleam gliding over all the soul, with such serenity and peace of mind as cannot be expressed; our conscience bearing us witness that we have been conversant in doing the pleasure of the Lord.[31]

There is evidence here, too, of the compatibility which Taylor felt existed between natural religion and Christianity, for as he says,

> Christianity is nothing else but the most perfect design that ever was, to make a man be happy in his whole capacity.[32]

Action and Knowledge

Out of this rich integration which constitutes the good life Taylor sees emerging the only solid truths which man is likely to find. He appeals to the same source to which Jesus appealed when he said, 'If any man will do his will, he shall know of the doctrine, whether it be of God, or whether I speak of myself.'[33] Taylor forthrightly puts the blame for man's intellectual difficulties upon his way of life.

> Our evil life is the cause of our controversies and ignorances in religion and of the things of God.[34]

He proposes therefore that man will have a better chance of arriving at truth if he lives life on the highest plane of which he is capable. His specific prescriptions coincide with that careful and intellectually honest approach which has characterized scepticism throughout its history.

> Diligence and care in obtaining the best guides, and the most convenient assistances, prayer, and modesty of spirit, simplicity of purposes and intentions, humility, and aptness to learn, and a

peaceable disposition, are therefore necessary to finding out truths, because they are parts of good life, without which our truths will do us little advantage, and our errors can have no excuse. But with these dispositions, as he is sure to find out all that is necessary, so what truth he inculpably misses of, he is sure is therefore not necessary, because he could not find it, when he did his best and most innocent endeavours. And this I say to secure the persons; because no rule can antecedently secure the proposition in matters disputable.35

As scepticism takes its start from an epistemological dilemma, so if it ever comes to rest, it is in the conviction that action and not speculation will save men. Taylor's determination 'to secure the persons' rather than to 'secure the proposition' is therefore genuinely sceptical. It stands under the shadow of 'the subtle knot.' As a churchman he held to 'that part of theology which is wholly practical; that which makes us wiser, therefore, because it makes us better.'36 Finally, intellectually and spiritually exhausted by lifelong pursuit of his ideal, he draws this honest and poignant self-portrait:

> I shall not be ashamed to say, that I am weary and toiled with rowing up and down in the seas of questions, which the interests of Christendom have commenced, and in many propositions, of which I am heartily persuaded I am not certain that I am not deceived; and I find that men are most confident of those articles, which they can so little prove, that they never made questions of them: but I am most certain, that by living in the religion and fear of God, in obedience to the King, in the charities and duties of communion with my spiritual guides, in justice and love with all the world in their several proportions, I shall not fail of that end, which is perfective of human nature, and which will never be obtained by disputing.37

As with all sceptics, it is the threat of finally missing the goal which gives both zest and pathos to the pursuit and which keeps the sceptic everlastingly humble.

Christianity, for Taylor, far from consisting of abstract propositions, finds its centre and justification in these perilous and always partially unredeemed Christian lives which nevertheless possess a distinguishing radiance. He refers to Christianity as 'a Divine frame and temper of Spirit'[38] and to theology as 'rather a Divine life than a Divine knowledge.'[39] In the cadences for which Taylor has become famous, he reaches the high point of his struggle with the problem of knowledge as it relates to religion:

> A good life is the best way to understand wisdom and religion, because by the experiences and relishes of religion, there is conveyed to them such a sweetness, to which all wicked men are strangers: there is in the things of God, to them which practise them, a deliciousness that makes us love them, and that love admits us into God's cabinet, and strangely clarifies the understanding by the purification of the heart. For when our reason is raised up by the Spirit of Christ, it is turned quickly into experience; when our faith relies upon the principles of Christ, it is changed into vision; and so long as we know God only in the ways of man, by contentious learning, by arguing and dispute,—we see nothing but the shadow of him; and in that shadow we meet with many dark appearances, little certainty, and much conjecture: but when we know him . . . with the eyes of holiness, and the intuition of gracious experiences, with a quiet spirit and the peace of enjoyment; then we shall hear what we never heard, and see what our eyes never saw: then the mysteries of godliness shall be opened unto us, and clear as the windows of the morning: and this is rarely well expressed by the Apostle, 'If we stand up from the dead, and awake from sleep, then Christ shall give us light.'[40]

CHAPTER VIII

JOSEPH GLANVILL, SELF-CONSCIOUS SCEPTIC

IN the writings of Joseph Glanvill the strong current of scepticism which had been flowing underground in many seventeenth-century English writers finally came into the open. Glanvill makes explicit the scepticism which can be seen sporadically in the writers who preceded him. The four other men in relation to whose works we have discussed the sceptic pattern either were known to Glanvill personally and admired by him or ally themselves with him by the coincidence of important phases of their thought with his.

For example, Basil Willey remarks that Glanvill echoes not only some of Sir Thomas Browne's vocabulary and his wit but also his 'peculiar mental poise.'[1] We know from Anthony à Wood and from the *Reliquiae Baxterianae* that in 1662 Glanvill felt such sympathy for Richard Baxter that he offered to write in his defence when he was accused of murder. Baxter, with his usual humility, says Glanvill was 'one that had too excessive estimation of me, as far above my desert, as the malicious Party erred on the other side.'[2] Glanvill's tribute to Baxter's technique of controversy is to be found in a letter quoted by Baxter in *A Second True Defence of the Meer Non-Conformist.*

There is a smartness accompanying your pen that forces what you write into the heart, by a sweet kind of irresistible violence; which is so proper to your serious way, that I never met it equal'd in any other writings. And therefore I cannot read them without an elevation, and emotions which I seldom feel in other perusals. And when you are ingag'd in doctrinal and controversial matters, I no less apprehend in them your peculiar excellencies. I find a strength, depth, cocinnity, and coherence in your notions, which are not commonly elsewhere met withall. . . . And methinks there is a force in your way of arguing, which overpowers opposition.3

Glanvill admired Baxter's reasoning concerning the authority of scripture and testified,

> I am not apt to rely on an implicit faith in things of this moment. But your performances in this kind brought relief to my staggering judgment, and triumph't over my hesitancy.4

Glanvill shared with both Browne and Jeremy Taylor the conviction that reason pushed to its limits may point toward faith and that the two are never fundamentally incompatible.5 Consequently, Glanvill was as persistent as Taylor in trying to formulate a reasonable basis for Christian unity. Both men felt that the truth by its very nature could never be divisive.

Nescience

Although most of a century separated Glanvill from John Donne, the two were equally impressed by the fallibility of human knowledge. However, the shift which had taken place during the century can be measured by the fact that the new philosophy which in Donne's day had 'called all in doubt' came to symbolize for Glanvill man's release from the blind dogmatism of the Aristotelians. It is illuminating to watch the same sceptic method which Donne advocated being employed by Glanvill and to see its success in liquidating those intellectual difficulties which had perturbed the late Renaissance. Indeed, there is a significant symbolism in the contrasting prose styles of the two men— Donne's by its paradoxes betraying the perplexity which led him to scepticism, and Glanvill's, after a rash of Browne-isms, exemplifying the calm clarity of one whose doubt has made him a fervent disciple of Descartes and then of Bacon and for whom philosophy clears the path leading toward the central truths of religion.

Of the principal phases of scepticism illustrated in the thought of these five men, Glanvill puts most emphasis upon the first, the recognition of man's essential ignorance. Whereas Donne's treatment of nescience takes the form of an agonized cry, Glanvill's has behind it the assurance of a man who has come to terms with this nescience and has made creative use of it. Perhaps his searching analysis of the psychology underlying dogmatism is somehow related to the temper of the man, as contemporaries have left us records of it. Anthony à Wood says of Glanvill that he was

> of a quick, warm, spruce and gay fancy, and was more lucky, at least in his own judgment, in his first hints and thoughts of things, than in his after-notions, examined and digested by longer and more mature deliberation.[6]

To reinforce this picture of a man who trusts his hunches, Anthony Horneck testifies to the worth of the resultant ideas.

> As he valued no notions, that were mean and trivial, so those, he hath sent abroad, savour of a more than ordinary genius. His Soul seemed to be spun of a finer thread than those of other mortals, and things look'd with another face, when they passed through the quicker fire of his Laboratory. Some curious Artists; though their work is materially the same with that of meaner Artificers, yet the shape they give it, and the neatness of the Fabrick, makes it seem a thing composed of different ingredients.[7]

Whatever this rare quality was which Glanvill possessed, it enabled him to throw an unusual light upon the 'vanity of dogmatizing' and upon its corollary, the unreliability of human knowledge.

One of his chief arguments against dogmatism he bases upon the late seventeenth-century version of the insight contained in the words of Isaiah, 'My thoughts are not your thoughts, neither are your ways my ways, saith the Lord.'[8]

> They are only Natures groser wayes of working, which are sensible; Her finer threads are out of the reach of our feeble *Percipient*, yea questionless she hath many hidden Energies, no wayes imitated in her obvious pieces: and therefore it is no wonder that

we are so often at a loss; an infirmity beyond prevention, except we could step by step follow the tracks and methods of *Infinite Wisdom*, which cannot be done but by him that owns it.[9]

Glanvill feels that unless a man recognizes that his knowledge is never coincident with that of God, he is in constant danger of succumbing to dogmatism. Although this dangerous situation is not likely to change, man's response to it can determine whether he will be a free and inquiring spirit or a circumscribed dogmatist. If he remains free and unopinionated, as Bacon had advocated, he stands a much better chance of moving toward infinite wisdom, even though he is destined never to reach it. In a style close enough to Browne's not to have lost touch with illuminating metaphors, Glanvill sets forth his main objection to dogmatism, its tendency to create agoraphobia of the spirit.

Dogmatizing shews *Poverty*, and *narrowness* of Spirit: There is no greater *Vassallage*, than that of being enslaved to Opinions. The *Dogmatist* is pent up in his Prison, and sees no Light but what comes in at those Grates. He hath no *Liberty* of *Thoughts*, no *prospect* of various *Objects*: while the *considerate* and *modest* Inquirer, hath a *large* Sphere of Motion, and the satisfaction of more *open* Light; He sees *far*, and injoys the pleasure of surveying the *divers* Images of the Mind. But the *Opiniator* hath a *poor shrivel'd* Soul, that will but just hold his little Set of Thoughts: His Appetite after Knowledg, is satisfied with his few Mushromes, and neither knows nor thinks of any thing beyond his Cottage and his Rags.[10]

Here is the usual sceptic indictment of dogmatism, not for its wickedness but for its narrowness. Glanvill goes beyond mere pity and contempt for such an attitude and calls 'opinionative ignorance . . . very *weak* and immoral.'[11] He will waste no energy upon such dogmatists until they 'have learn't that first principle of true *wisdome*, *To judge nothing till they thoroughly understand it, & have* weighed it in the ballance of impartial Reason.'[12] Such a cooling-off period might have the effect of setting men on the road to wisdom. They will think and examine and separate the true from the false.

In sum, I say, the *Free* and *Real* Philosophy makes Men deeply sensible of the Infirmities of Human Intellect, and our manifold hazards of *mistaking*, and so renders them *wary* and *modest*, *diffident* of the *certainty* of their *conceptions*, and *averse* to the *boldness* of *peremptory asserting.*[13]

This diffidence and tact and the careful handling of concepts is what must have convinced Glanvill's fellows that he was a person of more than ordinary parts. There is clear evidence here of a character trait having been transformed into an important component of his philosophical system.

Behind Glanvill's accurate description of what goes on when men set out toward truth there lay a keen analysis of his own and other men's experience.

So then, to direct all this to our end, the mind of man being thus naturally amorous of and impatient for *Truth*, and yet averse to, and almost incapacitated for, that diligent and painful search, which is necessary to its discovery; it must needs take up short, of what is really so, and please it self in the possession of imaginary appearances, which offering themselves to its embraces in the borrowed attire of that, which the *enamour'd Intellect* is in pursuit of, our impatient minds entertain these counterfeits without the least suspicion of their cousenage.[14]

Thus it is quite understandable that men should fall into error since they set out on an impossible quest for which they are ill-prepared. Glanvill holds that to recognize this situation clearly is to go part-way toward overcoming it. As soon as we are tempted to assert that the principles we hold are necessary and incontrovertible, we should check ourselves and remember how far we are from comprehending absolute truth.

And, me thinks, did we but compare the miserable scantiness of our capacities, with the vast profundity of things; both truth and modesty would teach us a *dialect*, more becoming short-sighted mortality.[15]

Glanvill does not neglect the power of ridicule to reinforce his serious conclusions regarding dogmatism.

How fond are men of a bundle of *opinions*, which are no better than a bagge of *Cherry-stones*? How do they *scramble* for their *Nuts*, and *Apples*, and how zealous for their pety Victories? Methinks those grave contenders about *opinionative trifles*, look like aged *Socrates* upon his boys *Hobby-horse*, or like something more ludicrous: since they make things their *seria*, which are scarce tolerable in their sportful *intervals*.[16]

Socrates comes naturally to Glanvill's mind in this connection, for he symbolizes a species of nescience which other men have rarely achieved. Even among those who acknowledge in theory the difficulties of knowing, there is a counterbalancing tendency to exempt their own convictions from the category of half-truths.

And though when they speak in the general of the weakness of our understandings, and the scantiness of our knowledge, their discourse may even justifie *Scepticism* it self; yet in their particular opinions are as assertive and dogmatical, as if they were omniscient.[17]

This is no doubt a variant of the above-mentioned paradox that we long for truth and yet are ill-equipped to seek it out. No matter how vigorously we assent to the omnipresence of ignorance and error, we reserve a charmed area about ourselves in which this general truth is inoperative.

And methinks 'tis very *strange*, that men should be so excessively confident of the *Truth*, and *Certainty* of their Opinions; since they cannot but *know* the *Weakness* of *Humane* understanding *in general*, and cannot but often have found the Fallibility of their *own*.[18]

Glanvill sees that one of the reasons men miss the truth is that they are sure they have already apprehended it. Cautious ignorance could have saved them from both error and absurdity. In proportion as we know ourselves, we will recognize the paucity of our valid knowledge of the world about us. 'The exercised understanding is conscious of its disability.'[19]

But what are the metaphysical antecedents of our nescience? Why is it that we can never see things as they truly are?

The Painter cannot transcribe a face upon a Transient view; it requires the information of a fixt and observant Eye: And before we can reach an exact sight of Truth's uniform perfections, this *fleeting Transitory* our *Life*, is gone. Thus we see the face of Truth, but as we do one anothers, when we walk the streets, in a careless *Pass-by*: And the most diligent observers, view but the backside o' th' *Hangings*; the right one is o' th' other side the *Grave*: so that our Knowledge is but like those *broken ends*, at best a most confused adumbration. Nature, that was veil'd to *Aristotle*, hath not yet uncover'd, in almost two thousand years.[20]

This poetic passage may hold the clue to Glanvill's being 'more lucky . . . in his first hints and thoughts of things, than in his after-notions.' Perhaps this is how men have to operate if they are to catch the expression on the face of truth before it has passed them by.

Unfortunately, there are more serious hindrances to the success of this venture than those resulting from the nature of the quest. Not only are men tempted to believe what they wish to believe, but they will defend their own opinions so vehemently that truth will be lost sight of.

So that the precipitancy of *disputation*, and the stir and noise of Passions, that usually attend it; must needs be prejudicial to Verity: Its calm insinuations can no more be heard in such a bustle, then a whisper among a croud of Saylors in a storm.[21]

Another obstacle on the road to truth is one that is more complicated and more involved with men's lives than those already mentioned. It is the predisposition to retain without examining them the first 'truths' of which one becomes aware.

Nor were there any hurt in this *innocent* easiness, did not most Men *all their lives* worship the *first* thing they saw in the *morning* of their days, and *ever after* obstinately adhere to those unexamined Receptions: But *this* is the *Mischief*, we infinitely *believe everything* when we are *Children*: and *most* examine little when they are *Men*, but *settle* in their *first Impressions*, without giving themselves the *trouble* to *consider* and *review* them. And *these prejudices*, by *custom* and *long acquaintance* with our Souls, get a *mighty* interest, and shut them up against every thing that is different from those *Images of Education.*[22]

It is this procedure which leads to one's supporting his beliefs by the statement that he was bred in them; but as a product of the same climate of opinion in which Locke was bred, Glanvill acknowledges that the child may be indoctrinated with any religion which his elders choose for him.

> For our initial age is like the melted wax to the prepared seal, capable of any impression from the documents of our Teachers. The *half-moon* or *Cross*, are indifferent to its reception; and we may with equal facility write on this *rasa Tabula*, Turk, or Christian. We came into the world like the unformed *Cub*, 'tis *education* is our Plastick: we are baptized into our opinions by our Juvenile nurture, and our growing years confirm those unexamined Principles.[23]

Here again Glanvill would invoke Socrates and his dictum that the unexamined life is not worth living. As he advanced from the imposed dogmatisms of his youth to the free reflection of later years, he realized that most believers, of whatever faith, were as confident as he in the truth of their positions, with little reason except their early indoctrination. Even those who try to exercise their reason are likely to find it entangled in fancy and imagination, from which state of affairs intellectual difficulties arise. Glanvill implies that if men would keep to the high road of reason, no such perplexities would be met, for they are 'but the toyings of our *Phancies*, no absurdities to our more defaecate faculties.'[24] These faculties are apparently the ones on which Glanvill depends to lead men as far as they are able to go along the path toward absolute wisdom, a path whose terminus they can never hope to reach in this life.

Within the first few pages of *The Vanity of Dogmatizing* Glanvill makes clear what he considers to be the origins of man's fundamental ignorance. Following the speculation of Augustine and Pascal, he makes the Fall responsible not only for the introduction of sin into the world but also for the ruin of man's understanding.

Man was never at odds with himself, till he was at odds with the commands of his Maker. There was no jarring or disharmony in the faculties, till sin untun'd them.[25]

Man struggles therefore to repair both the intellectual and the moral damage wrought by Adam and Eve. Thus, as John Owen points out, Glanvill combines 'the Philosophical doctrine of the weakness of human reason, and the Theological Dogma of the natural degeneracy of mankind.'[26]

That Glanvill maintained in his own thought and writing the same attitude of nescience which he urged on others is perhaps the best argument for the tenability of his position. He followed Montaigne in presenting his conclusions in 'essay' form, subject to modification with the coming of additional light. The foreword to *Scepsis Scientifica* is consistent with his whole position.

> *And really when I compare this* little *and mean* performance, *with the* vastness *of my* subject; *I am* discourag'd *by the* disproportion: *And me thinks I have brought but a* Cockle-shell *of water from the* Ocean. *Whatever I look upon within the* amplitude *of* heaven *and* earth, *is evidence of* humane ignorance; For all things *are a* great darkness *to us,* and *we are* so *unto our selves.*[27]

In introducing *The Vanity of Dogmatizing*, Glanvill strikes out a kind of motto for scepticism.

> The *knowledge* I teach is *ignorance*: and methinks the Theory of our own natures, should be enough to learn it us. We came into the world, and we know not how; we live in't in a self-nescience, and go hence again and are as ignorant of our recess.[28]

In elaborating this central tenet, Glanvill contributed to his age a much-needed clarification of scepticism and its method of seeking the truth.

Dualism

Closely related to the undependable nature of human knowledge is the dualistic character of all human experience. Wherever man goes beneath the sun, he must not expect to find oneness.

Do what we can, we shall be imperfect in our attainments; and shall we scornfully neglect what we may reach, because some things to mortality are denyed? 'Tis madness to refuse the Largesses of divine bounty on *Earth*, because there is not an *Heaven* in them. Shall we not rejoyce at the gladsome approach of day, because it's over-cast with a cloud, and followed by the obscurity of night? All sublunary vouchsafements have their alloy of a contrary; and uncertainty, in another kind, is the annex of all things this side the *Sun*.[29]

What is required of man, Glanvill implies, is never to lose sight of the difference between himself and God. As man cannot attain to infinite wisdom in this life, so he is fated to operate in a world whose composition includes light and shadow, body and spirit. His very manhood is dependent upon 'the subtle knot.'

He that looks for perfection, must seek it above the Empyreum; it is reserv'd for *Glory*. . . . He alone sees all things with an un-shadowed comprehensive Vision, who eminently *is All*: Only the God of *Nature* perfectly knows her, and light without darkness is the incommunicable claim of him, that dwells in *Light inaccessible*.[30]

Just as man, exulting in his own wisdom, is tempted to label his opinions 'truths,' so he will want to deny one half of a dualism for the sake of making more reasonable and orderly his intellectual universe. It is obviously simpler to eliminate either body or spirit from one's conception of the reality of things than to try fitting the two elements into a comprehensible system. But, as Glanvill points out, to succumb to this temptation is to diminish one's chances of ever arriving at the truth.

His generation valiantly, if somewhat blindly, insisted not only upon the fundamental dualism of body and spirit but also upon the subsidiary categories of good and bad spirits. It was at this point that it became necessary for them to assert the existence of witches, for doubt cast upon the being of such evil spirits might undermine the whole system and leave men nothing but the bare reality of matter.[31] Even though Glanvill's defence of witches appears reasonable from this point of view, nevertheless it in-

volved him in the kind of philosophical difficulties which usually
spring from basing a whole system, like an inverted pyramid,
upon a single all-important tenet. But for our purposes the
defence is significant because it shows Glanvill maintaining
dualism (in this case the dualism of body and spirit) at all costs
and thus proving himself a thorough-going sceptic.

> There is no one, that is not very much a stranger to the World
> but knows how *Atheism* and *Infidelity* have advanced in our days,
> and how openly they now dare to shew themselves in Asserting
> and disputing their vile Cause. Particularly the *distinction* of the
> *Soul* from the *Body*, the Being of *Spirits*, and a *Future Life* are
> Assertions extreamly despised and opposed by the Men of this
> sort, and if one lose those Articles, all Religion comes to nothing.
> They are clearly and fully Asserted in the Sacred Oracles, but those
> Wits have laid aside these Divine Writings. They are proved by
> the best Philosophy and highest Reason; but the Unbelievers,
> divers of them are too shallow to be capable of such proofs, and
> the more subtle are ready to Scepticize away those grounds.[32]

How Glanvill's use of the word *scepticize* is to be reconciled with
his advocacy of scepticism must be left in abeyance until later in
this discussion.

For the theologian the practical impact of a denial of spirit came
at the point where men were trying to avoid doing anything about
their deplorable spiritual condition. As Henry More says in introducing the second edition of *Sadducismus Triumphatus*,

> For these Wits, I say, have grown so brutish and dull as not to
> conceive or believe there are any such things as *Spirits*; or *Souls* in
> themselves to be saved.[33]

Glanvill maintained his dualism as a kind of faith, an insurance
that when the puzzle of existence was finally to be solved, some
of the important pieces should not have been misplaced. Good
Cartesian though he was, he saw the difficulties which stood in
the way of explaining rationally the co-existence of body and
spirit. That the device of 'animal-spirits' must not have been

completely satisfactory to him is evident by his continuing to marvel that one creature, man, can incorporate such opposites.

In the unions, which we understand, the extreams are reconciled by interceding participations of natures, which have somewhat of either. But Body and Spirit stand at such a distance in their essential compositions, that to suppose an uniter of a middle constitution, that should partake of some of the qualities of both, is unwarranted by any of our faculties, yea, most absonous to our reasons; since there is not any the least affinity betwixt length, breadth and thickness, and apprehension, judgement and discourse: The former of which are the most immediate results [if not essentials] of Matter, the latter of Spirit.34

The best Glanvill can do with this dilemma is to express its mystery poetically, as Donne did, by the use of metaphor. Indeed, there may lie an unguessed significance behind the fact that sceptics are so often driven to metaphor to express the truth they have grasped.

It is the saying of divine *Plato*, that Man is natures *Horison*; dividing betwixt the upper *Hemisphere* of *immaterial intellects*, and this lower of *Corporeity*: And that we are a Compound of beings distant in extreams, is as clear as noon. But how the purer Spirit is united to this *clod* is a knot too hard for our degraded intellects to unty. What *cement* should unite *heaven* and *earth*, light and darkness, natures of so divers a make, of such disagreeing attributes, which have almost nothing, but *Being* in common: This is a riddle, which must be left to the coming of *Elias*. How should a thought be united to a marble-statue, or a sunbeam to a lump of clay?35

The subtlety of this knot is far beyond man's understanding. Here is further proof, if he needed it, that his intellect is a broken reed, that existence far transcends his power to trail behind and reduce it to essence.

Reason and Faith

There can scarcely be a more accurate gauge of the distance between the scepticism of Glanvill and of Donne than a comparison of the two men's attitudes toward the outstanding dualism of their century, that of reason and faith. The best Donne could do was to enshrine in a metaphor his conviction that the two were not fundamentally incompatible.

> Reason is our Soules left hand, Faith her right,
> By these we reach divinity.[36]

Glanvill, on the other hand, like Bacon, puts in reason and science the same intensity of trust which other generations had reserved for religion. To those of his own generation whose disillusion led them to belittle science in self-defence, Glanvill said,

> I do not think, that all Science is *Tautology*: The last Ages have shewn us, what *Antiquity* never saw; no, not in a Dream.[37]

The question, then, is how to reconcile this genuine advance in scientific knowledge with the religious values already held. The Royal Society itself, of which Glanvill was a member, had a dual purpose,

> the improving the minds of Men in solid and useful notices of things, helping them to such Theories as may be serviceable to common life, and the searching out the true laws of Matter and Motion, in order to the securing of the Foundations of Religion against all attempts of Mechanical Atheism.[38]

These men had no doubt that the truth was one and that the very structure of the universe would be found to support their religious insights. Glanvill, it will be remembered, had least respect for those religious opinions which men took over unthinkingly from their parents. Reason, he felt, could help to sort out from this miscellaneous lumber the pieces which were strong enough to build with.

> 'Tis very proper and seasonable for the Age to represent the *Reasonableness* of *Religion*, both in the principles and duties of it; that Men may know upon what grounds they stand, and not hold their faith by meer Custom, and the Tradition of their Fathers.[39]

From being the plaything of the Renaissance, reason was being transformed toward the end of the seventeenth century into a solid foundation for men's faith.

The superstition regarding doctors which Sir Thomas Browne was trying to combat with *Religio Medici* extended also to philosophers, who were popularly supposed to be atheists. But of philosophy, Glanvill says, 'I dare say, next after the *divine Word*, it's one of the best friends to *Piety*.'[40] It is unbelievable, he holds, that the study of nature should prejudice the interests of religion. Only people whose zeal gets the better of their wisdom will see any necessary connection between the scientist and the atheist. In a world where such people abound it is well that the Royal Society should maintain a beacon.

> *Now it seems to me a signality in* Providence *in erecting your most* Honourable Society *in such a juncture of* dangerous Humours, *the very mention of which is evidence that* Atheism *is* impudent *in pretending to* Philosophy: *And* Superstition *sottishly* ignorant in *phancying, that the* knowledge of Nature *tends to* Irreligion.[41]

What, then, is behind this misconception which sees reason and faith as enemies? Glanvill clears the ground by stating,

> *The Difficulties* of *Religion* do not lye in the UNDERSTANDING. *Religion* is a *plain* thing, and *easie* to be *understood*.[42]

The villain of the piece was a force with which the age of reason was to find itself progressively less able to cope, the force of imagination and fancy.

> To say, *Reason* opposeth *Faith*, is to scandalize both: 'Tis *Imagination* is the Rebel; *Reason* contradicts its impious suggestions. Nor is our *Reason* any more accountable for the Errours of our *Opinions*; then our *holiness* for the vitiosity of our *Lives*: And we may as well say, that the *Sun* is the cause of the *Shadow*, which is the effect of the intercepting *opacity*, as either. *Reason* and *Faith* are at perfect *Unisons*: The disharmony is in the *Phancy*.[43]

What this kind of union always breeds is merely one more dualism. To solve the dualism of imagination and fancy set over against religion bolstered by reason, nothing less than the romantic revolution was to be required.

In *Lux Orientalis*, Glanvill sets down the blue-print for natural religion.

> And the *Right Reason* of a Man, is one of the *Divine* volums, in which are written the indelible *Ideas* of eternal Truth: so that what it dictates, is as much the voice of God, as if in so many words it were clearly *exprest* in the written *Revelations*.44

Man need no longer fear his own rationality as the instrument of the Devil. It had been baptized into the household of faith. There is no more valid evidence of this union than Glanvill's testimony that the truths of divinity and of mathematics are equally reasonable and certain.

> These are superstructed on principles that cannot fail us, except our faculties do constantly abuse us. Our *religious foundations* are fastened at the pillars of the *intellectual* world, and the grand *Articles* of our Belief as demonstrable as *Geometry*. Nor will ever either the subtile attempts of the resolved *Atheist*; or the passionate Hurricanoes of the *phrentick Enthusiast*, any more be able to prevail against the *reason* our *Faith* is built on, than the blustring *windes* to blow out the *Sun*.45

Paradox

Glanvill is less given to paradox than any of the sceptics we have treated in detail, with the exception of Jeremy Taylor, perhaps because the drift at the end of the seventeenth century was toward clarity and precision of expression. Men no longer luxuriated, as they had earlier, in the paradoxical nature of their existence. It was something they were trying to live down. Nevertheless, even Glanvill shows some sensitivity to paradox and thus further qualifies for a place among the sceptics. As seems appropriate for the author of *Scepsis Scientifica*, Glanvill's central paradox is this:

> All Opinions have their Truth, and all have what is not so; and to say all are *true* and none, is no absurdity.46

It will be noted that this paradox differs from many others uttered throughout the century in that it does not consist merely of a sinuous dilemma; rather is it the expression of an insight not capable of being set forth in simpler terms. Behind such a formulation lay years of experience in controversy with opinionated men.

The following passage, again through the use of paradox, lights up the arena of controversy so as to show truth being wrought out there.

> And indeed, if we do but impartially consider the grand inconveniences which each party urgeth against the others Conclusion, it would even tempt one to think, that both are right in their *opposition* and neither in their *assertion*. And since each side so strongly oppugns the other and so weakly defends itself, 'tis a shrewd suspicion that they are both mistaken. Wherefore if there be a *third* that can lay any probable claim to the truth, it deserves to be heard to plead its cause; and, if it be not chargeable with the contradictions or absurdities either of the one or other, to be admitted.47

In his book *Catholick Charity Recommended* Glanvill has documented the above paradox by drawing upon the experience of controversy.

> It is indeed very natural to most, to run into *extremes*: and when men are *fallen out* with a Practice, or Opinion, they think they can never remove to too great a distance from it; being frighted by the *steep* before them, they run so far back, til they fall into a *precipice* behind them. *Every Truth is near an Errour*; for it lies between two Falshoods: and he that goes far from *One* is apt to slip into the *other*; and while he flies from a *Bear*, a *Lyon* meets him. So that the best way to avoid the danger is to steer the *middle* Course; in which we may be *sure* there is *Charity* and *Peace*, and very probably, *Truth* in their company.48

The *via media* is for Glanvill the only satisfactory intellectual response to the keenly observed psychological pitfalls of controversy. It incorporates the essential dualism of existence and uses it creatively in the search for truth. In further analysing his method, Glanvill throws additional light on his use of the word *scepticism*.

> Thus I have in this last particular play'd with the *Dogmatist* in a personated *Scepticism*: and would not have the design of the whole *discourse* measur'd by the seeming tendency of this part on't. The *Sciolist* may here see, that what he counts of all things most absurd and irrational, hath yet considerable show of probability to plead its cause, and it may be more then some of his presumed *demonstrations*. 'Tis irreprehensible in *Physitians* to cure their Patient of one disease by casting him into another, less desperate. And I hope, I shall not deserve the frown of the Ingenuous for my innocent intentions; having in this only imitated the practice of bending a *crooked* stick as much the other way, to straighten it. And if by this verge to the other extream, I can bring the *opinionative Confident* but half the way, *viz.* that discreet modest aequipoize of Judgment, that becomes the sons of *Adam*; I have compast what I aim at.49

Here the way to truth lies through the apparently absurd and irrational, the realm of paradox. The ideal terminus is in the kind of judgment which befits a human nature tragically susceptible to dogmatism, a 'discreet, modest aequipoize,' always characteristic of the sceptic, the result of pulling a crooked stick straight.

The Sceptic Method

This figure proves most fruitful as a symbol of Glanvill's scepticism. As we have seen, he holds that scepticism can be misused to 'scepticize away' recalcitrant facts; but it can also prove useful as a check upon dogmatism. With the proper flexibility of mind, a thinker can '(play) with the *Dogmatist* in a personated *Scepticism*.' To maintain a healthy equilibrium, one must set over against the inevitable bass of his own dogmatism a counterbalancing treble of scepticism. As Glanvill says in *Scepsis Scientifica*, again resorting to paradox, 'Were I a sceptic I'd plead for Dogmatizing.'50 The balance is all. Let us mark out the steps of his sceptical method and so learn how he redefined the term *scepticism* so that it should become relevant to the intellectual problems of his own day.

First of all, the seeker after truth will require a free field of operation, and he must prove himself ready for such freedom by attempting to abandon dogmatism and by embracing intellectual humility. Glanvill shares with Milton a certain recklessness regarding truth. Both men believe that if free inquiry is allowed, truth will provide its own defences and will necessarily emerge the victor.

> But for those who are capable of *search* after *Truth*, and are provided with advantages for it, *Freedom* of *Judgment* is necessary in order to their success. . . . *Modest, impartial* enquiry is the *Foundation* of the *real, experimental* way of Philosophy. Not that it teaches *Scepticism* and *Neutrality* in all Things, but this *Caution* in our Disquisitions, That we do not *suddenly* give *firm* assents to Things not well understood or examin'd; which no doubt is very just and safe.[51]

There is still a loophole for limitation in the clause, 'those who are capable of *search* after *Truth*,' but Glanvill goes much farther than most of his contemporaries. The instrumental nature of his scepticism may be seen in the fact that he is not willing to stop at neutrality. That is only one station on the road to truth. The kind of philosophy which Glanvill recommends as an underpinning for theology is one which makes men cautious and cultivates their sensitivity to the presence of truth in unsuspected places.

> In sum, I say, the *Free* and *Real* Philosophy makes Men deeply sensible of the Infirmities of Human Intellect, and our manifold hazards of *mistaking*, and so renders them *wary* and modest, *diffident* of the *certainty* of their *conceptions*, and *averse* to the *boldness* of *peremptory asserting*.[52]

We have already explored the background of such a statement, Glanvill's conviction of the fallibility of human knowledge.

Two practical results of this approach to truth are that the seeker will never totally abandon any idea which might prove valuable and that he will hold all his conclusions subject to alteration in the light of a more comprehensive view of truth.

> I am an inquirer, and therefore not very forward of assent. Nor would I be rash in a sudden rejection of opinions that may prove serviceable to worthy purposes.53

This may account in part for Glanvill's retention of a belief in witches. But he made a real effort not to cling to any idea for its own sake.

> Whether this mine *Hypothesis* stand or fall, my Discourse is not at all concerned. And I am not so fond of my conjectures, but that I can lay them down at the feet of a *convictive* opposition.54

Another advantage of free inquiry was held to be its liberalizing of the mind. To have met and understood and tried to assimilate a diversity of ideas might confuse an individual, but it also provided insurance against a narrow and confined dogmatism.

> Opinions are the *Rattles* of immature intellects, but the advanced Reasons have out-grown them. . . . So they that never peep't beyond the common belief in which their easie understandings were at first indoctrinated, are indubitably assur'd of the Truth, and comparative excellency of their receptions, while the larger Souls, that have travell'd the divers *Climates* of *Opinions*, are more cautious in their *resolves*, and more sparing to determine.55

That a man might never feel sure he had arrived at any portion of truth was a risk Glanvill was prepared to take in the campaign against dogmatism. The enemy in this campaign Glanvill blasts with unsavoury metaphors.

> The *Opiniator* hath a poor *shrivel'd* Soul, that will but just hold his little Set of Thoughts: His Appetite after Knowledg, is satisfied with his few *Mushromes*, and neither knows nor thinks of any thing beyond his Cottage and his Rags.56

In *The Vanity of Dogmatizing* Glanvill expands this figure and shows his readers that to reach infallibility they must have abandoned all pretence to it.

It betrays a *poverty* and *narrowness* of *spirit*, in the Dogmatical assertors. There are a set of Pedants that are born to slavery. But the generous soul preserves the liberty of his judgement, and will not pen it up in an *Opinionative* Dungeon; with an equal respect he examins all things, and judgeth as impartially as *Rhadamanth*: When as the Pedant can hear nothing but in favour of the conceits he is amorous of; and cannot see, but out of the grates of his *prison*. The determinations of the nobler spirit, are but *temporary*, and he holds them, but till better evidence repeal his former apprehensions. He won't defile his assent by prostituting it to every conjecture, or stuff his belief with the luggage of uncertainties. The modesty of his expression renders him *infallible*; and while he only saith he *Thinks so*, he cannot be deceiv'd, or ever assert a falshood. But the wise Monseur *Charron* hath fully discourst of this *Universal liberty*, and sav'd me the labour of inlarging. Upon the Review of my former considerations, I cannot quarrel with his *Motto*: in a sense *Je ne scay*, is a justifiable *Scepticism*, and not misbecoming a Candidate of *wisdom*. *Socrates* in the judgement of the *Oracle* knew more then *All men*, who in his own knew the least of *any*.57

Again the paradoxical character of Glanvill's thought shows itself, and he admits the existence of a justifiable scepticism.

As he explains the inner workings of his philosophical method, he comes close to paralleling Richard Baxter's famous list of certainties in which he ranges truths in the order in which he is certain of them (cf. *supra*, p. 171).

For among a multitude of things carelessly received, many will be *false*, and many *doubtful*: and consequently a *mind*, not wholly *stupid*, will some time or other find reason to *distrust*, and reject some of it's receptions; upon review of which, perceiving that it imbraced *falshoods* for great *certainties*; and was as much assured of *them*, as of those it yet retains; it will be in great danger of staggering in the rest, and discarding all promiscuously: whereas if a man measure out the *degrees* of his *assent* to *Opinions*, according to the *degree* of *Evidence*, being more *sparing* and reserved to the more *difficult*, and not thoroughly examin'd *Theories*; and *assured* only of those that are *clearly apprehended*, and have been fully thought of, he stands upon a *firm Basis*, and his *Science* is not moved by the gusts of *phancy* and *humour*, which blow up and down the *multifarious Opinionists*. For the assent that is difficultly obtain'd, and sparingly bestowed, is better establish't, and longer retained. The mind of man is too light and narrow a bottom to bear much *certainty* among the ruffling windes, and tumultuary waves of *Passion*, *Humour* and *Opinion*: and if the *Luggage* be prized equally with the *Jewels*, none will be cast out, till all be lost and ship-wrack't.[58]

This is one more evidence among the sceptics of what Baxter called 'cutting by a fine thread.' To be sure, this process requires a complex discipline which is not easily achieved. It requires that the thinker separate the certain from the uncertain, that he guard his reason from the enticement of fancy, and that he maintain throughout a sense of his own fallibility. The equilibrium of forces thus achieved is reflected in his speech and in the quiet which he is able to achieve, a genuine sceptic *ataraxia*.

Thus he conceives *warily*, and he speaks with as much *caution* and *reserve*, in the humble Forms of [*So I think* and *In my opinion*, and *Perhaps 'tis so*—] with great deference to opposite Perswasion, and candour to *dissenters*, and *calmness* in *contradictions*, with *readiness* and *desire* to *learn*, and great delight in the Discoveries of Truth, and Detections of his *own* Mistakes. When he argues he gives his Reasons without *passion*, and *shines without flaming*, discourses without *wrangling*, and *differs* without *dividing*. He catcheth not at the *Infirmities* of his *Opposite*, but lays hold of his *Strength*, and weighs the substance without blowing the *dust* in his *eyes*. He entertains what he finds *reasonable*, and suspends his judgment when he doth not clearly *understand*. This is the Spirit with which men are inspired by the Philosophy I recommend.[59]

And this, as we shall see, forms the basis for Glanvill's irenic, about which, as a rational philosopher and a practical clergyman, he was as deeply concerned as was Jeremy Taylor.

Defining Scepticism

To watch Glanvill as he struggles with the variant meanings of the word *scepticism* in current use in his day is more than a lesson in semantics. It is at once a verification of the presence of sceptic thought throughout the century, even when unlabelled, and an object-lesson in the feasibility of rehabilitating the term for use in our own day. We have already seen that Glanvill disapproves of the kind of scepticism which ends in sheer *epoché*. He has a practical goal in mind from which he cannot be deterred to wander in the pleasant paths of Pyrrhonism.

> I desire it may be taken notice of once for all then, that I have nought to do with that shuffling Sect that love to doubt eternally, and to question all things. My profession is *freedom* of *enquiry*, and I own no more *Scepticism* then what is concluded in the *Motto* which the ROYAL SOCIETY have now adopted for theirs, NULLIUS IN VERBA.[60]

Scepticism was a necessary stage, but one could not with impunity rest in it.

Often the charge of scepticism could be reduced to mere name-calling, as in the case of those who accused their opponents of atheism.

> But besides I observe, That *narrow, angry* People take occasion to charge the *freer Spirits* with ATHEISM, because they move in a *larger* Circle, and have no such *fond adherence* to *some Opinions* which *they adore* and count *Sacred*.[61]

When he has explained the cautious reasonableness of his own position, Glanvill adds,

> This is the *Temper* of my *Genius,* and *this* some *warm* Folks, who have more *heat* than *light* are apt to call *Scepticism* and *cold Neutrality*.[62]

Often Glanvill observed that among his opponents *sceptic* was merely a polite synonym for *infidel* or *atheist*.

A graph which should chart the shiftings and turnings of

Glanvill's arguments would not only show the irenic philosopher following his own prescriptions but would further document the meaning of scepticism. Of Thomas White, Glanvill says,

> We differ in the Means and Method; For he thinks it is best promoted by perswading, that *Science* is not *Uncertainty*; and I suppose that men need to be convinc'd, that *Uncertainties* are not *Science*.[63]

This difference arose from opposite diagnoses of the sickness of their age. To another opponent Glanvill replies,

> If we differ, then 'tis only in *this*, that you think it more suitable to the requisites of the present Age, to depress *Scepticism*; and perhaps, I look on Dogmatizing and confident belief as the more dangerous and common evil: which *difference* supposed, there is yet no ground for a *Quarrel*; for the amount will be but this; that one writes against *Many*, and the other against *More*. So that though I grant you, that the evil of *Scepticism*, is greater and more general, then *that* which I am set down against, I do thereby but yield you the honour to conflict the more *formidable* enemy, while with my weak, and less instructed Forces, I venture on but the less *numerous mischiefs*. . . . It appears from the irreconcileable feudes of the numerous Factions in divided Christendom: that *Scepticism* is not so much the temper of the Age; and that *confident Opinion*, is none of the meanest of *modern* Evils; but without doubt hath infected the far greater numbers. . . . Unreasonable *confidence* in *doubtful* matters is the *raging Plague* of our times.[64]

No further evidence is required of the eminent tact of Glanvill as a controversialist. Sometimes this takes the form of saying to an opponent, 'How can I try to end a quarrel with you when from my point of view I cannot recognize one?'

Sometimes it is necessary for Glanvill to make clear that he is as wary of dogmatic incredulity as of dogmatic credulity and that he never gives his assent to the kind of neutrality which is static. Scepticism to be effective must be going somewhere.

> Between the slaves of *Interest, Humour, Superstition, Enthusiasm, Education* and *Authority* almost all the world are *Dogmatists*; while Scepticks are but a few *sculking Renagado's*, whose Intellects vice

hath debauched, or the *unreasonable* confidence of half-witted Opinionists hath made *so*. And indeed by striking at *Dogmatical presumptions*, I aimed at *Sceptical neutrality* also.[65]

In fact, Glanvill doubts whether, in view of the apparently ineradicable human tendency to prefidence, there can be any pure scepticism.

Glanvill treats scepticism like a powerful drug which in moderate doses has unquestioned therapeutic value but an overdose of which may ruin one's intellectual health.

> If this be enough to answer an *Argument*, to say, *for aught we know, it may be thus and thus*, when there is not the least sign or appearance of any such thing, then *nothing* can ever be *proved*, and we are condemned to *everlasting Scepticism*.[66]

In spite of Glanvill's courtesy and tact, there is a limit beyond which his controversial etiquette will not go. Intellectual honesty compels him to take a stand, even though he take it tentatively and subject to correction.

The thinkers whom Glanvill most admired were those who merited the title of 'inquirers,' chiefly Descartes and Gassendi. He approves completely of Descartes' attitude toward truth, call it what one may.

> And if that great Man, possibly one of the greatest that ever was, must be believed a Sceptick, who would not ambitiously affect the title? . . . For I am apt to think, that Mankind is like to reap more advantage from the *Ignorance* of *DesCartes*, then perhaps from the greatest part of the *science* was before him, and I cannot forbear pronouncing him the *Phosphoros* of that clear and useful *light*, that begins to spring in plentifully upon an awakened world.[67]

Elsewhere Glanvill calls this a scepticism which is the only way to science, but he continually emphasizes the fact that scepticism is a way and not a port of destination. His defence of Gassendi involves rehabilitating the reputation of a man whom his more dogmatic contemporaries had anathematized.

The *Scepticism* which the constancy of Christianity lay'd in its *Grave*, I dare say the Illustrious *Gassendus* would never have redeemed from *thence*. The *Scepticism* which consists in *Freedom* of *inquiry*, that noble pen recommended and adorned. . . . That *Gassendus* was no *Sceptick* in the *old* and *common* notion, is apparent from the voluminous pains he hath taken in the building up a *Body* of *Philosophy* upon the *Principles* of *Democritus* and *Epicurus*; and if he was not so fond of the *Principles* he undertook to illustrate, as to boast of their *certainty*; proposing them not in a confident and assertive form, but as *probabilities* and *Hypothesis*: I see no reason why his modesty should be made his *crime*, and be so severely animadverted on.[68]

In an essay, 'Of Scepticism and Certainty,' Glanvill points to the philosophical origins to clarify his definition and to show that the kind of scepticism he advocates is instrumental and not terminal in nature.

The word *Scepticism* is derived from ἐκέπτομαι, which signifies to *speculate*, to *look about*, to *deliberate*: An ancient Sect of Philosophers were call'd ἐκεπτιχοὶ, *Scepticks*; as also Ζητητιχοὶ, *Seekers;* Ἀπορητιχοὶ, *Doubters*; and Πυρρόνειοι, *Pyrrhonians*, from *Pyrrho* the first noted Author of this Sect. . . . The chief ground of *Scepticism* he saith, is this, πατι λογω λόγος ἰσος ἀντιχειται, That every reason hath an equal one opposite to it: So that they gave no assent to any thing. . . . Sextus Empiricus mentions divers others, who it seems were thought to be Scepticks, or very near them; as *Heraclitus*, because he taught that Contraries are in the same thing: *Democritus*, for denying Hony to be sweet or bitter. (etc.) . . . But all these he shews to have been *Assertors*, and very different from the *Pyrrhonian* Sect. . . . Though in his Gymnasticks, where *Socrates* is brought in deriding the Sophists, he hath the *Sceptick*, uncertain character; yet in declaring his Opinion, he was a *Dogmatist*. . . . Those of the New Academy say all things are *incomprehensible*, in which, saith *Sextus*, they differ from us, because they *assert this*; but we *do not know* but that they may be comprehended. . . . And indeed their *doubting* and *suspension* was not in order to the forming a *surer* Judgment, but a resolution to sit down for ever in despair of *Knowledg*.[69]

We cannot help wondering when we see the distinction which Glanvill draws between philosophy and religion, whether, judging from other pronouncements, he is being sincere or merely prudent in the following statement:

> Though I confess, that in *Philosophy* I'm a *Seeker*, yet cannot believe, that a *Sceptick* in *Philosophy* must be one in *Divinity*. *Gospel-Light* began in its *Zenith*; and, as some say the *Sun*, was created in its *Meridian* strength and lustre. But the beginnings of Philosophy were in a *Crepusculous obscurity*; and it's yet scarce past the *Dawn*.[70]

A Sceptical Irenic

The determination of the sense in which Glanvill is a sceptic appears as a scarcely relevant academic question in comparison with the practical use which he made of his distinctive approach to truth. His contribution toward a Christian irenic is the final justification of his scepticism.

One of the cardinal principles by which controversy may be avoided and divergent opinions reconciled is the principle of separating fundamental from unimportant beliefs. Glanvill commends the Church of England for the kind of latitude in such matters which underlies its doctrine of the *via media*.

> It is none of the least commendable indulgencies of our Church, that she allows us a latitude of judging in points of *Speculation*. And ties not up mens consciences to an implicit assenting to opinions, not *necessary* or *Fundamental*; which favourable and kind *permission*, is questionlesse a great obligation upon the ingenious, submissively to receive & observe her pious appointments for *peace* and *order*.[71]

It is in accord with Glanvill's perception of human nescience that he should distinguish between truths which are central and those which are peripheral. Farther on in *Lux Orientalis* he is discussing scriptural proof which he might, if he chose, bring to support a belief in pre-existence. The reason he does not bring such proof is that he is diffident about appealing to the authority of scripture in support of any but the barest essentials of his faith.

> I think the onely way to preserve the *reverence* due to the *oracles* of *Truth*, is never to urge their *Authority* but in things very momentous, and such as the whole *current* of them gives an *evident suffrage* to. But to make them speak every *trivial* conceit that our sick brains can imagine or *dream* of, (as I intimated) is to *vilifie* and deflowre them.[72]

There is a clue here to the use which Glanvill would make of scriptural authority when he implies he would accept only what 'the whole *current* of them gives an *evident suffrage* to.' This in itself reflects the tact and percipience of the sceptic, who would avoid petty controversy.

To a disregard of the principle enunciated above, Glanvill attributes the multifarious evils of religious wranglings in his day. The zeal which men should reserve for fundamental postulates, they expend upon mere opinions, and so they fill the atmosphere with smoke and darkness which obscure whatever light they might walk by. He implies that small men with their small minds busy themselves about inconsequential details and lose sight of what is at once fundamental and practical.

> If our Returning Lord, shall scarce find *faith* on earth, where will he look for *charity*? It is a stranger this side the Region of *love*, *blessedness*; bitter zeal for opinions hath consum'd it. . . . What a stir is there for *Mint*, *Anise*, and *Cummin controversies*, while the great practical *fundamentals* are unstudyed, unobserved?[73]

Men whose eyes were fixed steadily upon these fundamentals would possess the kind of intellectual stability which would allow them to weigh calmly a variety of opinions. They would not betray their own uncertainty by condemning all those who disagreed with them.

> Hence some innocent truths have been affix'd with the reproach of *Heresie*: into which, because contrary to the inur'd belief, the violent rejecters would not endure a patient inspection.[74]

One is reminded of the treatment accorded Shelley's *The Necessity of Atheism* in spite of the Oxford undergraduate's plea that whoever could refute his argument should undertake to correct him.

Glanvill observes also that the misdirected zeal of dogmatists on two sides of a controversy tends to cancel itself out. An onlooker is likely to conclude that the confidence of the two opponents is equally vain and that neither is on the way toward the truth. As we have seen before, Glanvill is convinced that dogmatists are essentially little people and that the farther they pursue their dogmatism, the less likelihood there is that they will ever be able to appreciate the perspective which is represented by scepticism.

> There are a sort of *narrow*, and *confin'd Spirits*, who account all Discourses *needless*, that are not for their particular *purposes*; and judge all the world to be of the *Size*, and *Genius* of those within the *Circle* of their Knowledge and Acquaintance; so that with a *pert* and *pragmatical Insolence*, they censure all the *braver Designs*, and *Notices* that lie beyond their Ken, as *nice* and *impertinent Speculations*. . . . And hence it comes to pass that the *greatest* and *worthiest* things that are written, or said, do alwayes meet with the most general *neglect*, and *scorn*; since the *little people* for whom they were not intended, are quick to *shoot* their *bolt*, and to condemn what they do not *understand*, and *because* they *do* not.75

Even though the situation as Glanvill presents it seems hopeless since it rests on a flaw in human nature, he nevertheless prescribes 'experimental learning' as a remedy on the chance that men will be able to embrace it and thereby avoid the evils of dogmatism.

> Thus the *Experimental Learning* rectifies the *grand abuse* which the *Notional* Knowledge hath so long foster'd and promoted, to the hinderance of *Science*, the disturbance of the World, and the prejudice of the Christian Faith. . . . *True Philosophy* is a *Specifick* against *Disputes* and *Divisions*.76

This statement throws additional light on the use which Glanvill would make of philosophy in solving the problems of religion.

Hovering in the background is the spirit of the Royal Society, which was to prevent eighteenth-century religious thinkers in England from falling into some of the pitfalls which yawned before theologians of the seventeenth century. Glanvill never lets his readers forget, even at moments when he seems about to grasp essential truths, that all he and they will ever seize is wrested from uncertainty at the price of a patience and a humility almost beyond the power of human achievement. The most practical advice he can give, then, is to prescribe the *via media*.

> *Study the moderate pacifick ways, and principles, and run not in Extremes*; both *Truth*, and *Love* are in the *middle*; *Extremes are dangerous*. After all the swaggering, and confidence of *Disputers* there will be *uncertainty* in *lesser* matters: and when we travel in *uncertain Roads*, 'tis *safest* to choose the *Middle*. In *this*, though we should miss a *lesser* truth, (which yet is not very likely) we shall meet with *Charity* and our *gain* will be greater than our *loss*. He that is extreme in his *Principles*, must needs be *narrow* in his *Affections*: whereas he that stands on the *middle path*, may *extend* the armes of his *Charity* to those on *both* sides.[77]

Again in the 'Essay Concerning Preaching' Glanvill extols this kind of charity, as if it were the only immediate goal which religionists had any possibility of achieving. Absolute truth might elude them, but they had every opportunity of maintaining charity, and out of that there might conceivably spring a kind of truth which men in their disputatious dogmatisms had ignored.

> *Catholick, Universal Charity* is a Doctrine exceedingly fit for these Times, in which divisions, and mutual animosities have produced so many fatal and deplorable effects. Peace and Love should be some of the Objects of our chief Care, Study and Indeavours, knowing that no Religion can thrive without them.[78]

Like other sceptics of his century, Glanvill moved from an appreciation of how little man can know to the conviction that religion cannot rest on knowledge alone.

> *Religion* consists not in *knowing many things*, but in *practicing* the *few plain things* we know.[79]

His own procedure in controversy implements this general principle. In describing in *Plus Ultra* his disputational method, Glanvill had said that he sought out not the 'infirmities' but the strength of his opponents and thus avoided blowing dust in their eyes and so advanced the cause of truth. This method, which *plus ultra* so fittingly symbolizes, is further elaborated in *Catholick Charity*.

> *Acknowledge worth in any man.* Whatever is *good* is from *God*, and *He* is to be *lov'd*, and owned in *all* things.[80]

Armed with this touchstone, a man would find it difficult to desert the *via media* of charity and to follow the false gods of his own dogmatism.

CHAPTER IX

THE EIGHTEENTH CENTURY: UNTYING
THE KNOT

NOW that we have seen at close range the operation of scepticism in the thinking of five representative men of the seventeenth century, it seems reasonable to ask what common results it can be said to have produced there. The answer to this question, however, is not simple, as it might be in the case of almost any other intellectual movement; for the question involves another: whether it is possible to evaluate scepticism on the basis of its end products alone. And the implications of this question reach into the history of scepticism subsequent to its apotheosis in the seventeenth century. An analysis of what happened to scepticism in the eighteenth century will be sufficient both to determine the technique of its evaluation and to account for the present status of the word.

The Products of Scepticism

We may, to be sure, call the roll of several admirable qualities which the five sceptics have in common, even though each man represents a separate variation of the sceptic theme. Somehow in reacting against dogmatisms they have lost whatever prefidence might have been a part of their normal human equipment, and they have gained instead an intellectual flexibility which enables them to handle with tact and poise divergent attitudes and beliefs until they can arrive at some satisfactory, though tentative, combination of them. This habit generates also the ability to perceive what is important in each position through considering the intention of its author and not the often clumsy trappings of his insight. Then, too, because the sceptic keeps his eye fixed upon the fundamental human complexity of body and spirit and so expresses himself in an oblique rather than in a simple and direct fashion, he achieves a richness which is of the same quality as significant human experience, though it can often be transmitted to the mind only by dualism and paradox. Thus it is that all the sceptics, at the end, come full circle to a recognition that what cannot be worked out intellectually may yet find expression in a life well lived, that if one does 'the will,' he may know of 'the doctrine.' This is a direct outgrowth of the perception that man by his very nature is a 'subtle knot' and that the truth about him must partake of the knot's complexity and obliqueness. If a man wants to clear his vision, say the sceptics, he must exemplify the highest kind of life he knows; then although he may not be able to settle fine points of doctrine, he will know what is most necessary to him as a human being. Out of this experience there emerges an individual who not only has an indestructible basis for tolerance of his fellows but who is forever reaching out after the larger and more inclusive truth and abandoning one after the other his partial insights, on the pattern of Holmes' chambered nautilus.

The fact that these results of scepticism cannot be stated as orderly propositions should perhaps warn us that by its very nature scepticism is not reducible to such terms; for essentially scepticism is a method, and its effects are therefore to be measured in dynamic rather than in static units. Those who shiver in fear or sigh in smug contentment when confronted with the phrase 'creative scepticism' equally misconceive the nature of scepticism. They have the idea that it consists of a set of conclusions rather than an on-going process. It is to be hoped that the readers of this book may have been hypnotized by the continual linking of *sceptic* and *scepticism* with the 'right' connotations to the point where for them the concept may have been partially restored to its original status.

But how can these gains be made permanent and widespread? A feasible method of doing this, one borrowed from psychoanalysis, would seem to be to discover what happened at the close of the seventeenth century not only to dissipate the original meaning of scepticism but to discredit the sceptical process itself, labelled or unlabelled; for it can be shown that our popular misconception of the word's meaning dates from the eighteenth century. Just as one can destroy a phobia or the bitter fruits of a frustration by bringing to light its psychological origins, so perhaps one can help to lay the ghost of this eighteenth-century misconception by showing it for what it is, in contrast with the rich and full-bodied scepticism which we have come to understand through watching its operation in the seventeenth century.

Cautions

A warning must be issued here which we hope will prove retroactive. It is always dangerous to generalize about a century or a trend of thought, and this book has been given over to generalizations about both. We realize that the seventeenth century might be looked at from another point of view and very different and equally important factors emphasized. But the sceptic would say that there is room in the world of criticism for both interpretations as well as for many others not yet conceived (on the supposition that out-worn interpretations will die off as fresh ones grow). If the tracing of one pattern falsifies the picture to a certain extent, this must be recognized as the risk inevitably assumed by all those who attempt to see a design in the changeable silk of human experience. The gains lie in the perception at one particular range of a design which makes it possible to return to the close-ups with greater percipience and with a conviction of ultimate order.

Likewise we shall talk of the eighteenth century as if it were of a piece and as if one character predominated. It should be recorded here that scepticism in the sense in which we have been considering it did not die out at the stroke of midnight on December 31, 1699 (old or new style), but that during the period from 1660 on it slowly went underground, and another point of view became the dominant one. The sceptics were thus the forgotten men of the eighteenth century, but their principles survived, notably in certain aspects of deism and of the scientific movement. Bishop Butler, for example, could be shown caught in this transition period. If his analogy between natural and revealed religion stressed the simplicity and reasonableness of the latter, his grounding of morality upon the ineffable complexity of human nature set him nearer the camp of his predecessors, the men of the knot. Among men in the early part of the eighteenth century Swift, Mandeville, and Shaftesbury could be shown to share large portions of the sceptic legacy. Those elements in deism which led its practitioners to transcend, successively, credal, national, and cultural boundary lines and to become truly citizens of the world are certainly related to the best sceptical thought of the seventeenth century. But what caused the shift in the climate of opinion between the two centuries was that other values came to the surface and another rider was in the saddle, a man on the whole much less disturbed and complex and venturesome than his seventeenth-century counterpart. One symptom which may be of great significance is that there is apparently a correlation between the decline of scepticism and the loss of the richness and power of religion, and it may be possible to show that the two derived from a single source. It may be that while many men of the eighteenth century were congratulating themselves on having relinquished superstition and narrow sectarianism, they had unwittingly lost the virtues corresponding to these vices and that our contemporary misunderstanding of scepticism is one symptom of this loss.

Untying the Knot

It is our contention that what went wrong with scepticism in the eighteenth century may best be symbolized by the untying of 'the subtle knot' in so far as that knot stands for an honest facing of the spiritual struggle to know—involving nescience and the other elements of scepticism which we have included in the pattern. This does not mean that the eighteenth century any more than the seventeenth repudiated the fact that man is a combination of body and spirit, but that it seemed often to drop out of this conception the subtlety of which the seventeenth century was always aware. The contrast then is frequently between a brash and a tentative statement of the same fact. The two positions illustrate perfectly the difference between the direct and the oblique approach to human experience—the one external, schematic, and relatively uncomprehending and the other internal, complex, and percipient. The fact that mysticism, which flourished in one form or another throughout the seventeenth century, nearly died out during the eighteenth, until it enjoyed a resurrection with the coming of romanticism, cannot be wholly unrelated, whether as cause or effect, to this phenomenon. Willey points up what was happening as the Enlightenment approached when he says that 'in the field of theology, then, we must expect to find the rationalizers largely concerned with putting an *idea*, an *abstraction*, where formerly there had been a *picture*.'[1]

To add still a third figure to those of the knot and the picture, on the theory that metaphor is more effective than an expository statement, it can be said that scepticism, as an on-going process, is comparable to tight-wire walking, which requires a continual balancing of opposites as the performer moves forward along the wire. On this analogy, we may say that the eighteenth century tended to repudiate the whole process and found it much more comfortable to drop lightly to the ground on one side or the other of the wire. Therefore there is commonly a safe and static quality about most eighteenth-century thought which distinguishes it from that of the seventeenth. Compare, for example, Pope's pronouncement, 'Whatever is, is right,' with Browne's or Baxter's anticipation of gradually moving into fuller and fuller knowledge. The eighteenth century was apt to over-simplify its problems and to shirk the responsibility of working out its own salvation. There is a consequent loss of verve and challenge in the most characteristic writing of the century, and the reader loses the feeling that he is looking on while great issues are being desperately decided.

Attitude Toward Scepticism

We may take a brief preliminary survey of the temper of the eighteenth century by reviewing what two of its spokesmen thought of scepticism. This indicates not merely that the legitimate meaning of the word had begun to shift but that the idea behind it was no longer a congenial one. Addison is far removed from the attitude of seventeenth-century seekers, for whom the only way to achieve the truth was to embrace opposites and battle one's way through their conflict to a certainty which lay above and beyond them.

> Those [he says, in *Spectator* No. 465] who delight in reading books of controversy, which are written on both sides of the question on points of faith, do very seldom arrive at a fixed and settled habit of it. They are one day entirely convinced of its important truths, and the next meet with something that shakes and disturbs them. The doubt which was laid revives again, and shows itself in new difficulties, and that generally for this reason, because the mind which is perpetually tost in controversies and disputes is apt to forget the reasons which had once set it at rest, and to be disquieted with any former perplexity when it appears in a new shape, or is started by a different hand. As nothing is more laudable than an enquiry after truth, so nothing is more irrational than to pass away our whole lives without determining ourselves one way or another in those points which are of the last importance to us. There are indeed many things from which we may withhold our assent; but in cases by which we are to regulate our lives, it is the greatest absurdity to be wavering and unsettled, without closing with that side which appears the most safe and the most profitable.[2]

The seventeenth-century sceptic assumed that the process of spiritual growth was dependent upon his perennially forgetting the reasons which had once set his mind at rest and pushing on to larger and more adequate ones. To be sure, there is an irresponsible intellectual trifling which Addison is quite justified in condemning, but one has the feeling that the wrong reasons lie behind his condemnation, especially when the deciding vote goes to the side which is 'the most safe and the most profitable,' and when the chief objective seems to be to set the mind at rest. He has by-passed his problem instead of solving it.

Likewise, Richard Blackmore in *Just Prejudices Against the Arian Hypothesis* shows that his age had no sympathy with scepticism and with its indomitable faith that 'truth is strong next to the Almighty.' Blackmore felt that man should be told what is true and thereafter protected from all 'impious Principles.'

> Unless some ways are discovered, and prosecuted with Vigour, to revive our languishing Religion and Vertue, which seem to be agonizing, and at the last Gasp, Vice and Impiety will inevitably bring about, if not the same, yet as great and perhaps more destructive Evils, than those that are now so sorely complain'd of. But this desirable Restoration can never be brought about, while impious Principles, that strike at the Foundations of Religion and Morality, are propagated with Success, and spread their Contagion among the deluded People, many of whom are grown Sceptical and embrace no Scheme of Religion.[3]

Can one imagine a Donne or a Baxter assuming thus that truth has been achieved once and for all and needs now only to be impaled and defended? Blackmore minces no words when it comes to pointing out just what it is that he fears. It is the very uncertainty and scepticism which we have seen co-existing with deep and powerful religious feeling.

> And as the Adversary's Assertion destroys entirely all religious Science and Belief of which there is not one Principle self-evident, so it utterly subverts all Knowledge whatsoever, and introduces again into the World, the Uncertainty of the *Pyrrhonian* Schools, and the Scepticism of the New Academy.[4]

Evidently Blackmore felt that since the scepticism of the Greeks had existed in the backward and abysm of time, to move in its direction would be to turn back history, with all its progressive achievements. His Renaissance and Puritan ancestors had known no such reverence for 'progress,' and therefore the spiritual legacy of Greece was made available to them.

Religious Controversy

The superficial nature of most religious controversy in the eighteenth century is another straw which shows the way the wind is blowing. Seventeenth-century controversialists might have been blind and narrow, but they could never have been accused of being light and insincere. According to Leslie Stephen, English preachers in the eighteenth century no longer spoke with authority because they themselves felt the insecurity of their intellectual bases, from which therefore no advances could be made. Yet they must reiterate a series of theological proofs as if they really believed them to be convincing.[5]

Addison, like many eighteenth-century writers, has a way of mouthing the same conclusions as his seventeenth-century predecessors, but on his lips they have lost their force because he bears the mark of a century which would untie 'the subtle knot' and make all clear and easy.

> Zeal for dogma he holds to be unusually mischievous, whether it be exercised on behalf of Calvinism or Atheism; he is for cheerful piety as opposed to austerity, for devotion as distinguished from enthusiasm, for reasonable worship but not for superstition.[6]

Most of these sentiments could be matched among our five sceptics, yet the very tone in which they are uttered in the eighteenth century betrays their shallowness. Seventeenth-century religionists often tried to avoid superstition, but when the superstition was only the by-product of an attempt to embrace a large and significant truth, they were not worried by it. Browne often recognized that some insights he clung to would have been considered superstitious by other men, but until he could find a better formulation of the truth, he was satisfied to risk misunderstanding rather than to 'be deaf unto the speaking hand of God.'[7]

Behind the cheap and mechanical devices often used by eighteenth-century apologists to counter the deep criticism of the deists was the kind of person who was determined to remain unmoved by controversy—not that he had achieved *ataraxia* but that he was committed to operating on the level of his mind alone and so had disengaged the whole of his personality from the struggle, in a kind of intellectual free-wheeling.

Scepticism and Freethinking

Before we explore farther the significance of the untied knot and show how on each count the eighteenth century inclined to falsify, because it tried to freeze, the sceptic pattern, it will be well to set over against the superficiality of many people in the eighteenth century the judgments of two men, one from the eighteenth and one from the nineteenth, who equate scepticism with freethinking and in trying to rehabilitate both words show their appropriateness to designate a process which has gone on wherever human beings have honestly sought the truth. Anthony Collins in *A Discourse of Freethinking* (1713) is forthright in his insistence that when men have been on the right track, they have always given evidence of freethinking.

> I will only add, That as I take it to be a difficult, if not impossible Task, to name a Man distinguish'd for his Sense and Virtue, and who has left any thing behind him to enable us to judg of him, who has not given us some proof of his *Free-Thinking*, by departing from the Opinions commonly receiv'd (as indeed every Man of Sense who thinks at all must do, unless it can be suppos'd possible, when Opinions prevail by mere *Chance* without any regard to Reason; that *Reason* and *Chance* should produce the same effect;) so I look upon it as impossible to name an *Enemy* to *Free-Thinking*, however dignify'd or distinguish'd, who has not been either Crack-brain'd and Enthusiastical, or guilty of the most Diabolical Vices.[8]

A statement such as this loses its dogmatism in proportion as the definition of freethinking deepens and expands. Unfortunately, however, the voice of men like Collins was often drowned out during the eighteenth century. What we have attempted to do thus far is to frame a definition of scepticism which would make claims such as his wholly justifiable.

In his *History of Freethought*, Robertson describes a process which coincides with what we have called scepticism and then proceeds to appraise its difficulty.

> But everything goes to show that freethinking normally proceeds by way of intellectual construction—that is, by way of effort to harmonize one position with another; to modify a special dogma to the general run of one's thinking. The attitude of pure skepticism on a wide scale is really very rare—much rarer than the philosophic effort.[9]

The kind of scepticism we have been discussing unites Robertson's scepticism with his freethinking and 'the philosophic effort,' for we hold that scepticism does not preclude the possibility of construction; scepticism only clears the way for it and finds ultimate justification in the nature of the structure. Thus both Collins and Robertson emphasize the normality and importance of the sceptical or freethinking stage in the development of human thought.

Support from the Critics

That such a stage was circumvented by the main stream of eighteenth-century thought accounts for what we have called the untying of the knot. It is evident from several estimates of the century that our symbol of the untied knot is a fitting one. Referring to the spread of rationalism, Jordan says, 'In area after area not only religious intolerance, but religious vitality yielded before it.'[10] Stephen elaborates the same idea in explaining, although he does not account for, the process by which the knot was untied.

> At the end of the seventeenth century, a serious criticism of the external evidences was scarcely in existence. What there was of grotesque and ignoble in the sacred records was hidden whilst faith still burnt brightly in the reflected glow of sanctity. The absurdities, which at a later period edged the sarcasms of Voltaire, till now had either escaped notice or been easily converted into symbols of a spiritual meaning. It was not till that magical splendour began to fade that the worshippers rose from their knees, and,

gazing coolly round them, made strange discoveries. The old worship first lost its spiritual meaning, and then men began to perceive that the shrines and the sacred images had their share of weakness and corruption.[11]

This is undoubtedly the right sequence of events. The pointing out of discrepancies and contradictions would have had no effect upon sturdier religious natures. Men like Browne, for example, embraced them enthusiastically. Why such men should have flourished in the seventeenth century and not in the eighteenth is somehow related, we feel, to the presence of scepticism in the seventeenth century. The contrast in spirit between the two centuries is sharpened by Tulloch when he sets Cudworth along-side Dryden.

> There is never anybody so unthinkingly orthodox as the clever man of the world, when he thinks it necessary to interest himself in religion. The broad open-eyed candour and large-mindedness of Cudworth were unintelligible to the definite, facile, and sharply moulding intellect of the author of the 'Religio Laici' and 'The Hind and the Panther.'[12]

God and Man's Mind

What the two centuries take for granted is a clue to their comparative scepticism. All the seventeenth-century sceptics we have investigated are prepared to discover that perhaps the real nature of things is very different from their conception of it. Browne is sure that if a man has done his best honestly to seek out the truth, he will receive his just reward, even though he eventually 'misses of the truth.' This is a part of what kept the sceptics humble, for they could not be at all sure that their ways were God's ways. This recognition also underlay their hospitality to paradox. Many eighteenth-century men, reproducing the self-assurance of Pope, have straightened out this difficulty. In the blasé confidence that God would not be so unreasonable as to work according to a plan man had not yet perceived or one he was ultimately incapable of perceiving, Blackmore concludes,

Had we a perfect and comprehensive View of the whole *Scheme* of the *Divine Oeconomy* in relation to all these *Parts* of his *Government*, and how in his *Administration* in the different Parts of it he promoted the *great* and *glorious Design* of the whole, we should have quite another *Apprehension* of *God's* Wisdom and Justice.[13]

All that is required, apparently, is a view of God's plan, and we should at once understand it and praise its author's wisdom and justice since we are the same kind of planners *in parvo*.

One wonders sometimes whether perhaps the missing ingredient in the eighteenth-century personality was a profound sense of humour, in spite of the fact that much of the literature of the century can be classified as humorous. Certainly the typical man of that century would not be able to perceive the vast joke of a God who could deceive him. He could not say with Augustine, 'Lord, if we are deceived, it is by thee!' Mandeville, who shows glimmerings of a sceptic sense, held, not without some reason, that ridicule was a test of truth, that whatever dogma could come out unscathed was not wholly false. Stephen accounts for the humour of Sir Thomas Browne in a way which implies the relation of Browne's humour to the basic intellectual pattern of the man.

Humour is the faculty which always keeps us in mind of the absurdity which is the shadow of sublimity. It is naturally allied to intellectual scepticism, as in Rabelais or Montaigne; and Sir Thomas shared the tendency sufficiently to be called atheist by some wiseacres. But his humour was too gentle to suggest scepticism of the aggressive kind. . . . He revels in the mental attitude of hopeless perplexity which is simply unendurable to the commonplace and matter-of-fact intellects. He likes to be balanced between opposing difficulties. . . . He could not have moved the tears or the devotional ecstacies of a congregation, for he has too vivid a sense that any and every dogma is but one side of an inevitable antinomy. Strong convictions are needed for the ordinary controversial successes, and his favourite point of view is the centre from which all convictions radiate and all look equally probable. But then, instead of mocking all, he sympathizes with all, and expresses the one sentiment which may be extracted from their collision—the sentiment of reverence blended with scepticism. It is a contradictory sentiment, one may say, in a sense, but the essence of humour is to be contradictory.[14]

The antinomies of the seventeenth century could not long remain unreconciled, and the method of their reconciliation in the eighteenth again partakes of the essence of simplicity. The bystander is at once shocked by and somewhat envious of the way men could disregard disturbing ideas.

The method by which the Deists contrived to believe at once both in the divine origin of truth and virtue, and in its basis in observation and experience, was by postulating the inevitable agreement of the will of God with the results of man's rational speculation. To them, therefore, there was no conflict between reason and religion; private judgment and revelation.[15]

We have seen the Cambridge Platonists heading toward a conclusion faintly resembling this, but with how much more complexity and respect for 'the subtle knot.' Kaye goes on to shed some light on the difference between the sceptic and the deist handling of the reason-religion dualism.

The Deists, as we have seen, held these forces in equilibrium by assuming the identity of the dictates of reason and the will of God. And this was a general position for the rationalists of the age. . . . Another, and opposite, method was seen in that scepticism— especially prevalent in the Renaissance—of which Montaigne's *Apologie de Raimond Sebond* was an example. The Sceptics argued that reason and religion were antithetical. Religion offers us absolute truth; but, they argued in detail, the human reason is incapable of reaching such final truth: its conclusions are never more than relative. Having elaborated thus far the conflict between reason and religion, the Sceptics then proceeded to solve the discord. Since, they said, reason is impotent to give us truth, reason itself, by its very impotence, shows us the need of religion to furnish us the truths we cannot find elsewhere. Thus the Sceptics developed elaborately the potential antithesis between reason and religion while yet holding them in unstable equilibrium.[16]

It is this very unstable equilibrium which preserves the nature of the knot. To the Platonists, who derived from scepticism, the lack of conflict between reason and religion did not imply their coincidence.

The Simple Truth

Willey stigmatizes the dominant eighteenth-century position out of the mouth of one of its own lay saints.

> The feeling that whatever can be clearly and distinctly conceived is 'true' means that the very structure of things is assumed to conform with the laws of the human mind—a capital instance of the Idola of the Tribe.[17]

That this thoroughly comfortable definition of truth rendered its followers insensitive to more than a very superficial layer of truths can be seen in Locke's reaction to Tertullian. Roberts notes that the eighteenth century usually had no place for beliefs which were in any way irreducible to words or which contradicted the facts of science.

> The intense conviction of the importance of intention and guidance, rather than scientific knowledge, that led a Christian to assert *Credo quia impossibile est* was ridiculed. ' "I believe because it is impossible" might, in a good man,' says Locke, 'pass for a sally of zeal, but would prove a very ill rule for men to choose their opinions or religion by.'[18]

It is obvious from this that Locke is not trying to understand Tertullian from the inside, on the basis of a common human struggle with imponderables, but rather condescends to him as if Tertullian were merely playing with prescriptions for 'how to win friends and influence people' instead of desperately wringing a truth from his heart's core. Surely Browne would have said that Locke had come into the pericardium but missed the heart of truth.

Even nearer to our purpose is the reaction of Locke to Glanvill's perception that how body and soul can be joined, 'how a thought can be united to a marble statue or a sunbeam to a lump of clay is a knot too hard for our degraded intellects to unty.'[19]

> The man [Locke] who writes 'remote from the nature of our ideas' where his predecessor wrote 'a knot too hard for fallen humanity to unty' is one who has tacitly agreed with his readers to keep the 'pure glass of the understanding' as free as possible from the 'gross dew' of imagination.[20]

If we are to judge by rich perceptions and by an approach to truth which is capable of infinite growth and expansion, let us pray for a double portion of this same dew, for is not the world globed in a drop of dew?

The use which Hume makes of the concept of the imagination marks him as a thinker at the far end of the eighteenth-century tether. Out there, as Willey says,[21] it was becoming more and more apparent that nature could not be accounted for by reason alone, that instinct and feeling were somehow inextricably woven with the rational, whether in the microcosm or the macrocosm. There was something in the scepticism of Hume which redressed the balance of his century. When he returned to his backgammon game, he set going an intellectual movement which was bent on retrieving the values of the subtle knot.

Douglas Bush sanely evaluates the gains and losses in that previous transition from the seventeenth to the eighteenth centuries.

> With superstition went the mythological and symbolic imagination, the capacity for 'an O altitudo.' With superstition, too, went the active belief in human life enveloped by divine power, and the whole traditional conception, in its old dynamic form, of man as a creature between the beasts and the angels, of man's relations with himself, with society, with the universe and with God. The year after Vaughan's death appeared Toland's Christianity Not Mysterious. Men had fought and died for their way of worshipping God; no one was called upon, or was ready, to die for deism. Nor did confident deism and mechanistic cosmology nourish the religious conviction of man's inescapable weakness and sin which, in times past, had sobered Platonic humanists as well as biblical Calvinists.[22]

Quite unwittingly Bush has touched on most of the elements of the sceptic pattern which suffered worse than destruction in the eighteenth century. They suffered the desecration of being reproduced in cheaper and less durable materials.

Nescience

Let us consider first of all, as our custom has been, the phenomenon of nescience. In so far as the eighteenth century was, after all, the child of the seventeenth, it could not repudiate all its heritage; and as we suggested above, there were in the century sporadic and repressed strains of genuine scepticism. One of the most noteworthy evidences of this is in the lines of Matthew Prior in 'Solomon on the Vanity of the World,' which are the eighteenth-century counterpart of Donne's concerning the 'new Philosophy.'

> Amid two seas on one small point of land
> Wearied, uncertain, and amaz'd we stand:
> On either side our thoughts incessant turn:
> Forward we dread; and looking back we mourn.
> Losing the present in this dubious haste:
> And lost ourselves betwixt the future and the past.[23]

Here the eighteenth century had a starting point in authentic nescience and might have gone on to even greater heights and depths of scepticism than the seventeenth century achieved. But for some reason the decision was reached that the struggle was not worth the candle, and so the eighteenth century found it easier to take over conclusions ready-made. It is depressing but true therefore that Stephen's picture of the spiritual dilemma of the age is more accurate than one we might conjure up from Prior's lines.

Where were men to turn? Follow the deists, and you are landed in an optimism contradicted by every fact before your eyes; follow the divines, and whilst they will in words ascribe the utmost perfection to their Deity, they will attack the works of his hands, pronounce human nature to be corrupt, and the world a scene of misery, and make their Deity reflect the worst human passions of cruelty and vindictiveness. Where were men bewildered by pretentious philosophy and revolted by the dry husks of an effete theology to turn for comfort?[24]

That eighteenth-century men turned to examine facts (without regard for their ultimate relationships) instead of looking straight into the heart of their own nescience perhaps accounts for their untying the knot.

The attitude of the early eighteenth century toward freethinking is most illuminating, for it reveals that the condemnation of freethinkers rested on three main counts: that such men constituted a disturbing element; that they lowered human dignity; and that they destroyed cheerfulness. The author of the *Guardian* dismisses freethinkers thus:

> There is not any character so hateful as his who invents racks and tortures for mankind. The freethinkers make it their business to introduce doubts, perplexities, and despair into the minds of men, and, according to the poet's rule, are most justly punished by their own schemes.[25]

Can one imagine what would have been the reaction to this smug pronouncement on the part of seventeenth-century sceptics who were struggling through nescience for their very spiritual existence?

Where the eighteenth-century man did admit his ignorance, it was with such fanfare and mock humility that the admission had lost its cutting edge. Dogmatisms he could not bear, but always for the wrong reasons.

> It is impossible for us, who live in the latter ages of the world, to make observations in criticism, morality, or in any art or science, which have not been touched upon by others. We have little else left us, but to represent the common sense of mankind in more strong, more beautiful, or more uncommon lights. . . . For this reason I think there is nothing in the world so tiresome as the works of those critics who write in a positive dogmatic way, without either language, genius, or imagination.[26]

The unruffled and world-weary tone of this *Spectator* signifies a man who is willing to make a feather-bed of his nescience until some Supreme Power chooses to pick him up and transport him to a point of vantage. For his part, he chooses not to move.

> But what I would chiefly insist on here is, that we are not at present in a proper situation to judge of the councils by which Providence acts, since but little arrives at our knowledge, and even that little we discern imperfectly.²⁷

The eighteenth century is often like a son inheriting his father's clothes which do not fit him, and for some of whose pockets he has no use. They are, to say the least, not functional, and neither was the nescience of the eighteenth century. Lovejoy diagnoses the situation admirably.

> But though this tone of becoming diffidence, this ostentatious modesty in the recognition of the disproportion between man's intellect and the universe, was one of the most prevalent intellectual fashions of a great part of the eighteenth century, it was frequently accompanied by an extreme presumption of the simplicity of the truths that *are* needful for man and within his reach, by a confidence in the possibility of 'short and easy methods,' not only with the deists, but with pretty much all matters of legitimate human concern. 'Simplicity, noblest ornament of truth,' wrote John Toland, characteristically; and one can see that to him, and to many of his time and temper, simplicity was in fact, not merely an extrinsic ornament, but almost a necessary attribute of any conception or doctrine which they were willing to accept as true, or even fairly to examine.²⁸

Certainly none of the seventeenth-century sceptics had the feeling that truth was simple, except with the simplicity of great profundity. Yet see how Mandeville tosses off the distinction between knowledge and belief.

> THIS then is call'd knowledge, but when we admit any Thing to be true or false, and our Judgment is perswaded that it is the one rather than the other, on an Authority from without, the Action is call'd believing: of this there are many degrees, and the Confi-

dence we believe with is either strong or slight, according to the good or indifferent Opinion we entertain of the Authority, which was the first Motive of our Belief.[29]

The dilemma into which the eighteenth century worked itself because it failed to see its nescience through is accurately delineated by Roberts.

> In their writings on religion, Hume and the eighteenth-century rationalists are continually evasive. Religion, they see, is ridiculous if taken 'literally.' At the same time they have an uncomfortable feeling that there is something in it. They pay lip service. And as they do so, they are conscience-stricken at the loss of their intellectual honesty. They solve the problem by writing ambiguously: they speak of Christianity in terms which they intend seriously one moment, and ironically the next. Whatever is the truth, they feel, their own writings are not wrong: they can be interpreted either way. But they themselves continue to wobble between a boisterous self-confidence and a pessimistic faith born of a reluctant recognition of the limits of the intellect.[30]

The two-fold fruit of this ambivalence, itself a caricature of seventeenth-century scepticism, is classified by Hunt in his *Religious Thought in England*, when he says concerning Hume,

> He follows experience till he finds there is something beyond experience. Then he either acknowledges that we must fall back upon natural instincts, and trust to reason, such as it is, or he gives way to despair, and with an easy indifference flings the problem aside as insoluble, bidding us be content with our ignorance, for all is an enigma, a riddle, and a mystery. These two states of mind are clearly distinguishable in Hume. They are both called Scepticism, yet they are so different that the one leads to inquiry, the other to indolence.[31]

This, like the lines from Prior quoted above, is another place where true scepticism might have been retrieved from oblivion. Indeed, it was perhaps this philosophical double-talk of Hume's which awoke Kant from his dogmatic slumber, with all the implications which that awakening had for nineteenth-century romanticism and the thinking which followed in its wake.

Lovejoy shows what the *esprits simplistes* came up with when they dove into the sea of nescience, certainly a less impressive haul than their fathers had accomplished.

It was nevertheless largely an age of *esprits simplistes*; and the fact had the most momentous practical consequences. The assumption of simplicity was, it is true, combined in some minds with a certain sense of the complexity of the universe and a consequent disparagement of the powers of man's understanding, which might at first seem entirely incongruous with it, but which in reality was not so. The typical early-eighteenth-century writer was well enough aware that the universe as a whole is physically an extremely large and complicated thing. One of the favorite pieces of edifying rhetoric of the period was Pope's warning against intellectual presumptuousness: . . . this pose of intellectual modesty was, in fact, an almost universally prevalent characteristic of the period, which Locke, perhaps, more than any one else had brought into fashion. Man must become habitually mindful of the limitations of his mental powers, must be content with that 'relative and practical understanding' which is the only organ of knowledge that he possesses.[32]

To have given up storming Heaven and to have been able to sit down contentedly with this cold intellectual comfort indicated what manner of men these heirs of the seventeenth century had turned out to be.

Dualism and Paradox

The most important dualism corollary to that of body and spirit is the sense of man's greatness and the sense of his insignificance. It is the mark of the sceptic that he tries to hold both elements in solution, but not so most eighteenth-century men. They will have none of man's smallness, except they can make a dramatic gesture of confessing it. The principal emphasis is upon man's dignity, and it was the freethinkers' alleged violation of this that called down all the wrath of the 'unco guid.'

And God said, *Let us make Man in our Image, after our Likeness.* This was a Declaration of the Dignity of Man's Nature, made long before any of your sagacious Moralists had a Meeting. As this Doctrine came thus early from Heaven, so in the several Ages of the World, God has had his *Oracles*, and *Prophets*, to raise Mens Thoughts to their first Original; to preserve a Sense of their Relation to God, and Angelick Natures, and encourage them to expect a State of Greatness suitable to that Image after which they were created.33

It was a similar type of thinking a century and a quarter later which refused to give Darwin a hearing, and what we have discovered in the realm of psychology since then makes us suspicious of people who insist upon having their dignity recognized.

That the eighteenth century in its blindness often started from the wrong end can be seen in the way it appreciated religion for its promotion of the dignity of man.

But there is nothing which favours and falls in with this natural greatness and dignity of human nature so much as religion, which does not only promise the entire refinement of the mind, but the glorifying of the body, and the immortality of both.34

No seventeenth-century sceptic was so impressed by the virtues of either his mind or his body that he craved their perpetuation into eternity, though he had hopes for his soul, which was somehow a projection of 'the subtle knot.'

It is one mark of the sceptic, too, that because of his own struggles with dualisms he is forever sympathetic with his fellows, no matter at what point along the road they have struck camp. But the *Tatler* has only contempt and ridicule for the atheist and anticipates the attitude of Theodore Roosevelt toward Tom Paine.

A wise man, that lives up to the principles of reason and virtue, if one considers him in his solutude, as taking in the system of the universe, observing the mutual dependence and harmony, by which the whole frame of it hangs together, beating down his passions, or swelling his thoughts with magnificent ideas of Providence, makes a nobler figure in the eye of an intelligent being, than the greatest conqueror amidst all the pomps and solemnities of a triumph. On the contrary, there is not a more ridiculous animal than an atheist in his retirement. His mind is incapable of rapture or elevation. He can only consider himself as an insignificant figure in a landscape, and wandering up and down in a field or a meadow, under the same terms as the meanest animals about him, and as subject to as total a morality as they; with this aggravation, that he is the only one amongst them, who lies under the apprehension of it.35

Unfortunately for the critic, he is afraid to abandon himself to a recognition that he may be on a level with the animals, for he doubts the strength of his conviction of greatness to draw him up again.

In welcome contrast is the far-sighted statement of Mandeville:

> It ought not to appear more strange to us that an Atheist should be a quiet moral man, than that a Christian should lead a very wicked life.36

But the majority, not endowed with Mandeville's insight, was unable to grasp the position of its opponents except in the simplest and most mechanical terms.

> For the *Deist's* Creed has as many Articles as the *Christian's*, and requires a much greater Suspension of our Reason to believe them. So that if to believe Things upon no Authority, or without any Reason, be an Argument of Credulity, the *Free-thinker* will appear to be the most easy, credulous Creature alive. In the first place, he is to believe almost all the same Articles to be false, which the Christian believes to be true.37

This kind of over-simplification, and hence falsification, is indicative of a mind to which every dualism presents a choice rather than a challenge to synthesis. This mind struggled to keep its world simple and in the process was overtaken by spiritual blindness, which was the price many thinkers in the eighteenth century paid for their clever avoidance of the dualistic dilemma.

As a consequence, paradox became unthinkable. So disciplined is the eighteenth-century man that he rarely even stumbles upon one unexpectedly. The nearest he gets is a colourless *via media*, but it has none of the pulsing vitality of the sceptic's, for it is a dwelling-place and not a road. It may not be too rash to suggest that the unemotional tone of the typical eighteenth-century sermon is traceable to the cool balance of the attenuated *via media*.

With regard to the dualism of reason and faith, we have seen enough of the eighteenth-century technique to understand what the results would be—a false simplification and almost never the one integrated into the other. Toland, in explaining why Christianity is not mysterious, proceeds thus:

> He maintains that, as nothing is contrary to reason, so there is nothing 'above reason' in the Gospel. We are required to believe nothing that is inconceivable as well as nothing that is contradictory. He argues at considerable length, and with much show of learning, that the word mystery, as used both in the writings of classical authors and in the Scriptures, does not signify a proposition inconceivable to our minds, but simply a proposition known to us by revelation alone. The veil once withdrawn, the mystery may be, and indeed must be, as simple as any other truth, and a mysterious doctrine is merely one which for some reason or other has been concealed from certain classes of mankind. In this sense the existence of America, for example, would be a mystery until Columbus had discovered it.[38]

This attitude is consistent with what we have seen previously in Pope and in Blackmore and precludes the possibility of there being truths of any other order than those recognizable by man at his present stage of development. In the matter of 'mysteries,' so long as the eighteenth century was saved from the terrifying prospects of dealing with a contradiction, it did not matter that salvation was by a semantic ruse.

Action and Knowledge

We have seen how seventeenth-century sceptics turned to the good life on the assumption that only its wholeness could give expression to truths which transcended intellectual formulation. Where they could not know, at least they could do; and perhaps knowledge would follow. In the eighteenth century this was transformed into the belief that religion was valuable to individuals because it assured them of 'the main chance' and to societies because it assisted in the maintenance of order. The emphasis in both cases was upon morality, but with what different purposes than in the seventeenth century. Tillotson in his preface to Wilkins' *Natural Religion* felt called upon to urge the adoption of religion not only as insurance against the perils of a future life but as security for the happiness of this life.

> *Thirdly*, To persuade men to the *Practice* of *Religion*, and the *virtues* of a good life, by shewing how natural and direct an influence they have, not only upon our *future* blessedness in another World, but even upon the happiness and prosperity of this *present* Life. And surely nothing is more likely to prevail with wise and considerate men to become Religious, than to be thoroughly convinced, that *Religion* and *Happiness*, our *Duty* and our *Interest*, are really but one and the same thing considered under several notions.[39]

The only men to whom such propaganda might appeal would be those who were already insensitive to any overtures on the basis of religion's light and spiritual power.

Samuel Clarke, writing his *Discourse Upon Natural Religion*, exalts morality as the heart of religion and therefore as the *raison d'être* of both the revelation and the institution.

> I have been the longer upon this Head, because Moral Virtue is the Foundation and the Sum, the Essence and the Life of all true Religion, for the Security whereof, all positive Institution was principally designed, for the Restoration whereof, all revealed Religion was ultimately intended, and inconsistent wherewith, or in opposition to which, all Doctrines whatsoever, supported by what pretence of Reason or Authority soever are as certainly and necessarily false, as God is true.[40]

This again is characteristic of the eighteenth-century over-simplification. The seventeenth century, as an extension of the

Renaissance, was striving primarily toward the attainment of truth.

It was in the seventeenth century that modern European thought seems first to have assumed, once more, that its appointed task was *La Recherche de la Vérité*, the discovery and declaration, according to its lights, of the True Nature of Things.[41]

Most thinkers of the eighteenth century, on the other hand, had abandoned this task as impossible and so went about trying to save morality when for what seemed to them inscrutable reasons theology had gone by the board, a theology with which they were perhaps relieved not to be involved. They were trying to save piecemeal a world whose core they did not have the energy either to understand or to fight for.

The Fate of Language

If we want to see this happening within the field of literature, we need go no farther than the striking change which took place in the use of language during the seventeenth century. Since we have undertaken to concentrate on literary scepticism, this is the proper area in which to take leave of our readers. We have had occasion to refer several times to the effect of the Royal Society's demands, during the Restoration, for a plain and simple style. Glanvill, who was at once a sceptic and one of the Society's spokesmen, gives evidence of what has been happening since Donne's day.

For I must confess that way of writing *to be less agreeable to my* present relish *and* Genius; *which is more gratified with* manly sense, *flowing in a* natural *and* unaffected Eloquence, *then in the* musick *and curiosity of* fine Metaphors *and* dancing periods.[42]

This is a part of the transition from pictorial to conceptual thinking, on which Willey lays great stress. Significant also is the fact that Glanvill scorns fine writing because it is unsuitable for instruction, implying that he is slowly moving away from his initial nescience.

For when men once ramble in the way of *phrases, metaphors,* and *conceits,* as they lose themselves, so they perfectly dazle, and amaze those others, whom they should instruct.[43]

This turn of events was more than a landmark in the development of modern prose style. It was a symptom of the changing temper of the times and serves as one more bit of evidence that the aim of the eighteenth century was to untie the knot which the seventeenth had insisted on preserving inviolate.

Roberts, among other critics, holds that the history of metaphor throughout the seventeenth century was a reflection of the history of thought.

For Andrewes, the truth of a statement depended as much upon intensity and sensuous vitality as upon 'scientific' accuracy; for Donne, far more sophisticated, the problem of a possible conflict between the demands of intensity and physical accuracy had already begun, and by the end of the century physical accuracy had become the sole criterion of truth, and metaphor and rhythm were compelled to apologise for their existence. 'A man,' said Dryden, 'should be learned in several sciences, and should have a reasonable, philosophical, and in some measure a mathematical head, to be a complete and excellent poet.' Long before this the poets had lost confidence in their own method and a more simple tribute seemed more honest and appropriate than all the riches of ingenious metaphor and sensuous description.[44]

Dryden was indeed the poet of the untied knot.

In the field of religious thought, Roberts feels that the gentle yielding of the Platonists to proponents of the plain style was the equivalent of allowing the camel's head under the edge of the tent.

The Cambridge Platonists could see that, whatever devotion to the Christian religion Hobbes might profess, his language and his emphasis on material things must lead in the end to a denial of the reality of *all* internal knowledge: intuitions and the products of the imagination are not derived from evidence of the senses, therefore they are not real. The unconscious argument was bound to run in this way, leading in the end to atheism or a purely intellectual deism, and to a morality of prudence. The Cambridge Platonists, concerned with the absolute morality and doctrine of religion, fought against that conclusion with all their power, using logic and authority and even popular superstition to support their cause; but by abandoning the poetic use of language, which alone is competent to deal with this internal knowledge, they themselves had made certain the defeat of their own cause.[45]

Something in the poetic use of language is forever bound up with the inscrutable complexity and subtlety of the knot. Indeed, Roberts holds that it was on the score of his poetic insensitivity that Hobbes was to be condemned.

The real, the crucial charge, against Hobbes (as we have seen) is not that he was an atheist, but that he was blind to poetry. Not that he denied its existence, but rather that he regarded it as trivial; it had no essential place in his scheme; there were no things which needed to be said which could only be said through the poetic use of language. Understanding only the scientific use of language, he interpreted theological doctrine as if it were scientific. Not recognizing that a concept is not necessarily valid beyond its own particular purpose he conceived of science as a universe of discourse in which all words and all rules of logic had universal validity, not validity relative to their purpose. Hobbes, like some other modern philosophers, believed in the universality and adequacy of an unrhetorical, unemotional descriptive language. In such a language rhetoric, the appeal to men's emotions, is impossible, and the function of theology, as a criticism of those appeals, disappears. Theology becomes an arbitrary code of morals and a pseudo-science of entities which cannot be known through the senses.[46]

This indicates not only the unbridgeable nature of eighteenth-century dualisms (perhaps that dissociation of sensibility which our critics have lamented) but also the loss of the seventeenth century's ability to understand the poetry of theological concepts, to interpret them not as counters but in the light of their capacity to clarify one small area of the truth.

Logan P. Smith, in commenting upon Donne's sermons,

laments the subsequent loss of whatever produced their brave energy and fire.

> This noble diction, this intensity, and what we might almost call inspiration of language, which gives so poetic a colouring to the English version of the Scriptures, was not the achievement of one man, but almost the universal birthright of the time: with the Elizabethan dramatists and translators, the preachers and theological writers had their share in this great utterance, which, whether due to linguistic causes which ceased to operate, or to an intensity of poetic vision which afterwards vanished, certainly grows fainter and thinner and gradually dies away as the seventeenth century advances, and the age of theology is superseded by the age of Reason and common sense.[47]

If Hume is right in his theory of causation (and certainly as a sceptic he made an important contribution by his questioning), it might be possible to account for the style by analysing the thought. Roberts speaks of 'the saving scepticism of the nominalist attitude toward language,'[48] and would have prescribed this for scientific philosophers who blithely asserted the reality of the material world. Another critic holds that this serfdom to matter was far more deadly than the mediaeval serfdom to spirit.[49] From our point of view, each was a violation of 'the subtle knot.' No doubt men of the eighteenth century seemed to themselves to be merely ordering their universe and so increasing their chances of comprehending it, but instead they were standing in their own light, and the shadow which they cast has darkened other centuries than their own.

As so often happened in the eighteenth century, when some individual did get an inkling of what was wrong with his age, he proposed a remedy whose very perverseness showed his own lack of insight. Such was the case with John Dennis, whose principal thesis, repeated *ad nauseam*, was that all would be well with eighteenth-century poetry if only poets would return to the use of religious themes and specifically to material taken from the Bible. Here is how he reasoned.

The more the Soul is mov'd by the greatest Ideas, the more it conceives them, but the more it conceives of the greatest Ideas, the greater Opinion it must have of its own Capacity. By consequence the more it is mov'd by the Wonders of Religion the more it values it self upon its own Excellences. Again, The more the Soul sees its Excellence the more it Rejoyces. Besides Religious Ideas are the most Admirable, and what is most Admirable according to the Doctrine of *Aristotle* is most delightful. Besides Religious Ideas create Passion in such a manner as to turn and incline the Soul to its primitive Object. So that Reason and Passion are of the same side, and this Peace between the Faculties causes the Soul to Rejoyce, of which we shall have occasion to say more anon.[50]

The last sentence comes very close to reproducing 'the subtle knot,' but in tissue paper rather than in hemp. The obverse of Dennis' contention here is that what religion needs to revivify it is more poetry, even though that has to be dragged in by the heels.

I believe that it would be an easie matter to prove, that it was the use of exalted Poesy, such as the lofty Hymn of St. *Ambrose*, that blew up the Flame of Christian zeal to such a transporting height, in the Primitive and Apostolical times, and that the neglect of so Divine an art, has not only in these latter Days considerably lessen'd the force of Religion, but has with some People among us gone a very great way towards the making Publick Worship contemptible.[51]

Could Dennis have seen around one more corner, he would have known that something far more serious had gone wrong in the heart of religion, and that no artificial respiration could save it. Roberts quotes Dennis as an illustration of the fact that at least some men in the eighteenth century knew the scientific use of language was being substituted for the poetic and left a record of their protest, inadequate as that proved to be.

The change that was creeping over poetry and religion did not pass unnoticed. It was noted, for example, by that neglected critic John Dennis. 'Poetry,' he said, 'is the natural language of Religion.' 'And I have reason to believe, that one of the principal Reasons that has made the modern Poetry so contemptible, is, That by divesting it self of Religion, it is fallen from its Dignity, and its original Nature and Excellence; and from the greatest Production of the Mind of Man is dwindled to an extravagant and a vain Amusement.'[52]

What could be more indicative of the untied knot than this plea that religion should come to the rescue of poetry? The seventeenth-century mind could never have conceived of their disparity.

CHAPTER X

CONTEMPORARY IMPLICATIONS OF SCEPTICISM

FROM one point of view this whole analysis has falsified the very concept we have been discussing. For scepticism is not static but dynamic and to be truly portrayed requires a hitherto undiscovered medium, which we can project even if we cannot produce —a kind of spiritual moving picture, a three-dimensional action-sequence which should provide a living and moving example of the operation of scepticism. The nearest we can come to such a desideratum, until human ingenuity has progressed farther, is to show scepticism being put to use in a particular situation by a great English writer of the seventeenth century who maintained the sensitivity of genius toward the intellectual currents of his day, and then, since it is the way of sceptics to unite the apparently irreconcilable, to glance briefly at contemporary insights, including existentialism, and show what would be the sceptic attitude toward these modern drives in the direction of truth. Milton and Sartre, for example, may not at first seem to have many points of contact, and we are certainly passing no judgment on their comparative literary worth when we link them; but perhaps their very juxtaposition may have for the reader the effect of shocking him, in a truly sceptic fashion, into a perception of unguessed truth. And thus he will have proved on his pulses the sceptic process. And once this is accomplished, we can do nothing further to rehabilitate the degraded concept of scepticism.

Since this is not the place to undertake a full-scale study of Milton's relation to scepticism, let us consider merely the 'Areopagitica' as perhaps the most widely known of the prose tracts and one in which many rays of Milton's thought come to a focus.

257

The Fruits of Nescience

One of the most important assumptions underlying Milton's argument in 'Areopagitica' is what we have chosen to call his confidence in a progr⸱⸱⸱ve revelation. That this is the positive correlate of nescience ⸱ an be seen from the following argument against censorship:

> That it will be primely to the discourag⸱ment of all learning, and the stop of Truth, not only by disexercising and blunting our abilities in what we know already, but by hindering and cropping the discovery that might be yet further made both in religious and civil Wisdom.[1]

Dogmatists, unless they have the saving grace of inconsistency, can never admit that truths greater and different from what they already possess may be forthcoming. Milton, as a Christian humanist, cleverly combines Egyptian and Christian legend to account by means of a parable for the fact that man must go on seeking endlessly for the truth. He says that after the death of Christ and his apostles, the truth which had come into the world with him was hacked to pieces like Osiris and strewn to the four winds. Since then 'the sad friends of Truth' have gone up and down the earth, imitating Isis and trying to recover and make one again the body of truth. This, he adds, recalling his Puritanism, will finally be accomplished at the second coming.

> He shall bring together every joint and member, and shall mould them into an immortal feature of loveliness and perfection.[2]

This was a particularly apt story for Milton's purposes because it met head-on the objections of his opponents that the unity of truth, which they would impose by force, was being destroyed by uncensored printing. He shrewdly observes that behind these objections lay the intellectual pride of men who considered that truth was a closed issue and that they had the only key.

> There be who perpetually complain of schisms and sects, and make it such a calamity that any man dissents from their maxims. 'Tis their own pride and ignorance which causes the disturbing,

who neither will hear with meekness, nor can convince, yet all must
be suppressed which is not found in their Syntagma. They are the
troublers, they are the dividers of unity, who neglect and permit
not others to unite those dissevered pieces which are yet wanting
to the body of Truth.3

Milton goes on to indicate his oneness with the sceptics by
exposing his own method of truth-seeking, which presupposes
a continual aggrandizement of the area of certainty until what
Browne calls 'the Arithmetick of the last day.'

> To be still searching what we know not, by what we know, still
> closing up truth to truth as we find it (for all her body is homogeneal,
> and proportional) this is the golden rule in Theology as well as in
> Arithmetic, and makes up the best harmony in a Church; not the
> forced and outward union of cold, and neutral, and inwardly
> divided minds.4

The echo of the whole seventeenth-century struggle between
Anglican and Puritan can be heard in this last sentence. Milton
reveals his own conception of the underlying purpose of education by allying himself with

> all those who had prepared their minds and studies above the vulgar
> pitch to advance truth in others, and from others to entertain it.5

Teaching, for him, was a reciprocal relationship, and as long as
it remained so, one need not fear that seductive error would get
the upper hand.

Since Milton's generation was still living under the lengthen-
ing shadow of the Reformation, it is understandable that the
highest name he could give to this continuous process of truth-
seeking was 'the New Reformation.' Like all sceptics, he was
unable to rest content with a reformation whose aims were
achieved once and for all. Why, then, in this continual search for
truth, asks Milton, should any of the seekers be handicapped by
restrictions? What if some of them are not obvious 'winners'?
Can the great and true man always be picked at a glance? Of

course, false teachers will arise, but so will those who are to advance the cause of truth.

> God then raises to his own work men of rare abilities, and more than common industry not only to look back and revise what hath been taught heretofore, but to gain further and go on, some new enlightened steps in the discovery of truth.[6]

One function the sceptics perform again and again is to remind their fellows that God has said, 'My ways are not your ways, nor my thoughts your thoughts.' This often becomes an important corollary of sceptic nescience. Milton's version is that God tempers his light in accordance with human tolerance and that when the balance is upset, man may misjudge the thoughts of God. To regulate the speaking and writing of men would be to assume that one possessed the full wisdom of God.

> Neither is God appointed and confined, where and out of what place these his chosen shall be first heard to speak; for he sees not as man sees, chooses not as man chooses, lest we should devote ourselves again to set places, and assemblies, and outward callings of men; planting our faith one while in the old Convocation house, and another while in the Chapel at Westminster; when all the faith and religion that shall be there canonized, is not sufficient without plain convincement, and the charity of patient instruction to supple the least bruise of conscience, to edify the meanest Christian, who desires to walk in the Spirit, and not in the letter of human trust, for all the number of voices that can be there made.[7]

'The letter of human trust,' the assurance of men that the truth, when known, will correspond to their blueprints of it, is exactly what the sceptics by their nescience have always protested against. Such a protest involves not only humility but a confidence that truth will win out in all encounters and that such encounters are necessary to its growth. Even the 'crackpot' notions are to be welcomed, for who knows (except the dogmatist) that they may not contribute just the ingredient we have been seeking, though in disguise.

No man who hath tasted learning, but will confess the many ways of profiting by those who not contented with stale receipts are able to manage, and set forth new positions to the world. And were they but as the dust and cinders of our feet, so long as in that notion they may yet serve to polish and brighten the armoury of Truth, even for that respect they were not utterly to be cast away.[8]

Even the intellectual slag is to be put to use.

An additional twist is given the concept of nescience when Milton argues that unless this free interplay of ideas is allowed, 'we are hindered and disinured . . . toward the true knowledge of what we seem to know.'[9] Like all creative sceptics, he is unwilling to rest in nescience but uses it as a base from which to operate as he pushes on to make his own the things which he only seemed to know. This requires humility and a sense of never having 'arrived'—difficult virtues for men to acquire but essential if they are even to glimpse the truth.

He who thinks we are to pitch our tent here, and have attained the utmost prospect of reformation, that the mortal glass wherein we contemplate, can show us, till we come to beatific vision, that man by his very opinion declares, that he is yet far short of Truth.[10]

Let us admit, then, that we do not know and thereby leave ourselves open to the intimations of truth, from no matter what direction, in the assurance that only by such a method will revelation gradually come to us.

The Fruits of Dualism and Paradox

Just as Milton exhibits courage in his conviction that man can afford to admit his nescience and rely upon the eventual appearance of a truth as yet unseen, so also in his acceptance of a series of paradoxes—from the belief that good use may be made of a bad book to the conviction that schisms are not a curse but a disguised blessing. In the famous passage in praise of 'the true, wayfaring Christian' Milton gives evidence of his sense of dualism by stating a conclusion which was to be elaborated in *Paradise Lost*, that good and evil are almost inseparably interwoven in this world and that since Adam we have known good only by evil. 'That which purifies us is trial, and trial is by what is contrary.'[11] Where books are concerned, he cites examples from both the ancients and the moderns of men who made distinguished use even of books containing errors. Chrysostom, he tells us, studied Aristophanes nightly and so 'had the art to cleanse a scurrilous vehemence into the style of a rousing sermon.'[12] Dionysius Alexandrinus, having been criticized by a Presbyter for reading heretical writings, was reassured by a vision from God that his judgment was strong enough so that, like Paul, he could 'prove all things, hold fast that which is good.' In the midst of the Parliament which he was addressing sat John Selden, who had followed the same advice and had demonstrated 'that all opinions, yea errors, known, read, and collated, are of main service and assistance toward the speedy attainment of what is truest.'[13] But paradoxically, the conclusion is that 'a wise man will make better use of an idle pamphlet than a fool will do of sacred Scripture.'[14]

The kind of men who have never known nescience and who therefore have no patience with paradox will see only spiritual disaster in the multiplying of sects and schisms. We have already noted the panic of despair into which this threw some seventeenth-century men. But Milton, with the insight of the sceptic, turns even this fact to good account. Characteristically, he shows by means of metaphors the necessity of schisms if construction is to go forward.

> These are the men cried out against for schismatics and sectaries; as if, while the Temple of the Lord was building, some cutting, some squaring the marble, others hewing the cedars, there should be a sort of irrational men who could not consider there must be many schisms and many dissections made in the quarry and in the timber, ere the house of God can be built.[15]

Again, it will be noted, the reference is to a process. Something is being built, as in Milton's next metaphor something is growing. Instead of taking the dim view of some of his contemporaries that 'the Adversary' is merely lying in wait to destroy piecemeal what he dare not attack as a whole, Milton turns the force of this argument back upon itself.

> Fool! he sees not the firm root, out of which we all grow, though into branches: nor will beware until he see our small divided maniples cutting through at every angle of his ill-united and unwieldy brigade. And that we are to hope better of all these supposed sects and schisms, and that we shall not need that solicitude honest perhaps though over-timorous of them that vex in this behalf, but shall laugh in the end, at those malicious applauders of our differences, I have these reasons to persuade me.[16]

Here again is the robust sceptic nonchalance which can wrest victory from defeat because, lacking timorousness, it judges intellectual movements by their highest potentialities as they reach out toward a certain but as yet unknown truth.

The most striking figure by which Milton presents the transformation which we have hitherto associated with the knot is that of the moulting eagle, and this he had led up to by the parallel figure which seems to represent England under the form of a snake,

> not degenerated, nor drooping to a fatal decay, but casting off the old and wrinkled skin of corruption to outlive these pangs and wax young again, entering the glorious ways of Truth and prosperous virtue destined to become great and honourable in these latter ages.[17]

Then comes the famous passage wherein England is compared to the eagle and her fearful detractors are shown to have no understanding of the process which is taking place before them.

> Methinks I see her as an Eagle mewing her mighty youth, and kindling her undazzled eyes at the full-mid-day beam; purging and unscaling her long-abused sight at the fountain itself of heavenly radiance; while the whole noise of timorous and flocking birds, with those also that love the twilight, flutter about, amazed at what she means, and in their envious gabble would prognosticate a year of sects and schisms.[18]

The Sceptic Process

Milton is equally ingenious in devising metaphors by which to convey the eternal vigilance which must be exercised if one is to make his way toward the truth. For it is possible, he reminds us, to be a heretic in the truth if one believes on another's authority.

> There is not any burden that some would gladlier post off to another, than the charge and care of their Religion.[19]

The man of implicit faith is one who 'resolves to give over toiling' in behalf of religious truth and so turn over his interests to an ecclesiastic, who takes himself off after breakfast 'and leaves his kind entertainer in the shop trading all day without his religion.'[20] Amid the confusion of controversy, England still represents the ideal proving-ground of truth.

> The shop of war hath not there more anvils and hammers waking, to fashion out the plates and instruments of armed Justice in defence of beleaguered Truth, than there be pens and heads there, sitting by their studious lamps, musing, searching, revolving new notions and ideas wherewith to present, as with their homage and their fealty the approaching Reformation: others as fast reading, trying all things, assenting to the force of reason and convincement. What could a man require more from a Nation so pliant and so prone to seek after knowledge.[21]

It is significant that Milton links pliancy with proneness to seek out knowledge, for he sees the two as equally necessary for the success of the enterprise. What he fears most, as a genuine sceptic, is the cessation of activity.

> Well knows he who uses to consider, that our faith and knowledge thrives by exercise, as well as our limbs and complexion. Truth is compared in Scripture to a streaming fountain; if her waters flow not in a perpetual progression, they sicken into a muddy pool of conformity and tradition.[22]

To such a muddy pool the coming of winter will be fatal, for most men are spiritually lazy and will not exert themselves to rewin their heritage but will prefer to take it over without a struggle.

> How goodly, and how to be wished were such an obedient unanimity as this, what a fine conformity would it starch us all into? doubtless a staunch and solid piece of framework, as any January could freeze together.[23]

Milton anticipated here the spiritual state of the eighteenth century, whose ideal was uniformity and which lost the saving scepticism of the preceding century through neglect and complacency.

Return to the Past?

It should have been obvious thus far that we would not advocate for our generation a mere return to the religious or philosophical opinions of the seventeenth century, even if that were possible. Fortunately or unfortunately, history cannot be run backward like a movie film. But what can be imitated with profit, just because it is not confined to any one historical period, is the attitude of mind represented by scepticism; for this, as we have seen, is experienced by all truth-seekers at some point in their development.

It would be interesting to discover whether at the heart of all proposed returns to the past—whether it be to the Middle Ages or to the Athens of Pericles or to a primitive Golden Age—there is not a similar urge to capture something like the sceptic pattern which has been fleetingly glimpsed in one of those settings. This may be the explanation for the success or failure of these various plans: the successful ones, such as that of the Renaissance, caught the spirit of the previous age while the unsuccessful ones, such as that of Augustan England, concentrated on the trappings of the period being imitated. Almost random dippings into the religious, philosophical, and artistic criticism of our day will reveal elements which might well become a part of the sceptic pattern but which, by the way they are being handled, are breeding, instead, new dogmatism and new despair.

A Theologian

When one emerges from an absorption in seventeenth-century scepticism and looks around him in the twentieth century, the after-image insures that for a little while he will see everything in terms of the sceptic pattern. He hears, for example, a famous American theologian preaching on the text, 'But the natural man receiveth not the things of the Spirit of God: for they are foolishness unto him: neither can he know them, because they are spiritually discerned' (I Cor. 2: 14). Our sceptic protagonist welcomes this as indicating perhaps a sensitivity to 'the subtle knot,' and he is further encouraged when the preacher insists that man must recognize both his greatness and his smallness. But then comes a part of the sermon in which it seems to him its potential scepticism goes awry. The preacher, who is driven by the fixed idea that man's sense of his own guilt is the most important fact about him, turns to condemn modern psychiatry for doing away with what he calls 'the responsible self.' He feels that psychiatry has gone beyond the stage of attaching praise or blame for one's actions. It sees, rather, the causes behind those actions and therefore understands them instead of passing judgment. This, to the preacher, is inexcusable, for it threatens his pet notion of guilt.

But the sceptic protagonist cannot help wondering why the preacher could not incorporate within his own thinking the insight of psychiatry since, looked at from the standpoint of its intention, it seems to reinforce such words of Jesus as 'Judge not, that ye be not judged' and 'Neither do I condemn thee.' The preacher, who starts out on the sceptic path, has fallen into the cleverly concealed trap of dogmatism through his unwillingness to let himself slip into complete nescience. What he is obviously afraid of is the theory of determinism, which threatens his dogmatism of the responsible self, without which it seems his world would fall apart. How deeply this is rooted in his personal life is seen when he asks, 'When I have prayed all day or all night over a decision and then have made it, am I to be told that circumstances being what they were, I could have done no other?'

It is here, among the unthinkables, that the sceptic meets his crucial test. If there is a single concept to which he is unwilling to give room, even as a transient, he fails to achieve real scepticism, for he has thus roped off a certain area and said, in effect, 'I will admit nescience everywhere but here. I simply cannot abandon my hold on all certainty.' If he could and if with the kind of humour characteristic of scepticism, he could say after having reached that momentous decision, 'I seem to have fought my way to a totally unpredictable resolution, but perhaps from another point of view I've merely been unrolling a scroll already written and sealed. Perhaps all my agonizing was to arrive at what I was inescapably bound to,' wouldn't this give a kind of spiritual flexibility to the man which would insure his moving out toward larger and more comprehensive truths? His very notion of 'the responsible self' might be raised to a higher level through combining it with the kind of non-judging understanding which comes from psychiatry. (Granted that the attitude of psychiatry also needs the corrective of his insight into guilt.)

The experience which the preacher has skirted here, for whatever reason, is the same one to which we have already referred as embodied in 'Eloi, eloi, lama sabachthani!' The mystical correlate would be the emptying of the soul in order that the High God may dwell therein. The practice of isosothenia, the matching of every theory with its opposite is the necessary prelude to the transvaluation of values which scepticism perennially effects. In the preacher there seems to be lacking the kind of faith which makes this possible, the faith by which Milton was encouraged to allow all shades of opinion to make themselves heard so that somehow the harmonious truth should arise out of their cacophony, albeit the harmony, for its unfamiliarity, might be at first unrecognizable.

An Art Critic

The sceptic protagonist turns from mid-twentieth-century religion to mid-twentieth-century art, and there he encounters a critic who is at once disturbed that in modern art man has lost his dignity and hopeful that an atomic age will reduce some of his cockiness and show him his 'true' position in the universe. Such a discussion seems a likely place to prospect for the raw materials of scepticism and so to augment our sceptical critique of the contemporary world.

The critic, Francis Henry Taylor, makes clear by means of a metaphor early in his *Atlantic Monthly* article that, like the preacher, he clings doggedly to one idea, that man is not now what he has been—that his sea-change has been for the worse and not for the better.

> Instead of soaring like an eagle through the heavens as did his ancestors and looking down triumphantly upon the world beneath, the contemporary artist has been reduced to the status of a flat-chested pelican, strutting upon the intellectual wastelands and beaches, content to take whatever nourishment he can from his own too meager breast.[24]

This is reinforced by the endorsement of C. E. M. Joad's diagnosis in his *Decadence*.

> [Ours is] an age which has no fundamental beliefs or convictions and, in particular, no beliefs in regard to the existence of an order of reality other than that which we can see and touch. It is an age which, having no religion, does not believe in God. Hence, it cannot write about Him as Milton did, make music about Him as Bach did or, like the cathedral makers of the early Middle Ages, build beautiful structures in His honour. Moreover, since it is an age whose mind has been largely formed by science, and which believes, therefore, only in the existence of what it can see and touch, and of things which are of the same kind as those which it can see and touch, it does not believe in the existence of beauty as an immaterial form which can manifest itself in man's handiwork and touch with surprise of its sudden glory his structures of sound and paint and brick. It does not aspire to make such structures. Finally, it is an age which does not believe in the dignity of man and does not seek, therefore, to assign him his place and prescribe for him his purpose in the developing scheme of a purposeful universe. In so far as it considers man at all, it thinks of him after the mode that science

has made fashionable; he is an accident of evolution, a complex of reflexes, a puppet twitched into love or war by the showman in his unconscious who pulls the strings, or, as the behaviourists would have us believe, a by-product of chemical and physiological processes, pursuing his course across a fundamentally alien and brutal environment and doomed ultimately to finish his pointless journey with as little significance as in the person of the amoeba his ancestors once began it.[25]

In relation to scepticism, this at once recalls Pascal's classic formulation of sceptic *epoché* and of 'the subtle knot' when he says it is dangerous for man to forget either his greatness or his smallness. We should always suspect the man who wrings his hands when either one or the other of these concepts is in the saddle; for while he may serve the purpose of 'pulling a crooked stick straight,' if he persists in pushing his one idea, he has no possibility of achieving the *ataraxia* of true scepticism. For the Joad of the 'twenties, when *Decadence* was written, we should have prescribed large doses of George Santayana.

In analysing the kinds of reality with which the modern artist deals, however, Taylor turns up elements which might be the building stones of a twentieth-century scepticism. In describing two kinds of realistic art he has laid bare an important dualism.

> We are confronted, therefore, with a conflict between two venerable truths inherited from the Renaissance, two types of reality: the one (dependent upon the concept of time and space) presents the picture of the world within the traditional limits of visual experience, and the other presents it from the point of view of personal emotion. Each of these truths is equally valid and equally circumscribed. Neither one attempts a teleological explanation of the universe. Man is the pivot about which the world revolves and he is absolved of any responsibility for its conduct.[26]

We have here the makings of 'the subtle knot,' and in another kind of reality related to the idea of time as the fourth dimension, he prefigures the notion of the moving and changing character of scepticism.

We are forced to bow before the 'dynamism of change.' Art might therefore conceivably become the illustration of energy rather than the illustration of form; the artist is thus presented with another reality or absolute as potential as electricity or atomic power.[27]

But instead of welcoming this tie-up with 'radar, television, and the rapid time-destroying projection of an airplane through space,' Taylor keeps on insisting upon 'the sterility and the intellectual vacuum of twentieth-century America or Europe,' and thus he indicates that he is clinging to a fixed point on the intellectual map instead of launching out even beyond the Pillars of Hercules. For one brief moment Taylor balances on the sceptic knife-edge, and one can hope that he will see the necessity of paradox with its 'subtle knot.'

> Picasso is at once the giant paradox and the towering genius of our day who has captured our imagination by exploiting the manic depression which has carried our generation through two world wars and is hurling us along the road to world revolution. He has caught our suicidal despair and laughed at it hysterically. Only history can determine whether Picasso, like the skeleton at the feast, is the last flowering of a civilization whose collapse amuses him, or whether there is latent in his extraordinary mobility of line and color the prophecy of a new world which is to come.[28]

Taylor reinforces this insight by recognizing 'the stalemate which now exists between the objective and the subjective attitudes,' but he relapses into a condemnation of Picasso and his 'utter contempt for the dignity of man' and thus shows that he is exalting a concept (in this case human dignity) above the complex and creative knot which is man and out of which, if contemplated long enough without preconceptions, there might spring a genuinely new truth.

With the sure instinct of children who eat plaster off walls because their diet lacks lime, Taylor, in accounting for the objective-subjective stalemate, goes straight to two outstanding sceptics for their statements of paradox.

John Donne, preaching before King Charles I at St. Paul's on Christmas Day, 1625, asked the question:

'What eye can fixe itself upon East and West at once? And he must see more than East and West that sees God, for God spreads infinitely beyond both: God alone is all; not only all that is but all that is not, all that might be if he would have it to be. God is too large, too immense, and then man is too narrow, too little to be considered; for who can fixe his eye upon an Atome; and he must see a lesse thing than an Atome, that sees man for man is nothing.'

Pascal echoed the same refrain: 'What is man in nature? A nothing in infinity, an everything in regard to nothing, a middle point between everything and nothing.'[29]

But what Taylor does not see is the necessity of holding fast to such statements as these and out of their complexity forcing a truth which we have not yet grasped. Instead, they mean to him only something like Eliot's 'dissociation of sensibility.'

It did not require a stock pile of Uranium 235 to convince the poet, the philosopher, and the prelate of the seventeenth century that, although the atom had not yet been split, fission had already taken place in man. The separation of the soul from the intellect could lead, they held, only to inevitable disaster. The atomic age had begun not with Hiroshima or Nagasaki but with Democritus and the earliest physicists of Greece. The medieval synthesis had been exploded, voyages of exploration on land and sea had produced new worlds to conquer. The Reformation as well as the Counter-Reformation of the Jesuits had concerned itself with the problem of the individual and his conscience—that spark of God within him—and its relation to the constantly expanding, yet at the same time increasingly particularized scientific universe.[30]

This is an excellent statement of the modern dilemma, and a man's scepticism might well be judged by the direction which he takes from this point.

To Taylor's credit are two insights which show he has at least crossed and recrossed the sceptic path. One is his recognition of the 'metaphysical anxiety and restlessness, so characteristic of the seventeenth century and its art,'[31] and the other is his endorsement of the words of H. T. Pledge:

> 'The infinities,' he adds, 'though not the pessimism of the Eastern religions, had been preserved by Christianity. For the step-by-step communion with the infinite by a series of sacraments, science had substituted the step-by-step communion with it by a series of hypotheses and experiments. But the infinity remains.'[32]

To see all the implications of this statement might be to unravel the relationship between scepticism and mysticism, but Taylor takes another turning and concludes that 'man and artist have become the victims of the scientific world they have created, and in their common fear for the future have lost contact with each other.'[33] He quotes Toynbee in support of his contention that the present state of the world represents a Slough of Despond rather than a Centre of Indifference. He cannot believe in the possibility of an Everlasting Yea and especially in its emergence from the same root as the Everlasting No. He would take his dualisms one half at a time, and thus he comes to rest with Joad in the conclusion that

> The Gods take their own revenge against man's impertinence. He is cast down and through suffering made to realize his true nature. In the chaos and confusion he recognizes the need for a higher reality than his own.[34]

That this repudiation of the oblique should end in rather commonplace and uninspired advice to the modern artist is understandable now that we have seen its origins. The artist is urged to try to communicate with his fellows, to resist propaganda, and to recognize his responsibilities of citizenship. The saving remnant of this advice is that the artist must remain free to create and the public to accept or reject. The larger freedom into which man is launched when he relinquishes the last of his pet theories and follows the ensign of paradox is somehow lost sight of.

A Philosopher

Remembering still our determination to keep to a discussion of literary rather than philosophical scepticism, let us likewise by-pass the philosophical existentialists such as Jaspers, Heidigger, and Kierkegaard and seek out in the popularization of Sartre what materials we can assemble for an assessment of sceptical thought in our own day. Perhaps we can carry on a kind of double-barrelled investigation whereby on the one hand we show the relevance of existentialism to scepticism and on the other we meet objections to it by putting sceptic criticism to work—the criticism which concentrates on the intention of a concept rather than on its objective validity.

In this necessarily superficial treatment of existentialism,35 we should like to emphasize chiefly the way in which it blunts the edge of modern despair by the characteristically sceptic technique (slightly reminiscent of the eating habits of the amoeba) of taking it in rather than shutting it out. Keats showed the same insight when he recognized the presence of 'veiled Melancholy' even in the Temple of Delight. Where people like Joad lament the passing of a belief in beauty as an immaterial form, Sartre counters with the classic existentialist formula, 'Existence precedes essence.' Granted that man may have lost his interest in beauty as an essence, that does not deter him from building an existence for himself which shall embody beauty, whether in one of the several art forms or in the quality of the living itself. Man creating the beautiful is as near as the existentialist hopes to come to an ideal of beauty in the abstract, for he has the sceptic suspicion of all that is static. Likewise, art as 'the illustration of energy rather than the illustration of form,' which Taylor can barely imagine, the existentialist takes in his stride, for he has no affection for disembodied forms.

What this anti-formalism heads up into, for the existentialist, is one more instance of men resolving to hold at the centre of their belief the inexplicable knot. Man exists first and is defined afterward, says Sartre, and this sequence accounts for philosophy's sometimes losing touch with experience. So by an emphasis on existence rather than essence, the existentialist hopes to avoid the debacle of eighteenth-century thought, which lost sight of the wholeness and moving quality of existence while worshipping a static essence.

We have noted previously that the sceptic in his search for truth somewhat resembles Abraham going out into a country he knew not. The result of an initial nescience has been to make him wary of ever boasting that he knows where he is going. Likewise the existentialist holds that man projects himself toward an unknown future and indeed creates that future by the very quality of his projection. His future is not out there somewhere for him to discover but rather is the world 'all before (him) where to choose,' and everything depends upon the quality of that choice.

In this respect existentialism reproduces the sceptic emphasis on action, for not only is man held responsible for what he is, but every individual decision involves all mankind. This is like the seventeenth-century formulations we have seen, in which a life is held of much higher value than a creed. There may be a historical connection between the two, traceable through Kant, whose question the existentialists keep asking themselves, 'What if all the world acted as I do?'

The existentialist does not welcome determinism any more than the theologian discussed above, but instead of making its rejection his primary aim, he circumvents it by putting the emphasis upon existence and so rejecting the possibility of any pattern according to which man can be determined. Man makes up his own pattern as he goes along. So also it becomes impossible for the existentialist to judge man, for he is always being made. 'Man is the future of man.' The analogy of the tight-wire walker is equally applicable to the existentialist and to the sceptic. Each is lost as soon as he stops moving forward. Are there not echoes here of the progressive revelation to which Milton was dedicated and for the sake of which he rejected the bonds of censorship?

The avowed atheism of Sartre's existentialism will be as

shocking to some readers as the notion that scepticism can be creative, but it is well to remember that the word *atheism* has had as chequered a career as *scepticism* and that what is designated by these words, like the man set upon by thieves, always deserves more than a passing glance and a shudder. In fact, it ought to be some recommendation for both scepticism and existentialism that they enable their followers to progressively rid themselves of fears and phobias. Serious atheism is always the outgrowth of a hypercritical attitude toward the prevailing concept of God. If we check our horror and look to see what unworthy elements the existentialists want to eliminate from the idea of God, we shall be in a far better position to understand them.

For one thing, they reject a God who has a preconceived notion of human nature, from which he patterns man. This, according to them, leaves too few creative possibilities for man. Again, they throw out with the concept of God the possibility of man's finding values within an unintelligible Heaven. They must be wrought out in his on-going life or not at all. So, too, if God does not exist, man will have no one to justify or excuse him, and he will have to assume the sole responsibility for his life, with all the anguish which that involves but likewise with all the creative possibilities.

We are well aware that these arguments are refutable and that the full-fledged sceptic would in his isosothenia set their opposites over against them and try to work out the truth from this *mélange.* Yet the truly creative attitude toward existentialism would be to appreciate the richness of its insights, the truth toward which it is aiming, and thus gratefully make the most of it instead of becoming panic-stricken and running for shelter to the nearest dogmatism. That way madness, not truth, lies.

It is not our purpose, then, to recommend existentialism as either the perfect contemporary form of scepticism or as a panacea for all our ills. It does contain, like most seriously conceived systems, a modicum of scepticism, and where it fails to come up to sceptic specifications, one can learn from its defections, without thereby condemning the whole system. The words which Milton quotes from Paul are applicable here, 'Prove all things, hold fast that which is good.' In this inquiring and critical spirit embodied, as we have shown, most effectively in scepticism, lies man's intellectual salvation—not that he should accept its conclusions but that he should walk in its ways.

THE DESPAIR OF GOD

OUT of the whole welter of sceptic theory and practice over the centuries, one formulation keeps ringing in our ears. It is the statement by a Hebrew prophet of his striking perception that man in his intellectual arrogance is infinitely removed from the God who made him. 'For my thoughts are not your thoughts, neither are your ways my ways, saith the Lord' (Isaiah 55: 8). In one form or another, all the sceptics have underscored this insight. They keep saying that God looks on things very differently from man. It may behoove us, then, following in their footsteps, to take these words literally and to speculate concerning the complete *bouleversement* of our prevailing notions which would result from our moving out in the direction of God's point of view. This operation ought to prove valuable as intellectual calisthenics, even if it lands us no nearer to the ultimate nature of things.

The agonies experienced by man in search of truth must be as nothing compared with the agonies of a God who is continually thwarted in his attempts to break through to man. Indeed, the whole history of humankind might thus be rewritten from the standpoint of a God who feels the almost unbearable weight of his frustration.

George Herbert in the seventeenth century made a beginning in the direction of revealing such a God when in 'The Sacrifice,' a poem tracing the events culminating in the crucifixion, he stresses the paradox of Christ's suffering for a world which rejected him. Each stanza ends with the refrain, 'Was ever grief like Mine?' and so reiterates the agony of a God whom men will not understand. The most pertinent stanzas for our purposes, those which reflect the knotted character of God's truth and which show the disparity between God and man, are the following:

Then they accuse Me of great blasphemie,
That I did thrust into the Deitie,
Who never thought that any robberie:
  Was ever grief like Mine? . . .

Yet still they shout, and crie, and stop their eares,
Putting My life among their sinnes and feares,
And therefore wish my bloud on them and theirs:
  Was ever grief like Mine? . . .

Why, Cesar is their onely king, not I.
He clave the stonie rock when they were drie,
But surely not their hearts, as I well trie:
  Was ever grief like Mine? . . .

Behold, they spit on Me in scornfull wise,
Who by My spittle gave the blinde man eies,
Leaving his blindnesse to Mine enemies:
  Was ever grief like Mine? . . .

They bow their knees to Me, and cry, 'Hail, King!'
What ever scoffes or scornfulnesse can bring,
I am the floore, the sink, where they it fling:
  Was ever grief like Mine?

Yet since man's scepters are as frail as reeds,
And thorny all their crowns, bloudie their weeds,
I, Who am Truth, turn into truth their deeds:
  Was ever grief like Mine? . . .

But, O My God, My God, why leav'st Thou Me,
The Sonne in Whom Thou dost delight to be?
My God, My God—
  Never was grief like Mine. . . .

In healing not Myself there doth consist
All that salvation which ye now resist;
Your safetie in My sicknesse doth subsist:
  Was ever grief like Mine?

Betwixt two theeves I spend My utmost breath,
As he that for some robberie suffereth:
Alas, what have I stollen from you? death:
    Was ever grief like Mine? . . .

But now I die; now all is finishèd;
My wo man's weal, and now I bow My head:
Onely let others say, when I am dead,
    Never was grief like Mine.[1]

From such verses can be reconstructed the spirit of a God who might soliloquize thus:

'I've tried almost everything in order to rouse man to some awareness of truth. I've hurled his own brash dogmatisms back into his face until I have made it almost impossible for him to avoid recognizing his own nescience; and yet he continues to pride himself upon his knowledge and to act as if it were absolute and incontrovertible. He even makes me in its image. I've bifurcated his world into so many dualisms that only a perverse and headstrong creature could cling to the comfortable illusion that his world is simple and static and all of one piece; yet man insists on tidying up his world so that he may sit down in it, blaspheming me as the Unmoved Mover.

'I've hurled paradoxes at him from every conceivable angle, by means of poets and prophets, in the hope of bombarding him into submission to life's knotted character; yet man has exercised his ingenuity in dodging, simplifying, and explaining away such paradoxes, where they were too barbed for him to ignore. In countless attempts I have spoken through the mouths of chosen prophets to point man back (or forward) to the inevitability of "the subtle knot," to the necessity for achieved truth to enthrone the complexity and mystery of the human being; but the prophets have been accused of uttering hard sayings, and man has settled for the direct and simple and static and easy and dogmatic as opposed to the oblique, the complex, the hard, the sceptical, and therefore the on-going. Eternal vigilance man has continually managed to circumvent, as if it were his deadly enemy, instead of his only saviour—so blind is he to his own deep needs.

'The succession of gadflies I have sent to earth to keep him disturbed and so help set him on the road to truth have invariably been misunderstood and then scourged and crucified—Buddha, Confucius, Socrates, Jesus, Mahomet. One I sent whose very crucifixion has been idolized; and even then I hoped that perhaps some Christian through the perspective of the ages might see its true significance. (For I can turn the most unpromising material to my own ends—witness what I have done with man thus far, even though he continues to resist the truth.) I hoped the crucifixion would shadow forth by the example of Christ the need for each of man's hard-won truths continually to lose itself. Man should be able to see that once an insight is elaborated until it approaches dogma as a limit, the inevitable destiny of that insight is to be neutralized by its opposite and so reabsorbed into the moving stream of human thought. How else can one account for that giant paradox, "He that loseth his life shall find it"? Meditated upon and acted upon, this might provide man a radical new approach to truth. Instead, this moving, breathing notion which centred in the crucifixion was stopped in its tracks. Man dessicated it, as South American natives shrink human heads, and made of it a museum piece.

'Man will not see, because it is simpler and less demanding not to see, that only if he admits he knows nothing and sets out to struggle honestly with his doubts and dualisms will he ever come within sight of the highway toward truth. Not through merely crossing and recrossing it once or twice in a generation nor through sitting down on it to chalk out proposed routes but only through going forward along this paradoxical way can he and I ever come to where truth has her dwelling place.

'I have not ceased to contemplate other devices which I might use, even though a less persistent God would have given up long ago. It's true that two world wars have to some extent shaken man's complacency and made it difficult for him to settle back into it again. It's true, also, that there may be some hope for him in the fact that his secularism, where it is positive and dynamic as in science, has often served to teach him the virtues of holding a hypothesis lightly, of veering and shifting his position, without threat of reprisals from an omnipotent absolute. Fear he has sometimes lost, but often humility along with it; and if this situation persists, he will be no nearer the way to truth than he was in any of his previous narrow dogmatisms.

'Perhaps another blow will turn the trick. Although he does not outwardly respect nor support his religious institutions, he has retained them in case they might prove to be the carriers of otherwise neglected aspects of the truth. This is perhaps encouraging as a sign of the spiritual economy of scepticism, which salvages all. Suppose, just when his fear is centred on the atom bomb, I were to scourge these institutions from the world. Suppose that whatever truths inhere in both his religion and his secularism were forced to merge, to relinquish the support of institutions, and to make their way alone—naked and splendid. Could I be sure that he would see, even then, that the highest destiny of a great institution is to destroy itself and so become one with the world it saves? Or would he only cling more tenaciously to his opinionative toys?

'Perhaps the risk is worth taking. Perhaps nothing short of this cataclysmic blow can rive the hard oak of dogmatism and leave extant only the germ within the acorn. Perhaps if I resort to this extreme action, the poets and prophets of all the ages may yet be justified. Perhaps before the twentieth century is over, man may yet make his chastened boast, "that they without us should not be made perfect." '

FOOTNOTES

CHAPTER I.   PROLEGOMENA TO THE DEFINITION
OF SCEPTICISM

1 Arthur O. Lovejoy, *The Great Chain of Being* (Cambridge, 1936), p. 16.

2 'The Apology,' *Works of Plato* (trans. Jowett), (New York, Tudor Pub. Co., n.d.), ii, 117.

3 *Oliver Cromwell's Letters and Speeches*, ed. Thomas Carlyle; vol. 16 of *Collected Works* (London 1870–1882), iii, 22; Letter cxxxvi.

4 *Lives of Eminent Philosophers* (trans. R. D. Hicks), (London, 1931), p. 487.

5 *History of Freethought Ancient and Modern*, 2nd ed. (New York, 1906), i, 4.

6 Bampton Lectures, 1862 (New York, 1863), p. v.

7 (London), p. xvi.

8 *Loc. cit.*

9 (London, 1891), no pagination in preface.

10 *The Advancement of Learning*, ed. G. W. Kitchin (London, 1861), p. 51.

11 *Adversaries of the Sceptic or the The Specious Present* (New York, 1901), p. 34.

12 'The Meaning of Scepticism,' *The Arena*, xl (1908), 395.

13 *Loc. cit.*

14 *Ibid.*, p. 306.

15 'Montaigne; or the Skeptic' in *Representative Men* (Boston, 1930), p. 181.

16 *Ibid.*, p. 182.

17 *The Religious Aspect of Philosophy* (Boston, 1885), p. 14.

18 'The Pensées of Pascal,' in *Essays Ancient and Modern* (London, 1936), p. 150.

19 'Scepticism,' *Westminster Review*, clxviii (1907), 547.

20 'Self-Reliance,' *The Complete Essays and Other Writings of Ralph Waldo Emerson*, ed. Brooks Atkinson (New York, 1940), p. 152.

21 *Religious Aspect . . .* , p. 20.

22 *Ibid.*, p. 21.

23 *Op. cit.*, p. 152.

24 *Ibid.*, p. 164.

25 *Op. cit.*, p. 152.

26 'Montaigne,' *op. cit.*, p. 186.

27 *Reasons of the Christian Religion* (London, 1667), p. 371.

28 'Concerning Skepticism' (unsigned), lxxv, 108.

29 George Santayana, *Scepticism and Animal Faith* (New York, 1923), p. 67.

30 *Ibid.*, p. 70.

31 *Ibid.*, p. 16.

32 *Ibid.*, p. 69.

33 *Op. cit.*, p. 309.

34 *Op. cit.*, p. 546.

35 Mitchell, *op. cit.*, p. 310.

36 Louis Robert, *De la Certitude et des formes recentes du Scepticisme* (Paris, 1880), p. vii.

37 *Op. cit.*, p. 193.

38 *Skeptics of the Italian Renaissance* (New York, 1893), p. xiv.

39 Cf. *supra*, pp. 6–7.

40 John 8: 32.

CHAPTER II.   AN HISTORICAL DEFINITION OF SCEPTICISM

1 Cf. *The Greek Philosophers* (London, 1914), p. 425.

2 Cf. *loc. cit.*

3 Eduard Zeller, *The Stoics, Epicureans, and Sceptics* (London, 1870), p. 521.

4 *Op. cit.*, p. 475.

5 Paul Elmer More, *Hellenistic Philosophies* (London, 1923), p. 309.

6 Jas. Hastings ed. (New York, 1920), 'sceptics,' xi, 228.

7 *Op. cit.*, p. 477.

8 *Loc. cit.*

9 *Ibid.*, p. 519.

10 *The Greek Sceptics* (New York, 1929), p. xiv.

11 *Op. cit.*, p. 483.

12 *Hellenistic Philosophies*, p. 374.

13 John Owen, *Evenings With the Sceptics* (London, 1881), i, 294.

14 Cf. Zeller, *op. cit.*, p. 552.

15 Cf. Eugene de Faye, 'The Influence of Greek Scepticism on Greek and Christian Thought in the First and Second Centuries,' *Hibbert Journal*, xxii (1924), 703.

16 Diogenes Laertius, *op. cit.*, p. 493.

17 Owen, *Religious Aspects* . . . , p. 6.

18 More, *Hellenistic Philosophies*, p. 347.

19 Zeller, *op. cit.*, p. 26.

20 Cf. Sextus Empiricus, *Outlines of Pyrrhonism*, Book I, (tr. Mary M. Patrick), (Henry Regnery Co., Chicago, 1949), p. 9.

21 Mary Patrick, *Sextus Empiricus and Greek Scepticism* (Cambridge, 1899), p. 29.

[22] *Op. cit.*, p. 426.

[23] John Donne, 'The Extasie,' *Complete Poetry and Selected Prose of John Donne and Complete Poetry of William Blake* (New York, 1941), p. 35.

[24] Cf. Basil Willey, *The Seventeenth Century Background* (London, 1946), p. 85.

[25] *Evenings . . .* , ii, 211.

[26] *Greek Sceptics*, p. 288.

[27] *Op. cit.*, p. 97.

[28] Margaret Leigh, 'A Christian Sceptic of the Fourth Century,' *Hibbert Journal*, xix (1921), 322.

[29] *Loc. cit.*

[30] *Ibid.*, p. 324.

[31] Owen, *Evenings . . .* , ii, 271.

[32] *The Modern Mind* (London, 1937), p. 16.

[33] *Op. cit.*, p. 84.

[34] Lovejoy, *op. cit.*, p. 93.

[35] Albert G. A. Balz, 'Dualism in Cartesian Psychology and Epistemology,' *Studies in the History of Ideas* (New York, 1925), ii, 87.

[36] Willey, *op. cit.*, p. 66.

[37] Owen, *Evenings . . .* , ii, 398.

[38] Lovejoy, *op. cit.*, p. 113.

[39] *Ibid.*, p. 83.

[40] Henry Bett, *Nicholas of Cusa* (London, 1932), p. 131.

[41] *Ibid.*, p. 204.

[42] Louis I. Bredvold, *The Intellectual Milieu of John Dryden* (Ann Arbor, 1934), p. 17.

[43] Cf. George Buckley, *Atheism in the English Renaissance* (Chicago, 1932), p. 118.

[44] Cornelius Agrippa, *De Incertitudine Scientiarum* (no title page; 1540?), p. aiii (verso).

[45] *Ibid.*, p. aiiii (recto).

[46] *Ibid.*, p. aiii (recto).

[47] *Op. cit.*, p. 29.

[48] *Orthodox Paradoxes Theoreticall and Experimentall, Or A Believer Clearing Truth by Seeming Contradictions* (London, 1650), p. 11.

[49] *Ibid.*, p. 23.

[50] Buckley, *op. cit.*, pp. 117–118.

[51] *Loc. cit.*

[52] Walter Raleigh was to reiterate this judgment of Talon.

> But for my self, I shall never be perswaded that GOD hath shut up all light of Learning within the Lanthorn of *Aristotle's* Brains: or that it was ever said unto him, as unto *Esdras, Accendam in Corde tuo Lucernam*

intellectus; that GOD hath given invention but to the Heathen; and that they only have invaded Nature, and found the strength and bottom thereof.

(*History of the World* (London, 1687), p. xxii.)

53 Buckley, *op. cit.*, p. 118.

54 Willey, *op. cit.*, p. 35.

55 Buckley, *op. cit.*, p. 118.

56 *Ibid.*, p. 117.

57 Douglas Bush, *English Literature in the Earlier Seventeenth Century* (Oxford, 1945), p. 278.

58 Buckley, *op. cit.*, p. 3.

59 *Ibid.*, p. 18.

60 Bush, *op. cit.*, p. 35.

61 *Ibid.*, p. 36.

62 Bredvold, *op. cit.*, p. 28.

63 *Sceptics of the Italian Renaissance* (New York, 1893), p. 179.

64 *Ibid.*, p. 204.

65 *Ibid.*, p. 115.

66 *Ibid.*, p. 121.

67 Quoted by Owen, *ibid.*, p. 125.

68 *Ibid.*, p. 299.

69 *Op. cit.*, p. 120.

70 *Skeptics of Italian Renaissance*, p. 321.

71 J. Huizinga, *Erasmus* (tr. F. Hopman), (New York, 1924), p. 148.

72 Willey, *op. cit.*, p. 21.

73 (London, 1651), p. 31.

74 *Ibid.*, p. 1.

75 'An Apologie of Raymond Sebond,' *Essayes of Montaigne* (tr. John Florio), (New York, n.d.), p. 449.

76 *Ibid.*, p. 451.

77 *Op. cit.*, p. xxiii.

78 Montaigne, *op. cit.*, p. 446.

79 *History of the World*, p. xxiii.

80 Montaigne, *op. cit.*, p. 448.

81 *Ibid.*, p. 450.

82 *History of the World*, p. xx.

83 *Op. cit.*, p. 389.

84 *History of the World*, p. xvi.

CHAPTER III.   SEVENTEENTH-CENTURY SCEPTICISM:
THE KNOT

[1] According to Descartes' theory, 'animal-spirits' were the linking elements uniting body and soul.

[2] *Op. cit.*, p. 16.

[3] W. E. H. Lecky, *History of the Rise and Influence of the Spirit of Rationalism in Europe* (New York, 1866), ii, 79.

[4] Bush, *op. cit.*, p. 2.

[5] *Ibid.*, p. 16.

[6] *Op. cit.*, p. 15.

[7] *Op. cit.*, p. 400.

[8] J. B. Leishman, *The Metaphysical Poets: Donne, Herbert, Vaughan, Traherne* (Oxford, 1934), p. 60.

[9] Farrar, *op. cit.*, p. 117.

[10] Morell, *op. cit.*, i, 249.

[11] *Op. cit.*, p. 307.

[12] *Ibid.*, p. 332.

[13] W. K. Jordan, *The Development of Religious Toleration in England . . .* (1603–1640) (Cambridge, 1936), p. 387.

[14] *Ibid.*, p. 378.

[15] Cf. John Tulloch, *Rational Theology and Christian Philosophy in England in the Seventeenth Century* (London, 1872), i, 128.

[16] Jordan, *op. cit.*, p. 399.

[17] *Ibid.*, p. 400.

[18] Ernest Barker, *Oliver Cromwell and the English People* (Cambridge, 1937), p. 53.

[19] C. E. Whiting, *Studies in English Puritanism from the Restoration to the Revolution, 1660–1688* (New York, 1931), p. 271.

[20] Jordan, *op. cit.*, p. 354.

[21] *Philosophical Poems of Henry More*, ed. Geoffrey Bullough (Manchester, 1931), p. xvi.

[22] Quoted by E. A. George, *Seventeenth Century Men of Latitude* (New York, 1908), p. 44.

[23] *English Devotional Literature* (1600–1640) (Madison, 1931), p. 216.

[23a] Morell, *op. cit.*, i, 267.

[24] *Ibid.*, i, 266.

[25] *Op. cit.*, i, 129.

[26] xxx (1932), 192.

[27] *Op. cit.*, p. 37.

[28] *Op. cit.*, p. 188.

[29] *Ibid.*, p. 171.

[30] (London, 1654), p. 220.

[31] *Ibid.*, p. 210.

[32] *Ibid.*, p. 218.

[33] *A Discourse of the Necessity and Usefulness of the Christian Revelation By Reason of the Corruptions of the Principles of Natural Religion Among Jews and Heathens* (London, 1705), p. 70.

[34] H. J. C. Grierson, *Cross Currents in Seventeenth Century Literature* (London, 1929), p. 20.

[35] P. Meissner, 'Rationalistische Grundlage der Englischen Kultur des 17. Jahrhunderts,' *Anglia*, lv (1931), 335.

[36] *Ibid.*, p. 323.

[37] L. S. Thornton, *Richard Hooker, a Study of His Theology* (London, 1924), p. 115.

[38] Leishman, *op. cit.*, p. 170.

[39] Clara Marburg, *Sir William Temple, a Seventeenth Century 'Libertin'* (New Haven, 1932), p. 17.

[40] Robert, *op. cit.*, p. 10.

[41] *Op. cit.*, p. 83.

[42] *Op. cit.*, p. 35.

[43] *Op. cit.*, p. 85.

[44] M. Kaufmann, 'Latitudinarianism and Pietism,' *Cambridge Modern History* (New York, 1934), v, 751.

[45] Tulloch, *op. cit.*, ii, 267.

[46] *Ibid.*, ii, 301.

[47] *Ibid.*, ii, 231.

[48] Cf. *ibid.*, ii, 283.

[49] Willey, *op. cit.*, p. 167.

[50] *Op. cit.*, p. 126.

[51] Introduction to *The Poems of John Donne* (Oxford, 1912), pp. xxxviii and xlii.

[52] Robert L. Sharp, *From Donne to Dryden* (Chapel Hill, 1940), p. 140.

[53] *Garland for John Donne* (1631–1931) (Cambridge, 1931), p. 8.

[54] Sharp, *op. cit.*, p. 22.

[55] Herbert Read, 'The Nature of Metaphysical Poetry,' *Criterion*, i (1923), 261.

[56] Donne, *op. cit.*, 'The Progresse of the Soule' ('Second Anniversary'), p. 188.

[57] W. J. Courthope, *A History of English Poetry* (London, 1903), quoted from *Poems of Raleigh, Wotton, etc.*, p. 114; iii, 120.

[58] *Ibid.*, quoted from *Christ's Death and Victory*, iii, 135.

[59] T. S. Eliot, 'The Metaphysical Poets,' in *Homage to John Dryden*, ed. Eliot (London, 1924), p. 26.

60 S. T. Coleridge, *Biographia Literaria* (London, 1894), p. 150.

61 Bush, *op. cit.*, p. 309.

62 *Ibid.*, p. 37.

63 *Ibid.*, p. 336.

64 *Loc. cit.*

65 Willey, *op. cit.*, p. 44.

66 Jordan, *op. cit.*, p. 399.

67 Sharp, *op. cit.*, p. 141.

68 Tulloch, *op. cit.*, ii., 14.

69 *Ibid.*, ii, 191.

70 *Op. cit.*, p. 86.

71 Tulloch, *op. cit.*, ii, 113.

72 S. P. of Cambridge, *A Brief Account of the New Sect of Latitude Men*. This may be Simon Patrick, but the evidence is not conclusive.

73 *Ibid.*, ii, 41.

74 Roberts, *op. cit.*, p. 113.

75 Quoted by Tulloch, ii, 184.

76 *Ibid.*, ii, 415.

77 *Ibid.*, ii, 116.

78 Quoted, *ibid.*, ii, 101.

79 *Ibid.*, ii, 233.

80 *Op. cit.*, p. 386.

81 *Ibid.*, p. 387.

82 Bush, *op. cit.*, p. 347.

83 *Op. cit.*, pp. 292, 293.

84 Willey, *op. cit.*, p. 122.

85 Bush, *op. cit.*, p. 322.

86 *Ibid.*, p. 340.

87 Cf. *ibid.*, p. 323.

88 *Op. cit.*, p. 441.

89 Bush, *op. cit.*, p. 321.

90 *Loc. cit.*

91 Tulloch, *op. cit.*, i, 166.

92 *A Worke Concerning the Trunesse of Christian Religion*, 4th ed. (London, 1617), p. B5 verso.

93 *Loc. cit.*

94 Tulloch, *op. cit.*, ii, 258.

95 Jordan, *op. cit.*, p. 318.

96 Tulloch, *op. cit.*, i, 52.

97 Sharp, *op. cit.*, p. 144.

98 Cf. Jordan, *op. cit.*, p. 394.

99 *Ibid.*, p. 352.

100 M. Kaufmann, *op. cit.*, v, 748.

101 (London, 1675), p. iii.

[102] Willey, *op. cit.*, p. 73.

[103] 'The American Scholar,' *op. cit.*, p. 49.

[104] Willey, *op. cit.*, p. 135.

[105] *Ibid.*, p. 129.

[106] Paul R. Anderson, *Science in Defense of Liberal Religion: A Study of Henry More's Attempt to Link Seventeenth Century Religion With Science* (New York, 1933), p. 48.

[107] Tulloch, *op. cit.*, ii, 230.

[108] *A Discourse of the Use of Reason in Matters of Religion* (London, 1683), p. 35.

[109] *Practical Treatise Concerning Humility* (London, 1707), p. 138.

[110] Willey, *op. cit.*, p. 73.

[111] *The Modern Mind* (London, 1937), p. 107.

[112] Bush, *op. cit.*, p. 343.

[113] Roberts, *op. cit.*, p. 85.

[114] *Ibid.*, p. 105.

[115] Bush, *op. cit.*, p. 348.

[116] Roberts, *op. cit.*, p. 102.

[117] Rufus Jones, *Spiritual Reformers in the Sixteenth and Seventeenth Centuries* (London, 1914), p. 317.

[118] Tulloch, *op. cit.*, ii, 110.

[119] *Ibid.*, ii, 115.

[120] F. J. Powicke, *A Life of the Rev. Richard Baxter (1615–1691)* (London, 1924), p. 54.

[121] G. D. Boyle, *Richard Baxter* (London, 1883), p. 39.

[122] F. J. Powicke, 'Baxter and Comprehension,' *Constructive Quarterly*, vii (1919), 350.

[123] *The Rise of Puritanism* (New York, 1938), p. 198.

[124] *Ibid.*, p. 197.

[125] Cf. Tulloch, i, 34.

[126] Jordan, *op. cit.*, p. 339.

[127] *Ibid.*, p. 357.

[128] Willey, *op. cit.*, p. 38.

[129] Jones, *op cit.*, p. 286.

[130] Bush, *op. cit.*, p. 342.

[131] *Ibid.*, p. 324.

[132] Jordan, *op. cit.*, p. 377.

[133] Tulloch, *op. cit.*, ii, 104.

[134] *Ibid.*, i, 439.

[135] *Ibid.*, ii, 58.

[136] *Ibid.*, ii, 91.

[137] *Op. cit.*, p. 46.

[138] *Op. cit.*, p. B8 verso.

[139] *Op. cit.*, p. 226.

CHAPTER IV.   JOHN DONNE AND THE POETRY OF
SCEPTICISM

[1] C. M. Coffin, *Donne and the New Philosophy* (New York, 1937), p. 252.
[2] W. J. Courthope, *History of English Poetry* (London, 1903), iii, 150.
[3] 'Donne in Our Time,' *Garland for John Donne* (1631–1931), ed. Theodore Spencer (Cambridge, 1931), p. 8.
[4] Coffin, *op. cit.*, p. 286.
[5] Introd. to *The Complete Poetry* . . . , p. liii.
[6] H. J. C. Grierson ed., *The Poems of John Donne*, ii, x.
[7] *The Complete Poetry* . . . , p. 171.
[8] *Ibid.*, p. 188.
[9] *Loc. cit.*
[10] *Ibid.*, p. 189.
[11] Geoffrey Keynes ed., *Works of Sir Thomas Browne* (London, 1928), i, 86.
[12] *Ten Sermons*. Selected by Geoffrey Keynes (London, 1923), p. 115.
[13] *Ibid.*, p. 8.
[14] *Ibid.*, p. 115.
[15] *The Complete Poetry* . . . , pp. 472, 473.
[16] Grierson ed., i, 193, 'To the Countesse of Bedford.'
[17] *Ibid.*, i, 157.
[18] *Ten Sermons*, p. 23.
[19] Coffin, *op. cit.*, p. 280.
[20] Grierson, ed., i, 225.
[21] *The Complete Poetry* . . . , p. 461.
[22] E. M. Simpson, 'Donne's *Paradoxes and Problems*,' in *Garland for John Donne*, p. 43.
[23] *Ten Sermons*, p. 2.
[24] Grierson ed., i, 368.
[25] *Ibid.*, i, 331.
[26] *Ibid.*, i, 319.
[27] *Loc. cit.*
[28] *Ibid.*, i, 353.
[29] *Ibid.*, i, 331.
[30] *Ibid.*, i, 328.
[31] *Ibid.*, i, 157.
[32] *Ibid.*, i, 189.
[33] *Ibid.*, i, 267.
[34] *L Sermons* (London, 1649), p. 324.
[35] Grierson ed., i, 340.
[36] *The Complete Poetry* . . . , p. 455.

THE SUBTLE KNOT

37 *L Sermons*, p. 324.
38 *Ibid.*, p. 326.
39 *Essayes in Divinity* (London, 1651), p. 37.
40 *Ten Sermons*, p. 97.
41 *Ibid.*, p. 62.
42 Grierson ed., i, 299.
43 *Donne's Sermons*, ed. L. P. Smith (Oxford, 1920), p. 85.

CHAPTER V.   SIR THOMAS BROWNE AND THE
GENESIS OF PARADOX

1 *Works of Sir Thomas Browne*, ed. Geoffrey Keynes (London, 1928), i, 9.
2 *Loc. cit.*
3 *Ibid.*, i, 12.
4 *Ibid.*, i, 39.
5 *Ibid.*, ii, 19.
6 *Ibid.*, iii, 206.
7 *Ibid.*, i, 86.
8 *Loc. cit.*
9 *Loc. cit.*
10 Quoted by Robert Sencourt, *Outflying Philosophy* (London, 1923), p. 250.
11 *Puritan and Anglican* (New York, 1941), p. 46.
12 Keynes ed., i, 4.
13 *Loc. cit.*
14 *Ibid.*, i, 35.
15 *Ibid.*, i, 28.
16 *Biographia Literaria* (New York, 1939), p. 64.
17 Keynes ed., ii, 69.
18 *Ibid.*, i, 58.
19 *Ibid.*, iv, 42.
20 *Ibid.*, i, 58.
21 *Ibid.*, i, 97.
22 *Ibid.*, i, 88.
23 *Ibid.*, i, 23.
24 *Ibid.*, i, 26.
25 *Ibid.*, i, 115.
26 *Ibid.*, i, 83.
27 *Ibid.*, i, 43.
28 *Ibid.*, i, 72.
29 *Ibid.*, iv, 42.
30 *Ibid.*, i, 40.
31 *Ibid.*, i, 9.
32 *Ibid.*, i, 114.

33 Keynes ed., i, 9.
34 *Ibid.*, i, 7.
35 *Ibid.*, i, 9.
36 *Ibid.*, i, 26.
37 *Ibid.*, ii, 40.
38 *Ibid.*, i, 13.
39 *Ibid.*, iii, 173.
40 *Ibid.*, i, 14.
41 Louis I. Bredvold, *op. cit.*, p. 43.
42 Keynes ed., i, 85.
43 *Ibid.*, i, 122.
44 *Ibid.*, i, 67.
45 *Ibid.*, i, 66.
46 *Ibid.*, i, 65.
47 *Shelburne Essays*, 6th series (New York, 1909), p. 167.
48 *Op. cit.*, p. 452.
49 (New York, 1909), p. xii.
50 *Sir Thomas Browne, a Study in Religious Philosophy* (Menasha, 1926), p. 46.

CHAPTER VI.   RICHARD BAXTER AND THE PROBLEM
OF CERTAINTY

1 This very useful word, which has become obsolete, means 'over-confidence,' the holding of a position (usually dogmatically) before one has a rational basis for judgment.
2 *Reliquiae Baxterianae*, ed. Matthew Sylvester (London, 1696), p. 125.
3 *Practical Works*, ed. Wm. Orme (London, 1830), 'A Treatise of Knowledge and Love Compared,' xv, 120.
4 *Ibid.*, p. 138.
5 *Loc. cit.*
6 *Autobiography of Richard Baxter* ed. J. M. Lloyd Thomas (London, 1925), p. 131.
7 *Loc. cit.*
8 *Practical Works*, xv, 121.
9 *Ibid.*, p. 120.
10 *Apology Against the Modest Exceptions of Mr. T. Blake* (London, 1654), p. 3.
11 *Practical Works*, xv, 33.
12 *Essays in Ecclesiastical Biography* (London, 1853), p. 4.
13 *Practical Works*, xv, 89.
14 *Ibid.*, xv, 132.
15 *The Reasons of the Christian Religion* (London, 1667), p. 496.
16 For all Baxter's tolerance of Protestant points of view

opposed to his own and in spite of his sympathetic understanding of atheists and infidels, he was the implacable foe of
Roman Catholicism. He looked far beyond his own day to a
possible agreement among Protestants, but he saw no means of
enlarging the circle to take in the Papists.

[17] *Practical Works*, xv, 131.

[18] *Reasons of Christian Religion*, p. 448.

[19] *Ibid.*, p. 371.

[20] *The Saints' Everlasting Rest*, 12th ed. (London, 1688),
p. 154.

[21] *The Unreasonableness of Infidelity* (London, 1655), preface,
4th page after C4.

[22] *Ibid.*, p. C4.

[23] *Reliquiae*, p. 21.

[24] *Ibid.*, p. 128.

[25] *Ibid.*, p. 24.

[26] *Autobiography*, p. 26.

[27] *The Reasons of the Christian Religion*, p. 416.

[28] P. 128.

[29] J. T. Wilkinson, *Richard Baxter and Margaret Charlton,
a Puritan Love Story* (London, 1928), p. 151.

[30] *Reasons . . .*, p. 241.

[31] *Ibid.*, p. 157.

[32] 'Knowledge and Love,' *Practical Works*, xv, 37.

[33] *The Unreasonableness of Infidelity*, p. 59.

[34] Grierson ed., i, 267.

[35] *Reasons . . .*, p. 259.

[36] *A Saint or a Brute* (London, 1662), p. 353.

[37] *Ibid.*, p. 375.

[38] 'Knowledge and Love,' *Practical Works*, xv, 43.

[39] *Autobiography*, p. 109.

[40] William Orme, *The Life and Times of Richard Baxter*
(Boston, 1831), ii, 19.

[41] John Hunt, *Religious Thought in England from the Reformation to the End of the Last Century* (London, 1870), i, 464.

[42] *Unreasonableness of Infidelity*, p. 194.

CHAPTER VII.   JEREMY TAYLOR, THE SCEPTIC AS
CHURCHMAN

[1] *The Whole Works of the Right Rev. Jeremy Taylor*, ed.
Reginald Heber (London, 1828), ix, ccccvii; from which all
subsequent quotations are also taken.

[2] vii, 468; 'Liberty of Prophesying.'

[3] vii, ccccxxxv; Epistle Dedicatory to same.

[4] iv, 86; *The Rule and Exercises of Holy Living*.

5 iv, 103.

6 iii, 500; 'Contemplations of the State of Man.'

7 ii, lvii; preface to *Life of Christ*.

8 ii, ix; Dedicatory Letter to same.

9 *Loc. cit.*

10 vi, 376; 'A Sermon Preached to the University of Dublin.'

11 iv, cccxxxii; Dedication to *The Rule and Exercises of Holy Dying*.

12 vi, 267; Sermon iii, 'Fides Formata; Or, Faith Working by Love.'

13 i, 116; *Christian Consolations*.

14 i, 165.

15 vi, 203; 'The Miracles of the Divine Mercy.'

16 ii, 442; *Life of Christ*.

17 vi, 374; 'A Sermon Preached to the University of Dublin.'

18 vi, 197; 'The Miracles of the Divine Mercy.'

19 iv, 180.

20 x, 16; *The Real Presence*.

21 x, 18.

22 ii, xli; preface to *Life of Christ*.

23 xi, 461.

24 xi, 462.

25 vii, 495; *The Liberty of Prophesying*.

26 Grierson ed., i, 189.

27 Taylor, *op. cit.*, xi, 459.

28 i, 112; *Christian Consolations*.

29 xi, 349; preface to *Doctor Dubitantium*.

30 ii, xxxiv; preface to *Life of Christ*.

31 i, 124; *Christian Consolations*.

32 ii, xxxvi; preface to *Life of Christ*.

33 John 7: 17.

34 Taylor, *op. cit.*, vi, 387; 'A Sermon Preached to the University of Dublin.'

35 viii, 116; *The Liberty of Prophesying*.

36 ii, xii; Dedicatory Letter to *Life of Christ*.

37 *Loc. cit.*

38 vi, 266; 'The Christian's Conquest Over the Body of Sin.'

39 vi, 379; 'A Sermon Preached to the University of Dublin.'

40 vi, 393.

CHAPTER VIII.   JOSEPH GLANVILL, SELF–CONSCIOUS
SCEPTIC

1 *Op. cit.*, p. 171.

2 *Reliquiae Baxterianae*, p. 378.

3 (London, 1681), p. 180.

4 *Ibid.*, p. 181.

5 Taylor, Browne, Glanvill, and Baxter also had in common the dubious distinction of believing in witches. This, as we have seen, was an understandable corollary of their conviction that spirit is as real as matter.

6 *Athenae Oxonienses* (London, 1817), iii, 1245.

7 Joseph Glanvill, *Some Discourses, Sermons and Remains* (London, 1681), preface to reader by Anthony Horneck, p. A3 recto.

8 Isaiah 55: 8.

9 *The Vanity of Dogmatizing* (London, 1661), p. 68.

10 *Essays on Several Important Subjects in Philosophy and Religion* (London, 1676), 'Against Confidence in Philosophy and Matters of Speculation,' p. 32.

11 *Lux Orientalis* (London, 1662), p. C4 verso.

12 *Loc. cit.*

13 *Essays . . .* , 'The Usefulness of Real Philosophy to Religion,' p. 26.

14 *The Vanity of Dogmatizing*, p. 112.

15 *Ibid.*, p. 193.

16 *Ibid.*, p. 231.

17 *Ibid.*, p. 15.

18 *Catholick Charity Recommended* (London, 1669), p. 33.

19 *The Vanity of Dogmatizing*, p. 225.

20 *Ibid.*, p. 66.

21 *Ibid.*, p. 164.

22 *Essays . . .* , 'Modern Improvements of Useful Knowledge,' p. 50.

23 *The Vanity of Dogmatizing*, p. 128.

24 *Ibid.*, p. 102.

25 *Ibid.*, p. 4.

26 'Essay on Glanvill,' *Scepsis Scientifica*, ed. John Owen (London, 1885), p. xix.

27 (London, 1665), p. c2 verso.

28 P. A6 recto.

29 *The Vanity of Dogmatizing*, p. 237.

30 *Ibid.*, p. 238.

31 Richard Baxter says in *A Second True Defence of the Non-Conformist* (London, 1681), 'It grieved me to hear of Mr. Glanvill's death, for he was a man of more than ordinary ingeny, and he was about a Collection of Histories of Apparitions, which is a work of great use against our Sadducees, and to stablish doubters, and the best mans faith hath need of all the helps from sense that we can get.' (P. 175).

32 *Sadducismus Triumphatus* (London, 1681), part ii, p. 1.

33 *Ibid.*, p. 15.

34 *The Vanity of Dogmatizing*, p. 20.

35 *Scepsis Scientifica* (London, 1665), p. 15.
36 Grierson ed., i, 189.
37 *The Vanity of Dogmatizing*, p. 188.
38 *Scepsis Scientifica*, 2nd ed. (London, 1703), p. a2 recto.
39 *An Essay Concerning Preaching*, 2nd ed. (London, 1703), p. 31.
40 *The Vanity of Dogmatizing*, p. 248.
41 *Scepsis Scientifica*, (1665) p. a4 recto.
42 *The Way of Happiness* (London, 1670), p. 6.
43 *The Vanity of Dogmatizing*, p. 103.
44 P. 115.
45 *The Vanity of Dogmatizing*, p. 209.
46 *Ibid.*, p. 65.
47 *Lux Orientalis*, p. 2.
48 P. 28.
49 *Scepsis Scientifica* (1885 ed.), p. 192.
50 *Ibid.*, (1703) p. a3 recto.
51 *Essays . . .* , 'The Usefulness of Real Philosophy to Religion,' p. 22.
52 *Ibid.*, p. 26.
53 'Letter to Baxter on Preexistence,' *Bibliotheca Platonica*, May–June 1890, p. 187.
54 *The Vanity of Dogmatizing*, p. B4 verso.
55 *Ibid.*, p. 226.
56 *Essays . . .* , 'Against Confidence in Philosophy and Matters of Speculation,' p. 32.
57 P. 233.
58 *Scepsis Scientifica*, (1703) p. a3 recto.
59 *Plus Ultra: the Progress and Advancement of Science Since the Days of Aristotle* (London, 1668), p. 146.
60 *Scepsis Scientifica*, (1703) p. 3.
61 *Plus Ultra*, p. 139.
62 *Ibid.*, p. 140.
63 *Essays . . .* , 'Of Scepticism and Certainty,' p. 45.
64 *Scepsis Scientifica*, (1703) p. a verso.
65 *Ibid.*, p. a2 verso.
66 *Lux Orientalis*, p. 83.
67 *Scepsis Scientifica*, (1703) p. 5.
68 *Ibid.*, p. 12.
69 *Essays . . .* , pp. 39 ff.
70 *The Vanity of Dogmatizing*, p. 186.
71 *Lux Orientalis*, p. 1 of preface.
72 *Ibid.*, p. 109.
73 *The Vanity of Dogmatizing*, p. 230.
74 *Ibid.*, p. 131.
75 *A Blow at Modern Sadducism* (London, 1668), p. A3 recto.

76 *Plus Ultra*, p. 148.
77 *Catholick Charity*, p. 28.
78 P. 33.
79 *Catholick Charity*, p. 29.
80 *Ibid.*, p. 21.

CHAPTER IX.   THE EIGHTEENTH CENTURY:
UNTYING THE KNOT

1 *Op. cit.*, p. 133.
2 W. J. Courthope, *A History of English Poetry* (London, 1903), v, 75.
3 (London, 1721), p. 6.
4 *Ibid.*, p. 71.
5 Cf. *A History of English Thought in the Eighteenth Century* (New York, 1927), ii, 335.
6 Courthope, *op. cit.*, v, 77.
7 *Religio Medici and Christian Morals* (London, 1940), 'Christian Morals,' p. 143.
8 (London, 1713), p. 177.
9 *Op. cit.*, i, 18.
10 *Op. cit.*, p. 423.
11 *Op. cit.*, i, 186.
12 *Op. cit.*, ii, 223.
13 *A Paraphrase on the Book of Job* (London, 1700), p. h recto.
14 *Hours in a Library* (London, 1899), i, 295.
15 F. B. Kaye, preface to Bernard Mandeville, *The Fable of the Bees or Private Vices, Public Benefits* (Oxford, 1924), i, xxxix.
16 *Ibid.*, p. xli.
17 *Op. cit.*, p. 87.
18 *Op. cit.*, p. 125.
19 *Scepsis Scientifica* (London, 1665), p. 15.
20 Willey, *op. cit.*, p. 270.
21 Cf. Willey, *The Eighteenth-Century Background* (London, 1949), p. 111.
22 *Op. cit.*, p. 401.
23 *The Poetical Works of Matthew Prior*, ed. R. B. Johnson (London, 1892), ii, 177.
24 *English Thought* . . . , i, 183.
25 Alex Chalmers, 'British Essayists' (Boston, 1866), *Guardian*, 169, xv, 240.
26 *Ibid.*, viii, 117. *Spectator* No. 253.
27 *Ibid.*, viii, 43. *Spectator* No. 237.
28 *Op. cit.*, p. 9.

[29] *Free Thoughts on Religion, the Church, and National Happiness* (London, 1720), p. 64.

[30] *Op. cit.,* p. 132.

[31] John Hunt, *Religious Thought* . . . , iii, 198.

[32] *Op. cit.,* p. 7.

[33] William Law, *Remarks Upon a Late Book, Entituled, The Fable of the Bees* (London, 1724), p. 7.

[34] Chalmers, *op. cit.,* iii, 18. *Tatler* No. 108.

[35] *Ibid.,* iii, 33. *Tatler* No. 111.

[36] *Free Thoughts on Religion,* p. 4.

[37] Law, *op. cit.,* p. 65.

[38] Stephen, *English Thought* . . . , i, 107.

[39] John Wilkins, *Of the Principles and Duties of Natural Religion,* 4th ed. (London, 1699), p. vii.

[40] Selby-Bigge (L.A.) *British Moralists* (Oxford, 1897), p. 50.

[41] Willey, *The Seventeenth Century Background,* p. 1.

[42] *Scepsis Scientifica,* p. c4 recto.

[43] *An Earnest Invitation to the Sacrament of the Lord's Supper* (London, 1681), p. 8.

[44] *Op. cit.,* p. 95.

[45] *Op. cit.,* p. 115.

[46] *Ibid.,* p. 101.

[47] *Reperusals and Re-collections* (New York, 1937), p. 228.

[48] *Op. cit.,* p. 66.

[49] Cf. M. P. Ramsay, 'Donne's Relation to Philosophy,' in *Garland for John Donne, op. cit.,* p. 118.

[50] *Grounds of Criticism in Poetry* (London, 1704), p. 82.

[51] *Ibid.,* 4th page of preface.

[52] *Op. cit.,* p. 126.

CHAPTER X. CONTEMPORARY IMPLICATIONS OF SCEPTICISM

[1] *Milton's Prose,* ed. Malcolm W. Wallace (London, 1925), p. 279.

[2] *Ibid.,* p. 311.

[3] *Ibid.,* p. 312.

[4] *Loc. cit.*

[5] *Ibid.,* p. 306.

[6] *Ibid.,* p. 321.

[7] *Loc. cit.*

[8] *Ibid.,* p. 322.

[9] *Ibid.,* p. 310.

[10] *Ibid.,* p. 311.

[11] *Milton's Prose*, ed. Malcolm W. Wallace (London, 1925), p. 290.

[12] *Ibid.*, p. 281.

[13] *Ibid.*, p. 289.

[14] *Ibid.*, p. 293.

[15] *Ibid.*, p. 314.

[16] *Ibid.*, p. 315.

[17] *Ibid.*, p. 316.

[18] *Loc. cit.*

[19] *Ibid.*, p. 308.

[20] *Loc. cit.*

[21] *Ibid.*, p. 313.

[22] *Ibid.*, p. 307.

[23] *Ibid.*, p. 309.

[24] 'Modern Art and the Dignity of Man,' *Atlantic Monthly*, clxxxii (1948), 30.

[25] *Ibid.*, p. 31.

[26] *Loc. cit.*

[27] *Ibid.*, p. 32.

[28] *Ibid.*, p. 33.

[29] *Ibid.,* p. 35.

[30] *Loc. cit.*

[31] *Loc. cit.*

[32] *Loc. cit.*

[33] *Ibid.*, p. 36.

[34] *Loc. cit.*

[35] This section is based upon Jean Paul Sartre's *L'Existentialisme est un Humanisme* (Paris, 1946).

POSTSCRIPT: THE DESPAIR OF GOD

[1] *The Poems of George Herbert* (Oxford, 1913), pp. 30–35.

INDEX